We may live without poetry, music and art,
We may live without conscience, and live
without heart,
We may live without friends,
We may live without books,
But civilized man cannot live without cooks.

He may live without books — what is knowledge
but grieving?
He may live without hope — what is hope,
but deceiving?
He may live without love — what is passion,
but pining?
But where is the man who can live without
dining?

"Bluenose II (Photo by Maurice Crosby)."

Canadian Cataloguing in Publication Data

Bluenose cook book

Compiled by the Ladies' Auxiliary of the Yarmouth YMCA.
ISBN 1-55109-028-7

1. Cookery, Canadian -- Nova Scotia style.
2. Cookery -- Nova Scotia -- Yarmouth. I.Young
Men's Christian Association (Yarmouth, N.S.).
Ladies' Auxiliary

TX715.6.B48 1992   641.5971631   C92-098614-5

cookscountry.com/tv

Some Handy Metric Conversion Hints

Liquid Measure

Present measuring cup graduated 1 cup, ½ cup, ¼ cup, will in metric = 250 millilitres, 125 ml, 50 ml or 1 cup - approx. 250 ml.

Small amounts 1 tbsp, 1 tsp, ½ tsp, ¼ tsp will be metric 15 millilitres, 5 ml, 2 ml, 1 ml.

Mass

1 oz = 28.45 grams
1 pound = 0.454 kilograms
1 gram = 0.035 oz.
1 kilogram = 2.205 lb.

Volume

1 tablespoon = 14.21 millilitres
1 fluid ounce = 28.412 millilitres
1 cup = 0.227 litres
1 quart = 1.136 litres
1 gallon (Imp.) = 4.546 litres
1 millilitre (ml) = 0.0704 tbsp. or .0352 fluid oz.

Present Day Weights & Equivalents

3 tsp. = 1 tbsp.
2 tbsp. = 1 liquid oz.
4 tbsp = ¼ cup
2 cups = 1 pt.
½ c butter = ¼ lb.

1 sq. chocolate = 1 oz. or 1/3 c dry cocoa
16 oz = 1 lb.
2 c. white sugar = 1 lb.
2 2/3 c. icing sugar = 1 lb.
4 c. flour = 1 lb.

Celsius Degrees for oven reading

Very slow oven	120-150 celsius
Slow oven	150-170 celsius
Moderate	170-190 celsius
Moderately hot	190-200 celsius
Hot	200-230 celsius

"Superior Milk" is a brand name for regular milk

The Ladies Auxiliary of the Yarmouth YMCA take this opportunity of thanking all those who have supported our Cook Book in the past - making this 4th printing of the 4th Edition necessary. We are sure that our "Famous Yarmouth Recipes" will please all of you and we'd appreciate you telling your friends about us. Additional copies may be obtained from Mrs. Irving Pink, 9 Seminary Street, Yarmouth, Nova Scotia, Canada.

Contents

ROLLS

Quick Rolls

Scald 1 cup Superior Brand Milk, add 3 tablespoons butter or shortening. Let cool.

Dissolve 1 yeast cake or 1 pkg. dry yeast in ½ cup lukewarm water, with 1 tsp. sugar.

Beat 2 eggs in bowl; add 3 tbsp. sugar, 1 tsp salt. Add this to cool milk, then add yeast mixture. Add flour and knead well. Let stand ¾ of an hour, in a warm place. Then make up into rolls. Let rise about 1 hour. Bake ½ hour in a 350°F. oven.

Mable Patten, Arcadia

Goofy Rolls

Shortening size of egg	1 cup cold water
⅓ cup sugar	1 cup flour with 1 tsp. baking
1 egg	powder and 1 tsp. salt
1 yeast cake (quick acting — not	1 cup cold water
dissolved)	4 cups of flour (approx.)

Add ingredients in order. Place in refrigerator and use as necessary, or let rise once in bowl, then put in pans or muffin tins, let rise until double in bulk.

Bake 375° oven 15 minutes or until golden brown.

B. MacDonald

Rolls (White)

1 yeast cake	2 cups lukewarm water 98°F.
1 scant tablespoon salt	½ cup melted shortening
⅓ cup sugar	6 - 7 cups all-purpose flour
1 egg	

METHOD: Break yeast cake into large mixing bowl, add salt, sugar, egg, and water. Beat well with rotary beater. Mix and beat well 3 cups of flour into first mixture; then add remaining flour and shortening, mixing until dough is smooth and of an elastic consistency. Allow to raise in a warm pleace free from draughts until double in bulk. Punch down and form into about 6 - 7 dozen small rolls. Place rolls on well buttered pans and allow to raise until double in size.

Bake in 370° oven until brown, about 20 minutes.

P.S. — Above dough may be used in any desired shape.

If you have difficulty raising yeast dough, simply place a pan of boiling water in the bottom of your oven (electric or gas) and place your dough in container well covered beside or above the hot water. Raising time usually 1½ - 2 hours.

Mary Sperry

Cinnamon Rolls

5 cups all-purpose flour
½ cup Mazola oil
3 eggs (well beaten)

1 yeast cake
1½ cups lukewarm water
¾ cups sugar

Prepare yeast cake with a little warm water and teaspoon sugar in glass. Let stand a few minutes. Pour flour in a large bowl, add sugar and mix well together. Make a well in the centre, add the well beaten eggs, yeast cake, oil and water. Mix well and knead, let rise until double in bulk. Knead down a second time and let rise. Cut dough into parts, roll and sprinkle with cinnamon and sugar. Roll as a jelly roll and slice. Let rise in pan before baking — 400° about 20 minutes.

Corinne Pink

Cinnamon Pinwheels

2 pkgs. dry yeast
2 cups warm water
½ cup sugar
6½ - 7 cups flour

1 egg
¼ cup soft shortening
2 tsp. salt

Dissolve yeast in water, add sugar, salt and ½ of flour, beat 2 minutes, add egg and shortening, then add remaining flour. Mix with hands until smooth, let rise. Punch down, roll on lightly floured board, spread with brown sugar cinnamon, sprinkle with raisins and chopped nuts. Roll as jelly roll. Slice ½ - 1 inch. Place on cookie sheet, let rise, bake in 350° oven about 15 - 20 minutes.

Mrs. Austin Churchill

Hot Cross Buns

½ cup hot mashed potatoes
¼ cup butter
½ cup each, milk and water
3 tbsp. sugar
1 tsp. salt
1 tsp. grated orange or lemon
   rind
1 pkg. yeast

1 tsp. sugar
1 tsp. cinnamon
½ tsp. allspice or nutmeg
3 cups sifted all-purpose flour
1 egg, well-beaten
½ cup each, raisins and chopped
   peel

Combine first seven ingredients, stir and heat until butter melts. Cool to lukewarm. Dissolve yeast and sugar in ¼ cup warm water. Sift one cup flour with spices. Beat into potato mixture. Add yeast, egg and fruit. Stir in sufficient flour for a soft dough. Knead until smooth. Place in greased bowl and let rise until double in bulk. Knead down and shape in rolls. Place on greased baking sheet. Again allow to rise until double in bulk. Bake in hot oven for about fifteen minutes

Mrs. Bernard Strong

Crusty Rolls

Soften 1 pkg. dry yeast or 1 cake yeast in ¼ cup water. Add 1 tbsp. sugar, 1 tsp. salt, and 2 tbsps. salad oil to ¾ cup lukewarm water. Stir in 1 cup flour, yeast mixture and 2 egg whites beaten until frothy. Mix in 3 cups flour. Knead smooth. Place in greased bowl; cover; let rise till double. Punch down; let rise again until double. Brush shaped rolls with mixture of 1 egg yolk and 1 tbsp. cold water. Bake at 375° for 35 minutes. Place pan of boiling water in oven during baking. Makes about 12.

Ruth Urquhart

Brown Rolls

½ cup rolled oats	2 cups boiling water
½ cup corn meal	1 pkg. yeast
½ cup brown sugar	¼ cup lukewarm water
1 tbsp. shortening	5½ cups flour
1 tsp. salt	

Pour boiling water over rolled oats, corn meal, sugar and salt. Mix thoroughly and cool. Dissolve yeast cake in lukewarm water and add. Then add flour and mix well. Let rise until double in bulk. Make into rolls and let rise until double in size. Bake about 20 minutes in 400 degree oven.

Mrs. H. M. Langille

Hot Cross Buns

1½ cups Superior Brand Milk	5 cups flour
8 tbsp. sugar	1 pkg. yeast
2 tsp. salt	2 tbsp. lukewarm water
1 tsp. nutmeg	2 eggs, beaten
1 tsp. cinnamon	½ cup raisins
6 tbsp. shortening	½ cup currants

Heat milk to scalding point, and pour over sugar, salt, cinnamon, nutmeg, shortening, raisins and currants, stir until sugar is dissolved and shortening melted. Cool to lukewarm. Sift flour and measure. Dissolve yeast in water and add to cooled mixture. Add beaten eggs and flour, beat until smooth. Cover and let rise until light. Place dough on floured board and roll to ½ inch thick. Cut out with cookie cutter and place on greased cookie sheet. Brush with melted shortening, cover and let rise until double in bulk. Cook in hot oven 15 minutes. Brush with fat and sprinkle with sugar. Put cross on each with icing sugar. Makes 2 dozen.

Mrs. Gard Nickerson, Carleton

Upside Down Rolls

Combine and heat until shortening has melted:

½ cup Superior Brand Milk   ¼ cup shortening
¼ cup sugar   1 tsp. salt

Cool and add 2 eggs beaten, 1 yeast cake dissolved in ¼ cup warm water. Gradually add 3 cups flour. Let rise. Then drop small rolls of dough into muffin tins that have been prepared with melted butter, 1 tsp. brown sugar and 1 tbsp. drained fruit cocktail. Let rise and bake in a hot oven, 425 degrees for ten to fifteen minutes.

Mrs. Austin Churchill

Sinkers

1 pkg. dry yeast   ½ cup shortening
½ cup lukewarm water   2 well beaten eggs
1 teaspoon white sugar   1 teaspoon vanilla
1½ cups Superior Brand Milk   2 cups whole-wheat flour
½ cup liquid honey   Bread flour for a stiff dough
½ cup white sugar   (approximately 4½ cups)
1½ teaspoons salt

Dissolve yeast in lukewarm water. Add 1 teaspoon sugar and let stand 10 minutes. Scald milk and add shortening, sugar, honey and salt. Cool mixture to lukewarm. Combine milk and yeast mixtures. Add eggs and vanilla. Stir in 2 cups white flour (sifted) and beat until smooth. Add 2 cups wholewheat flour and enough more white flour to make dough that will handle easily. Knead lightly on floured board until smooth and elastic. Place in greased bowl. Cover with damp cloth. Set in warm place to rise to double in bulk. Punch down dough. Then roll to ½ inch thick on floured board and cut with doughnut cutter. Let rise again and fry in deep hot fat (375 to 400 deg. F.) Turn doughnuts as soon as they rise in the hot grease and continue turning till they are browned. Drain on absorbent paper and while still hot dip in warm Honey-Dip mixture and set on a cake rack to cool. Yields 3 to 4 dozen.

HONEY-DIP

Combine ½ cup butter, ½ cup liquid honey, ½ cup white sugar and ½ cup milk in saucepan. Stir and let boil for 1 minute. Cool to lukewarm and add 1 cup icing sugar, ½ teaspoon salt, 1 teaspoon vanilla and 1 teaspoon cinnamon.

Mrs. D. F. Macdonald

Cinnamon Ring

¼ cup butter	½ yeast cake
¼ cup sugar	1 tsp. salt
1 cup Superior Brand Milk	4 cups flour
1 egg	½ tsp. cinnamon

Soak yeast in ¼ cup lukewarm coffee, cream butter and sugar and add egg, milk, yeast and dry ingredients. Let rise until double in bulk. Knead down and place in a cool place for one hour. Roll dough 14" x 5", brush with melted butter and sprinkle with brown sugar and cinnamon, roll lengthwise, place in tube pan or cookie sheet and let rise. Bake 400 degrees for 15 to 20 minutes. Glaze top by combining egg white slightly beaten and cold water.

Mrs. Earle Churchill

Sugar Plum Loaf

Dissolve 1 yeast cake in:

1 cup lukewarm Superior Milk   1 tsp. sugar

Add 1 cup flour and let this sponge raise until bubbly, 10 or 15 minutes.

Cream:

½ cup shortening	1 cup raisins
½ cup sugar, add	1 cup currants
2 eggs and beat	½ finely cut citron or mixed peel
1 tsp. salt then sponge and 4 cups flour, add fruit	½ cup maraschino Cherries cut in half

Knead, put in greased tube pan, let rise until double. Bake one hour in moderate oven.

Mrs. David Corning

Sweet Rolls Many Varieties

BASIC DOUGH:	1 tsp. salt
1¼ cups scalded Superior Brand Milk	1 pkg. yeast
	2 well beaten eggs
½ cup shortening	5 cups flour
⅓ cup sugar	

Combine Superior Milk, shortening, sugar and salt, cool to lukewarm. Add softened yeast. Add eggs and beat thoroughly. Add flour, knead lightly. Let rise in warm place until double in bulk. Roll as desired. Let rise again until double. Bake in 400° oven 15 minutes.

FOR ORANGE BOWKNOTS

Add ¼ cup orange juice and 2 tbsp. orange peel to above before adding flour. Cut dough in strips. Tie each in a knot and proceed. When baked spread with a thin orange icing.

FOR CHERRY NUT ROLLS

Use basic dough. Roll dough into rectangle. spread with softened butter, brown sugar, chopped nuts and maraschino cherries. Roll as for jelly roll. Cut 1½" thick. Place cut side down on greased pan which has dabs of butter, brown sugar and maraschino cherry juice as a base. Proceed to let rise and bake.

FOR FRUIT BREAD

Mix 1 lb. mixed fruit into dough before adding flour. When raised first time form into 2 rolls. Twist together. Place on greased pan, then proceed as above.

FOR CHEESE ROLLS

Mix 1 small bottle grated cheese into dough. When ready to shape make individual rolls or shape as one loaf. Then proceed as above.

(I often double the Basic Dough and make up several varieties at one baking.)

Mrs. D. F. Macdonald

RAISED BREADS

White Bread

2 cups Superior Milk (scalded). Add 2 cups cold water. Take out ½ cup liquid, dissolve in it 1 tsp. sugar, 1 yeast cake. Add 4 tsps. shortening, 8 tsps. sugar, 4 tsps. salt to first mixture. Add 10 cups flour when above mixture is cool.

Knead dough well. Let rise once in bowl. Put in pans. Let rise until double in bulk. Bake 15 mins 350° oven, then ½ hour at 300° oven.

Mrs. Russell Cleveland

"Royal George" Brown Bread

(No kneading required)

Pour 2 cups boiling water over 1 cup rolled oats
Let stand until cooled.

Add:
2 tsps. salt
2 tbsps. shortening
½ cup Silver Lasses molasses

1 yeast cake dissolved in
½ cup warm water
5 cups flour

Beat well. Let rise in bowl until double in bulk. Beat again and spoon into loaf pans. Let rise until double in bulk. Bake 1 hour at 375°. Slices well the next day.

Can be made using ½ cup corn meal and ½ cup rolled oats. Other ingredients and method the same.

Margaret W. Quickfall

Helen's Brown Bread

Mix:
1 cup rolled oats
½ tbsp. shortening

2/3 cup Silver Lasses molasses
2 cups hot water
1 tbsp. salt

Pour hot water over rolled oats and add to rest of mixture. Allow to cool.

Dissolve 1 yeast cake in ½ cup warm water and 1 tsp. sugar. Cool. Add to above mixture.

Add about 6 - 7 cups of flour or enough to handle. Knead well.

Divide dough in half and either make 2 small loaves or 1 double loaf. Let rise in pans once until double in bulk.

NOTE: This dough does not have to raise in bowl first.
Bake in 350° oven for 1 hour.

Mrs. E Clarke

French Style Bread

4 pkgs. active dry yeast
2½ cups lukewarm water
1 tbsp. salt
1 tbsp. sugar
6 - 7 cups flour

Corn meal
1 egg white beaten slightly with
 1 tbsp. water
Poppy seeds

Dissolve yeast in the lukewarm water. Add the salt and sugar, enough flour to make a stiff dough. Turn out on a floured board and let rest 5 minutes.

Knead the dough until smooth and elastic, at least 10 minutes. Place in a clean basin and cover with a damp cloth. Let rise in a warm place until double in bulk, about 1 hour. Knock down dough, let rest 10 minutes.

Divide into 3 parts, and shape each part into a sausage-shaped loaf. Place the loaves on a baking sheet sprinkled with cornmeal. Make three or four slashes ½ inch deep at an angle along loaf.

Brush with egg white mixture. Cover with a damp cloth supported over two glasses, so that cloth will not tuoch dough. Let rise about one hour. Brush the loaves again with egg mixture, sprinkle with seeds. Place in a preheated oven of 400 degrees. Bake 15 minutes.

Brush again with egg white mixture. Return to oven for 10 - 15 minutes or until golden brown. Cool slightly, but best eaten while still warm. These loaves can be reheated in a moderate oven, wrapped in foil if a soft crust is wanted, or uncovered for that crisp crust typical of french bread.

Mrs. Irving Pink

Brown Bread

1 cup oatmeal
Scant tbsp. salt

⅓ cup corn meal
Shortening size of large egg

Pour over 2½ cups boiling water, cooking slowly for a few minutes.

Cool, add:
good cup Silver Lasses molasses
one yeast cake or 1 pkg. dry yeast
 which has been dissolved with

½ cup lukewarm water and
1 tsp. sugar

Mix well, then add:
1 cup graham flour or
 whole wheat flour

and enough bread flour for quite
 stiff dough (about 4 - 5 cups)

Let rise double its size, then put in pans, let rise again, bake in rather slow oven. (About 1 hr.)

Dorothy Robbins

Shredded Wheat Bread

2 shredded wheat	¾ cup Silver Lasses molasses
1 pt. Superior Brand Milk	1 tsp. salt
1 pkg. dry yeast, 1 tsp. w. sugar,	4 small tbsp. shortening (melted)
⅓ cup warm water	6 cups unsifted flour

Soak wheat in warm milk and shortening. Add molasses, salt and yeast, which has been dissolved in ⅛ cup lukewarm water to which has been added 1 tsp. white sugar, and last, knead in the flour.

Let raise in warm place about 2½ - 3 hours. Knead down and put in pans. Raise again for ¾ - 1 hour. Bake in 350° - 375° oven for ¾ hour.

Makes two 9 x 5½ loaves.

(Mrs. Merle) Gladys Allen

Swedish Limpa Bread

1½ cups lukewarm water	2 tbsp. shortening
2 tsp. sugar	grated rind of 1 orange
2 pkg. dry yeast	2½ cup sifted rye flour
¼ cup Silver Lasses molasses	2½ to 3 cups sifted all-purpose
⅓ cup sugar	flour
1 tbsp. salt	

Dissolve 2 tsp. sugar in ½ cup lukewarm water. Sprinkle yeast on top and let stand ten minutes, then stir. Combine remaining water, molasses, sugar, salt, shortening and orange rind in large bowl. Add yeast. Mix in flour, turn on board, cover and let stand 10 minutes. Knead until smooth. Place in greased bowl, cover and let rise until double in bulk. Punch down, round up and let rise again 45 minutes. Punch down and form into 2 long loaves. Place on greased baking sheet, cover with damp cloth and let rise until double in bulk. Bake 35 minutes at 375°. Brush top with shortening.

Good with cheese or for sandwiches made with smoked salmon and egg.

Ruth M. Rideout

Cheese Caraway Twist

1 pkg. active dry yeast	1 tbsp. sugar
¾ cup warm water	1 tsp. salt
1 cup grated sharp cheese	1 egg, beaten
2 tbsp. caraway seeds	2½ cups flour

In large bowl sprinkle yeast over warm water. Stir until dissolved. Stir in everything but flour. Stir in half of flour. Blend well. Then rest of flour. Turn dough out on lightly floured surface. Knead about 10 minutes or until smooth and satiny. Place in greased bowl. Cover, let rise until double in bulk (1 hour). Punch down. Let rise 30 minutes more. Divide dough in half. Shape each piece into a 12" roll. Twist two rolls together. Seal ends. Place on greased baking sheet. Brush with melted butter. Let rise 1 hour. Bake at 375° 30 - 35 minutes. Brush with more butter. Yield: one large twist.

R. Pink

Kugelhoff

1 pkg active dry yeast	2 tsp. grated lemon peel
¼ cup warm water	1 tsp. vanilla extract
¾ cup scalded Superior Milk	1 tsp. almond extract
4 cups flour	5 eggs
½ cup butter	1½ cups dark or golden raisins,
¾ cup sugar	coarsely chopped
1½ tsp. salt	1 cup pecans, chopped

Sprinkle yeast into warm water in warm bowl. Let stand 5 minutes, then stir until dissolved. Add cooled scalded milk. Beat in 1 cup flour to make a smooth, thick batter. Cover and let rise in warm place 45 minutes, or until light. Cream butter, sugar, salt, lemon peel, vanilla and almond extract until light and fluffy. Beat in eggs one at a time. Add yeast mixture and remaining flour. Beat well. Stir in raisins and nuts. Turn into well greased 10 inch tube pan. Let rise until double in size. About 1½ hours.

Bake at 350 degrees 50 to 60 minutes, until richly browned. Turn out on wire rack to cool quickly. Sprinkle loaf with confectioners sugar.

Anna Durkee,

Keystone No. 5, O.E.S.

Christmas Fruit Bread

2 tsp., plus ½ cup sugar	1 tsp. mace
2 envelopes yeast	4½ cups (approx.) sifted all-
1½ tsp. salt	purpose flour
¼ cup soft butter	1 cup chopped mixed candied
½ cup Superior milk, scalded	fruits
2 eggs, well beaten	1 cup sultana raisins

Dissolve yeast in warm water and the two tsp. sugar. Combine remaining ½ cup sugar, salt and butter in large bowl. Add milk. Then cool. Add yeast to warm mixture. Stir in eggs, mace and 2½ cups of flour. Beat mixture with wooden spoon until smooth. About five minutes. Stir in fruit. Then add remaining flour to make soft dough. Turn out on board and knead until smooth and elastic, about five minutes. Let rise, 1¼ hours, or until doubled. Punch down and knead again. Let rise ten minutes. Make loaves and rise again for an hour. Bake in 375° oven for about 35 minutes. Makes two loaves. Can be iced.

Mrs. C. Fry

Dilly Casserole Bread

No. 1
1 pkg. dry yeast
¼ cup warm water
No. 2
1 cup cottage cheese, cream and
  heat to lukewarm
2 tbsp. sugar
1 tbsp. instant minced onion

OR celery seed
1 tbsp. butter, melted
2 tsp. dill seed
1 tsp. salt
¼ tsp. soda
1 unbeaten egg
2¼ to 2½ cups flour

Method:

(1) Soften yeast in water

(2) Combine ingredients in order given. Add flour gradually, beating well after each addition.

Cover and let rise until light and double in bulk. (Takes about 50 minutes). Punch down. Place into well greased 8 inch casserole. Let rise (about 40 minutes). Bake at 350° oven 40 - 50 minutes.

Brush with butter — sprinkle with salt.

Bea Koon

QUICK BREADS

Dark Nut Bread

3 eggs (beaten)
1 cup sugar
¼ cup shortening (melted)
2/3 cup Silver Lasses molasses
1 cup sour milk
1½ cups flour

1 tsp. salt
1 tsp. soda
1½ cups whole wheat OR
  graham flour
1 cup seedless raisins
½ cup walnuts (chopped)

Beat eggs and sugar together until thick. Add shortening and molasses. Mix well. Add sour milk, white flour, graham flour, raisins and nuts last. Beat until smooth. Bake 350° oven, 1 hour.

(Mrs. E. L.) Dot Brown

Date Bread

2 cups dates
1 cup brown sugar
1 tsp. soda
Over this pour:
1 cup boiling water.
Stir well. Add:

1 tbsp. butter
1 egg, unbeaten
Mix well. Add:
2 cups flour
1 tsp. salt

Bake in moderate oven 50 minutes approximately. Add 1 cup chopped walnuts, if desired.

Madeline Durkee

Date Bread

Cook in ¾ cup hot water:
  ½ - ¾ lb. dates & 1 tsp. soda
1 tsp. baking powder
½ tsp. brown sugar
1½ cups flour
METHOD:

½ tsp. salt
1 egg
Add ½ cup melted shortening
  last
A little vanilla makes a difference

Mix all dry ingredients, add egg, then dates and melted shortening. Put into greased pan and bake in 350° oven 55 - 60 minutes.

T. O. Breen

Banana Bran Bread

1½ cups sifted flour
2 tsp. baking powder
½ tsp. soda
½ tsp. salt
¼ cup shortening
1 cup white sugar

1 egg
1 cup bran flakes
1½ cups mashed bananas
1 tbsp. grated orange rind
2 tbsp. water
½ tsp. vanilla

Cream shortening, gradually blend in sugar. Add egg and beat until fluffy. Mix in bran flakes. Combine mashed bananas, orange rind, water, vanilla and add alternately with flour to creamed mixture. Combine only enough to blend the ingredients. Turn into greased loaf pan and bake 1 hour - 1¼ hour 350° oven.

Mrs. Archie Brannen

Banana Loaf (Bread)

½ cup butter
1 cup white sugar
2 eggs
3 mashed bananas (1 cup)

1½ cups flour
½ tsp. soda
1 tsp. baking powder
pinch of salt

Mix in order given, put in loaf pan. Let raise for a few minutes (15 - 20 minutes). Bake 45 minutes in moderate oven.

Mrs. Raymond Dease, Arcadia

Cinnamon Bread

¼ cup shortening
1 cup white sugar
2 eggs
2 cups flour
½ tsp. soda
1 tsp. baking powder

1 cup sour Superior milk (can use vinegar to sour milk)
1 tsp. vanilla
½ tsp. salt
Mix together:
2 tbsp. white sugar
1 tbsp. cinnamon

Cream shortening and sugar, add eggs, sour milk and vanilla. Sift flour, soda, baking powder and salt and add to creamed mixture.

Grease loaf pan, then add layer of batter on bottom and layer of cinnamon mixture, another layer of batter, finish with cinnamon mixture.

Bake 40 minutes at 350°

Pubnico Womens Institute

Carrot Bread

1 cup grated raw carrots (about 3 carrots)
2 eggs
½ cup sugar
¼ cup Silver Lasses molasses
¼ cup salad oil

2 cups sifted flour
1 tsp. soda
1 tsp. baking powder
½ tsp. salt
1 tsp. cinnamon
½ cup nuts

Line the sides and bottom of an 8 x 2¼ in. loaf pan, or two 5 x 2 in. pans. Grate the carrots. Beat the eggs until thick, beat in sugar, and continue beating until the sugar is dissolved. Fold in carrots, molasses and oil. Sift the dry ingredients together and add nutmeats, stirring to coat them with flour. Fold dry ingredients into carrot mixture. Pour in prepared pans and bake at 350° for forty minutes for the small loaves, and fifty minutes for large loaf. Cool the bread, then wrap for freezing.

If you like, the pan may be lined with aluminum foil, left about 9 ins. longer than the pan. When the bread has baked and cooled, wrap it by folding the ends of foil to cover the top of loaf. Bake for 5 minutes less than if the pan is liner with wax paper. This bread may be frozen from for two months in advance of need, which makes it very palatable.

Good luck to the users

Mrs. John Doucette

Carrot Loaf

¼ cup butter
1 cup white sugar
2 eggs
1¾ cups flour
1 tsp. baking powder
1 tsp. baking soda

pinch of salt
1 tsp. vanilla
1½ cups shredded carrots
½ cup chopped raisins
2 tsp. lemon juice
rind of 1 lemon

Mix in order given. Bake 50 minutes at 350°.

Mrs. H. B. Stackhouse

Coconut Bread

Cream together:
1 tbsp. butter
1 cup white sugar and add
  1 beaten egg

3 cups once sifted flour
4 tsp. baking powder

1 tsp. salt

Add alternately with:
1 cup Superior milk
1 tsp. vanilla
1 cup dessicated coconut

Bake 1 hour, 350° in small loaf tin.

Mrs. John Green

Christmas Orange Bread

½ cup shortening
¾ cup sugar
3 eggs
½ cup mashed bananas (choice)
½ cup orange juice
4 tsp. baking powder

¾ tsp. salt
2½ cups flour
1½ cups mixed fruit
¼ cup raisins
¾ cup nuts

Cream first two. Add beaten eggs. Combine bananas, fruit juice. Add alternately with dry ingredients and fruit and nuts. Loaf pan 9 x 5 x 3. Bake 1 hour, or more if necessary, oven temp. 350°.

Mrs. J. M. MacDonald, Hebron

Orange Nut Bread

1¾ cups flour
1½ tsp. baking powder
1 tsp. salt
¼ cup butter
¾ cups sugar

2 eggs
2 tsp. orange rind
⅓ cup chopped nuts
½ cup Superior milk

METHOD:

Mix flour, baking powder, salt together. Cream butter. Add sugar gradually. Beat in eggs one at a time. Add orange rind, then dry ingredients alternately with milk, mixing well.

Pour into greased loaf pan. Bake in oven 350°, 50 or 60 minutes. Cool 10 minutes.

Glaze top with 2 tbsp. orange juice and 1 tbsp. sugar. Return to oven for 1 minute. Cool.

Mrs. G. M. MacDonald

Blueberry Nut Bread

2 eggs	1 tsp. salt
1 cup white sugar	4 tsps. baking powder
1 cup Superior milk	½ tsp. cinnamon
3 tbsp. melted butter	1 cup blueberries
3 cups flour	½ cup walnuts (chopped)

Beat eggs. Add sugar and butter. Sift dry ingredients. Add alternately with milk, ending with flour. Add blueberries and nuts. Bake 50 - 60 minutes at 325° oven.

(Mrs. E. L.) Dot Brown

Allie's Fruit Bread

Sift into large bowl:	1 pkg. mixed fruit
¾ cups (scant) white sugar	½ cup chopped walnuts (optional)
4 tsp. baking powder	Beat:
¼ tsp. salt	2 eggs
2 cups flour	Add: 1 cup Superior milk
Add:	3 tbsp. melted butter

Add latter to flour mixture. Let stand in pan 30 minutes before baking in moderate oven 1 hour.

Peggy Cann

Pineapple Nut Bread

2¼ cups flour	¾ cup chopped nuts
¾ cup sugar	1½ cup undrained crushed pineapple
3 tsp. baking powder	apple
1 tsp. salt	1 beaten egg
½ tsp. soda	3 tbsp. butter
1 cup All Bran	

Sift dry ingredients, add remaining ingredients in order given. Bake in moderate oven 50 to 60 minutes. Better kept a few days to moisten.

Mrs. Austin Churchill

Orange Pecan Bread

3 cups sifted flour	2 eggs, well beaten
4 tsp. baking powder	½ cup Superior milk
½ tsp. baking soda	½ cup orange juice
½ tsp. salt	1 tbsp. grated orange rind
1 cup chopped pecans	¾ cup orange marmalade

Mix and sift dry ingredients, stir in chopped pecans. Combine well beaten eggs, milk, orange juice, orange rind and marmalade. Stir in dry ingredients. Mix well. Turn into greased 9 x 5 loaf pan and bake in moderate oven (350°) for 1 hour or until done. Cool in pan 10 minutes. Remove.

Mary Clulee

Raisin Bran Bread

1½ cups All Bran
½ cup Silver Lasses molasses
1¼ cups Superior milk
1 egg, well beaten
2 cups flour

1½ tsp. salt
1 tsp. soda
3 tsp. baking powder
½ cup sugar
1 cup raisins or nuts

Add All-Bran to molasses and milk. Soak 15 minutes. Stir in beaten egg. Sift flour, soda, salt, baking powder and sugar. Add flour mixture to bran mixture. Stir until just blended. Bake in moderate oven (350°) 1 hour.

Ann Rodney

Apple Sauce Nut Bread

2 cups sifted flour
¾ cup sugar
3 tsp. baking powder
1 tsp. salt
½ tsp. cinnamon

1 cup chopped nuts
1 egg
1 cup apple sauce
2 tbsp. melted shortening

METHOD:

In mixing bowl beat egg, add apple sauce and melted shortening. Add sifted ingredients. Stir just enough to blend. Pour in greased loaf pan. Bake in moderate oven (350°) 40 minutes to 1 hour.

Mrs. Austin Churchill

Lemon Bread

¾ cup white sugar
½ cup margarine (scant)
1½ cups all purpose flour
2 eggs

½ cup Superior milk
2 tsp. baking powder
½ tsp. salt
grated rind of 1 lemon

Mix sugar, margarine, eggs and salt together, then add flour, baking powder, lemon rind and Superior milk. Put in pan. Bake 1 hour in 350° oven. When done, take bread out. Leave in pan and pour mixture of: ½ cup white sugar dissolved in juice of 1 lemon and rind of 1 lemon, over bread and let set in pan 10 - 15 minutes.

Mrs. George Killam

Cranberry Bread

2 cups flour
½ tsp. salt
1½ tsp. baking powder
½ tsp. soda
1 egg

¾ cup white sugar
2 tbsp. butter
1 cup chopped walnuts
1 cup chopped raw cranberries

Put juice and rind of orange in measuring cup and enough water to make ¾ cup of liquid. Proceed as for quick bread. Bake one hour at 350°.

Mrs. Gordon Hughes

Cherry Coffee Bread

2 eggs, beaten
½ cup sugar
1 cup Superior milk
1 cup cornmeal
2 cups sifted bread flour
   OR 2¼ cups sifted pastry flour

4 tsp. baking powder
1 tsp. salt
2 tbsp. melted shortening
⅓ cup chopped maraschino
   cherries, drained

Line loaf pan with waxed paper. Grease paper. Heat oven to 350 deg. Beat eggs with rotary beater until light. Add sugar and milk. Beat until well blended. Add sifted dry ingredients and beat mixture about 1 minute. Lightly stir in the melted shortening and cherries. Bake in prepared pan in moderate oven for about 1 hour. Cool for 5 minutes before removing from pan.

BISCUITS

Basic Tea Biscuit Mix

6 cups all-purpose flour
2 tsp. salt
4 tbsp. baking powder
1 tbsp. sugar
½ lb. + 4 tbsp. shortening

Sift flour, salt, baking powder and sugar. Cut in shortening. Store in covered container in refrigerator.

If dough is to be rolled out, use ¼ cup Superior milk to 1 cup mix. Add milk all at once. Stir lightly. Knead 10 seconds.

Dot Lonergan

Pin Wheel Scones

2 cups flour
2 tbsp. sugar
shortening size of egg
½ tsp. salt
3½ tsp. baking powder
1 egg
½ cup Superior milk, or more

Mix dry ingredients, cut in shortening, add beaten egg and milk. Knead until smooth, roll into a rectangle.

Spread over rectangle a mixture of 4 tbsp. butter, melted, 1 cup brown sugar mixed. Roll like jelly roll, cut into slices and bake in muffin tins.

Mrs. Wm. Muir, Halifax, N.S.

Cloud Biscuts

2 cups sifted all-purpose flour
1 tbsp. sugar
4 tsp. baking powder
½ tsp. salt
½ cup shortening
1 beaten egg
2/3 cup Superior milk

Sift together dry ingredients, cut in shortening till mixture resembles coarse crumbs. Combine beaten eggs and milk; add to flour mixture all at once. Stir till dough follows fork around bowl. On a lightly floured board, knead gently with heel of hand about 20 times, dip cutter in flour, cut straight down — no twisting. Place on ungreased baking sheet (apart for crusty biscuits, touching for soft). Chill 1 - 3 hours. Bake in hot oven 450° for 10 - 14 minutes.

Mrs. Charles Robbins
Mrs. R. W. Balmanno

Tomato Cheese Biscuits

2 cups flour
4 tsp. baking powder
1 tsp. salt
4 tbsp. shortening
½ cup grated cheese
2/3 cup strained tomato juice

Mix dry ingredients, chop in shortening, add tomato juice and cheese. Pat out on floured board and cut. Bake in hot oven 450° 10 to 15 minutes.

Mrs. Gertrude Baker

Quick Cinnamon Buns

2 cups sifted flour
3 tsp. baking powder
½ tsp. salt
4 tbsp. sugar
6 tbsp. shortening

2/3 cup Superior Brand milk
2 tbsp. butter, melted
1 tsp. cinnamon
¼ cup sugar
½ cup raisins

Sift together flour, baking powder, salt, and sugar. Blend in shortening, add milk gradually, working it in with a knife to form soft dough. Turn out on lightly floured board, knead 30 seconds and roll to ¼ inch thickness. Brush over the top with melted butter, sprinkle with combined sugar and cinnamon. Sprinkle raisins on top of this and roll up like jelly roll. Cut in 1 inch pieces and place cut side down on greased pan. Bake in a hot oven 425° 15 to 20 minutes. Makes about 12. For variation use this same recipe and make Butterscotch Buns as follows: Melt 4 tablespoons butter on pan, add 4 tablespoons brown sugar, mix well. Spread over bottom of pan and sprinkle with ¼ cup of nutmeats. Place buns in pan cut side down. Bake in hot oven 425° 15 minutes, then reduce temperature to moderate 350° and bake 15 minutes longer.

Mrs. J. K. Taylor

MUFFINS

Tomato Luncheon Muffins

Sift once, measure:
2 cups all-purpose flour
Sift with:
3 tsp. baking powder
2 tbsp. sugar

1 tsp. salt (scant)
Combine:
1 egg, beaten
1 tin tomato soup (1¼ cups)
¼ cup shortening (melted)

Make a well in centre of dry ingredients, add the combined liquids all at once. Stir until just mixed. Fill greased muffin tins two-thirds full. Bake in hot oven 425°F about 20 minutes.
Yield: 12 - 16 muffins.

Mrs. Harold Langille

Blueberry or Date Muffins

2 cups sifted flour
4 tsp. baking powder
½ tsp. salt
¼ cup sugar
¼ cup or ½ stick margarine,
butter or Mazola oil

(I use Mazola oil)
1 beaten egg
1 cup Superior milk
1 cup washed and well drained
blueberries OR
½ cup cut-up dates

Sift flour, etc., in mixing bowl. Add shortening. Beat egg and mix with milk. Add to dry ingredients and mix only until dry ingredients are well dampened. Fold in berries or dates lightly. Bake in muffin pans in 450° oven about 20 minutes.

Blanche A. Larkin

Applesauce Bran Muffins

1¼ cups sifted all-purpose flour
3 tsp. baking powder
½ tsp. salt
2 tbsp. sugar
1 cup cooking bran

1 egg, stiffly beaten
⅓ cup Superior milk
¾ cup thick applesauce
¼ cup melted fat

Grease well 12 medium size muffin cups. Heat oven to 350 deg. F. Into a mixing bowl sift flour, baking powder, salt and sugar. Mix in bran. Combine egg, milk, applesauce and melted fat. Add to dry ingredients all at once, stirring only enough to moisten. Half fill cups. Bake 15 to 20 minutes.

Marguerite Atkinson

Walnut Muffins

1½ cups flour
½ tsp. salt
4 tsp. baking powder
1 tbsp. sugar
METHOD:

¾ cup Superior milk
2 well beaten eggs
¼ cup melted shortening
½ cup chopped walnuts

Sift flour with salt, baking powder and sugar. Combine remaining ingredients; add all at once. Stir just until dry ingredients are

moistened, but not smooth. On the last 4 or 5 stirs, add nuts. Fill greased muffin pans 2/3 full. Sprinkle muffins with mixture — 1 tbsp. sugar, ⅛ tsp. cinnamon and 2 tbsp. chopped nuts.
Bake in hot oven (425°) 25 minutes.

Helen G. Clarke

Melt In Your Mouth Blueberry Muffins

1st Mixture:
Cream well:
½ cup shortening
1 cup sugar
2 well beaten egg yolks
Beat whites of 2 eggs stiffly

2nd Mixture:
Sift together 3 times:
1½ cups sifted flour
1 tsp. baking powder
½ tsp. salt

Add 2nd mixture to 1st mixture alternately with ⅓ cup Superior milk. Fold in egg whites, 1 tsp. vanilla and lastly 1½ cups floured blueberries. Bake at 350° in muffin tins 20 - 25 minutes. You can sprinkle batter with sugar before baking.

Marguerite Atkinson

Grape Nut Muffins

2 cups sifted flour
3 tsp. baking powder
½ tsp. salt
4 tbsp. sugar

½ cup grape nuts
1 egg well beaten
1 cup Superior milk
7 tbsp. shortening

Sift flour once, measure and add baking powder, salt and sugar and sift again. Add grape nuts and mix well. Combine eggs, milk and shortening. Add to flour mixture and beat only enough to dampen all flour. Turn into greased muffin tins, filling only about 2/3 full. Bake in hot oven 425° about 25 minutes.

Mrs. Arthur Cosman

Spiced Apple Muffins

2 cups pastry flour
½ tsp. cinnamon
½ cup sugar
4 tsp. baking powder
¼ tsp. salt

1 beaten egg
1 cup Superior Milk
4 tsp. melted butter
1 cup chopped apples

Sift dry ingredients. Beat egg, add milk and melted butter and mix with dry ingredients, stirring only enough to wet all the flour. Do not beat. Fold in chopped apples, put in greased muffin tins, sprinkle tops with a mixture of 2 tsp. sugar and 1½ tsp. cinnamon. Bake in hot oven until done.

Mrs. Percy Hood

QUICK COFFEE CAKES

Cherry Streusel Coffee Cake

1½ cups all purpose flour
3 tsp. baking powder
½ tsp. salt
¾ cup sugar
½ cup shortening
2 eggs
1 tsp. vanilla

½ cup Superiod milk
1 15 oz. tin pitted red cherries
  packed in syrup, drained
½ cup all purpose flour
¼ cup brown sugar
¼ cup butter

Measure flour (without sifting))onto a square of waxed paper. Add baking powder and salt. Stir to blend.

Cream sugar, shortening, eggs and vanilla until light and fluffy. Add blended dry ingredients alternately with milk. Mix until smooth.

Spread half the batter in bottom of well-greased 9-inch square pan. Arrange drained cherries evenly over batter. Spread remaining batter evenly over cherries.

Combine flour (not sifted) and brown sugar in bowl. Cut in butter until particles are the size of small peas. Sprinkle evenly over batter.

Bake at 350°F. (moderate) for 40-45 minutes. Serve warm.

Yield: 9 or 12 servings.

Note: Coffee cake can be made a day ahead and reheated before serving.

R. Pink

Quick Coffee Cake

¾ cup sugar
1 egg
¼ cup shortening
½ tsp. salt

1½ cups flour
2½ tsp. baking powder
½ cup Superior milk

Mix in order given. Put in greased 8 x 12 x 2 inch pan. Top with following:

6 tbsp. flour
2 tbsp. cinnamon

½ cup brown sugar
6 tbsp. butter

Grated rind of one orange and chopped walnuts may be added. Sprinkle over dough and bake in 375° oven for 15 to 20 minutes.

Mrs. H. D. MacLeod

Maple Nut Coffee Cake

1¾ cups sifted pastry flour or
  1 2/3 cups sifted all-purpose
  (bread) flour or instantized
  flour
¾ tsp. salt
3 tsp. baking powder
⅓ cup shortening
1 tbsp. grated lemon rind

1 egg
3 tbsp. Superior milk
2/3 cup maple syrup
Topping:
2 tbsp. butter or margarine,
  melted
2 tbsp. maple syrup
¼ cup sliced almonds, toasted

Heat oven to 350 degrees. Grease an 8-inch square cake pan.

Sift into mixing bowl, the flour, salt and baking powder. Beat in shortening. Add lemon rind.

Beat together egg, milk and syrup. Gradually add to flour mixture. Beat thoroughly. Pour batter into prepared pan.

Combine topping ingredients and spread over top of batter. Bake in moderate oven 30 to 35 minutes. Serve warm with butter, if desired.

Note: When using glass cake pan, bake at 325 degrees for 35 to 40 minutes.

Y. Auxiliary

Orange Coffee Cake

A fluffy, light, flavorsome cake.

Topping:
⅓ cup sifted pastry flour
⅓ cup brown sugar
1 tbsp. grated orange rind
1 tbsp. melted butter or
  margarine
Cake:
1 cup + 2 tbsp. sifted pastry
  flour
2 tsp. baking powder

½ tsp. salt
¼ cup shortening
⅓ cup granulated sugar
1 egg
2 tsp. grated orange rind
⅛ tsp. almond flavoring
½ cup ready-to-eat bran
¼ cup orange juice
¼ cup Superior milk

To Make Topping: Sift together flour and brown sugar. Mix in rind and melted butter with a fork until crumbly.

To Mix Batter: Blend shortening and sugar. Add egg, grated rind and flavoring. Beat well. Stir in bran, juice and milk, then sifted dry ingredients. Mix only enough to combine ingredients. Pour into greased 8-inch square cake pan. Sprinkle with topping. Bake in moderately hot oven of 375 degrees for 25 minutes. Serve warm.

Y. Auxiliary

CAKES

Plain Cake Tried And True

1½ cups all purpose flour, warmed & sifted 2 or 3 times
1 tsp. baking powder
¼ tsp. salt

1 cup butter, worked into flour until creamy
Beat 4 eggs until very light
Add: 1 cup sugar

Combine the two mixtures, adding a little of egg mixture at a time, and beat vigorously after each addition. Flavor with lemon extract. Put in loaf pan and bake in 350° oven about 50 minutes.

Pubnico Women's Institute

Cream Cake

Beat 2 eggs well
Add:
1 cup sugar
1 cup thick Superior whipping cream

¼ tsp. salt
1 tsp. vanilla
Add:
1½ cups cake flour, sifted with 2 rounded tsp. baking powder

Bake in 8 x 8 pan 350° for 35 minutes. Makes a small, delicate cake. Delicious frosted or as an accompaniment to fresh berries.

Mae Ladd

California Cake

2 eggs, beaten until light
1 cup white sugar
1 cup flour
1 tsp. baking powder

pinch of salt
½ cup hot Superior milk
1 tbsp. butter in milk

Beat all together and bake 20 minutes in 400° oven. Remove from oven.

Mix:
3 tbsp. butter
5 tbsp. brown sugar

2 tbsp. Superior cream or can milk
½ cup coconut

Pour on top of cake and return to oven until brown.

Mrs. Edmund Boudreau

Beatrice Shane's Sponge Cake

7 eggs
1 cup sugar
½ tsp. salt

juice of small lemon
1 cup Swansdown flour

Beat whites a little stiff and then add ½ cup of sugar and beat for 10 minutes. Beat 7 yolks with rest of sugar and beat until thick and lemon colored. Add sifted flour to yolks with lemon juice, then add the yolk mixture to whites, folding in. Bake at 350° oven 1 hour or until brown and firm to the touch.

Gold Cake

2 cups sifted cake flour	3 egg yolks, beaten until thick
2 tsp. baking powder	and lemon colored
½ cup butter	¾ cup Superior milk
1 cup sugar	1 tsp. vanilla or ½ tsp. orange
	extract

Sift flour once, measure, add baking powder and sift together three times. Cream butter thoroughly, add sugar gradually and cream together until light and fluffy. Add egg yolks and beat well. Add flour alternately with milk, a small amount at a time, beating after each addition until smooth. Add flavoring and beat thoroughly. Bake in greased pan 8x8x2 375° 50 minutes.

Mrs. T. A. M. Kirk

Silver Cake

2 cups sifted cake flour	1 cup sugar
2 tsp. baking powder	2/3 cup Superior milk
¼ tsp. salt	1 tsp. vanilla
½ cup butter	3 egg whites stiffly beaten

Sift flour once, measure, add baking powder, and salt, and sift together three times. Cream butter thoroughly, add sugar gradually, and cream together until light and fluffy. Add flour alternately with milk, a small amount at a time, beating after each addition until smooth. Add vanilla. Fold in egg whites quickly and thoroughly. Bake in moderate oven 375° 50 minutes.

Mrs. T. A. M. Kirk

Potato Flour Cake

4 eggs	½ cup potato flour
¾ cup sugar	½ tsp. salt
1 tsp. lemon flavoring	1 tsp. baking powder

Separate eggs. Beat yolks until light, add sugar. Beat 3 egg whites until stiff (use 4th for frosting), and fold into yolk mixture. Lightly fold in sifted dry ingredients.

Bake in 8 x 8 pan 350° 35 - 45 minutes. Frost with fluffy boiled icing tinted pale pink.

For a decorative touch, cut off very thin layer of cake. Frost cake, then replace cut layer of cake. This gives a lace effect to the frosting.

Nina Slade

Fluffy Orange Cake

2½ cups cake flour
2½ tsp. baking powder
¾ tsp. salt
1½ tsp. grated lemon peel
1 tbsp. grated orange rind
2/3 cup shortening

1½ cup sugar
3 eggs
2 tbsp. lemon juice
¼ cup orange juice
¼ cup Superior milk

Sift together flour, baking powder and salt. Add lemon and orange rind to shortening and cream well with sugar until light and fluffy. Add eggs, one at a time. Beat well. Add flour mixture alternately with juices, then milk, a small amount at a time. Bake in two 9 inch round pans in 375° oven for 30 minutes. When cool frost with 7 minute icing.

Tested

Pineapple Parfait Cake

2½ cups sifted cake flour
1½ cups sugar
3½ tsp. baking powder
1 tsp. salt
2/3 cup butter

½ tsp. grated lemon rind
¾ cup canned pineapple juice
¼ cup water
4 egg whites, unbeaten

Sift flour, sugar, baking powder and salt into mixing bowl. Drop in butter and lemon rind. No pre-creaming with butter. Add about 2/3 of combined pineapple juice and water and beat 150 strokes. Takes only a minutes or so. Scrape bowl and spoon often. Add egg whites unbeaten and mix well. Bake in two 9" well greased pans in moderate oven 20 to 30 minutes.

Frost with Pineapple Parfait Frosting (See frosting section).

Virginia Ross

Golden Chiffon Cake

1 cup cake flour sifted several
    times
¾ cup sugar

1½ tsp. baking powder
⅛ tsp. salt

Measure above and sift together in mixing bowl. Make a well and add:

¼ cup Mazola oil
3 egg yolks
⅜ cup (¼ cup plus 2 tbsp.) cold
    water or orange juice

1 tsp. vanilla or
1 tsp. grated orange rind

Beat above with spoon until smooth. In another bowl measure:

½ cup egg whites (3 or 4)   ¼ tsp. cream of tartar

Whip until very stiff. Pour egg yolk mixture gradually over egg whites, gently folding until just blended. Pour into ungreased angel cake or 9 inch square pan and bake at 300° for 30 - 40 minutes.

Invert pan as soon as taken from oven so that cake does not touch, and let stand until cold. The success of this cake depends on slow baking.

Pubnico Women's Institute

Coffee Pecan Chiffon Cake

Sift together:
1 cup pre-sifted pastry flour
or ⅞ cup sifted all purpose
flour

1½ tsp. baking powder
½ tsp. salt
2 tbsp. instant coffee
⅞ cup white sugar

Make a well in these dry ingredients and add
5 tbsp. cooking oil
3 egg yolks

⅓ cup water
1 tsp. vanilla

Stir until well blended. Stir in
¼ cup finely chopped pecans
Sprinkle 4 egg whites at room

temp. with:
¼ tsp. cream of tartar

Beat until very stiff. Fold first mixture into egg white, ¼ at a time. Fold gently until well blended. Pour into ungreased 8 inch tube pan. Bake in 325 deg. oven for one hour. Allow to hang upside down until cold. Remove from pan gently. Frost if desired.

Mrs. Irving Pink

Heavenly Pink Chiffon Cake

2 2/3 cups sifted cake flour
1½ cups sugar

1½ tsp. salt
4 tsp. baking powder

Mix the above dry ingredients and add:
2/3 cup Mazola
4 egg yolks
¾ cup water
1 tsp. vanilla
2 tsp. cherry juice

few drops red food coloring
Beat 4 egg whites with
¼ tsp. cream of tartar, until
stiff

Fold into mixture. Bake in tube pan 1 hour at 325°.

Mrs. J. D. Cohen

Banana Cream Chiffon Cake

Step 1:
Measure and sift together:
1⅛ cups (1 cup plus 2 tbsp.)
sifted cake flour
¾ cup sugar
1½ tsp. baking powder
½ tsp. salt
Step 2:
Make a well and add in order:

¼ cup salad oil such as Wesson
2 unbeaten egg yolks
3 tbsp. cold water
½ cup crushed very ripe bananas
1 tsp. vanilla
Beat with spoon until smooth.
Beat 4 egg whites,
¼ tsp. cream of tartar
until it forms stiff peaks

Pour into egg mixture, gently folding until blended. Do not beat. Pour into ungreased 9 in. tube pan immediately. Bake 50 to 55 minutes in 325° oven. When cool split cake crosswise into 2 or 3 layers (whatever desired). Spread whipped cream between layers and over top and sides. Garnish with banana slices.

Mrs. Russell Cleveland

Carrot Cake

4 eggs	1 tsp. vanilla
2 cups sugar	½ cup chopped nuts
2 cups grated carrots	Topping:
3 cups sifted all-purpose flour	2 tbsp. melted butter
1 tsp. salt	½ cup brown sugar
3 tsp. baking powder	¼ cup chopped nuts
½ tsp baking soda	2 tbsp. Superior milk
1 cup salad oil	

Heat oven 350°. Grease and flour 9½" tube pan. Beat eggs, gradually blend in sugar, then grated carrot. Sift dry ingredients and add alternately with the oil to egg mixture. Blend in vanilla and nuts Bake 45 minutes.

Remove from oven and quickly spread on topping which has been mixed together and return to oven for 15 minutes.

Emily Doucette

Toasted Sesame Seed Cake

2¼ cups cake flour (sifted)	½ cup toasted sesame seeds
1½ cups sugar	⅓ cup soft shortening
1 tbsp. baking powder	1 cup Superior milk
¾ tsp. salt	2 eggs
¼ tsp. mace	

Sift first 5 ingredients into mixing bowl. Stir in sesame seeds. Add shortening and ¾ cup of the milk. Beat 2 minutes with electric mixer at low speed or 300 strokes by hand. Add remaining milk and eggs. Beat 1 minutes with mixer at low speed or 150 strokes by hand. Scrape bowl and beater often. Pour into greased and floured 9" tube pan. Bake 1 hour at 350° oven.

Tested

Blueberry Cake

1 cup sugar	2 tsp. baking powder
½ cup shortening	½ tsp. salt
1 egg	½ cup Superior milk
2 cups flour	1 cup blueberries

Cream shortening and add sugar a little at a time, add the beaten egg. Add flour, salt and baking powder alternately with the milk. Fold in the washed berries. Bake in a 350° oven for 35 minutes.

Mrs. Gertrude Wathen
Peggy Cann

Cherry Loaf Cake

Cream:
⅓ cup butter
1 cup brown sugar
Add: 1 egg, unbeaten, and
   cream again
Sift together:
2 cups sifted all purpose flour

2 tsp. baking powder
¾ tsp. salt
30 maraschino cherries, cut in
   quarters
1 cup liquid (cherry juice and
   Superior milk)

Sprinkle some of the measured flour over the cut cherries before adding them to the batter.

Bake in oven 350°, less than 1 hour in a pan 9 x 5 x 2¾ deep.

Lois Sweeny

Spice Cake

2 cups all purpose flour
1⅓ cups white sugar
1¼ tsp. baking powder
¾ tsp. soda
1 tsp. salt
2 tsp. cinnamon
¼ tsp. cloves

¾ tsp. nutmeg
¼ tsp. allspice
¼ tsp. ginger
½ cup Crisco
¾ cup sour Superior milk
1 tsp. vanilla
2 unbeaten eggs

Sift dry ingredients together into mixing bowl, and add Crisco. Add milk (may be soured with 1 tsp. vinegar), and beat 2 minutes at No. 3 speed. Add vanilla and eggs and beat 2 minutes at low speed (No. 2). Bake in 9x9 pan at 350 degrees 1 hour. Frost with coffee icing made by adding one tbsp. instant coffee to butter icing — only a drop of vanilla, if any.

Mrs. J. T. Balmanno

Macaroon Cake

½ cup butter
½ cup sugar
3 egg yolks, well beaten
½ cup Superior milk
1 cup flour

3 tsp. baking powder
¼ tsp. salt
1 tsp. vanilla
1 tsp. almond

Mix as in order given, place in 9 x 9 pan.

Beat 3 egg whites until stiff
Fold in:

½ cup sugar
1 cup coconut

Spread on cake mixture. Bake at 350° about 45 or 50 minutes.

Anna Porter

Graham Wafer Cake

25 single graham wafers, rolled
    fine
1 cup dessicated coconut
2 tbsp. butter
1 egg

¾ cup white sugar
2 tbsp. flour
1½ tsp. baking powder
1 cup Superior milk
1 tsp. rum flavoring

Combine graham wafers, flour and baking powder. Mix butter, sugar and egg. Add milk and flavoring, then dry ingredients. Bake 25 minutes at 350°.

Mrs. H. B. Stackhouse

Mystery Cake

1 pkg. Duncan Hines golden
    cake mix
1 pkg. lemon instant jello
    pudding

½ cup Mazola oil
4 eggs, room temperature
1 cup cold water

Put cake mix and jello powder in large bowl. Add rest of ingredients and beat well. Bake in 9" tube pan 45 to 60 minutes at 350°

Mrs. A. E. Ford

Chocolate Cake

1⅓ cups all purpose flour
1 tsp. baking powder
1 tsp. baking soda
½ tsp. salt
½ cup soft shortening (part
    butter)

1 cup sugar
½ tsp. vanilla
2 eggs
2 sqs. Bakers unsweetened
    melted chocolate
1 cup Superior milk

Preheat oven to 350°F. Grease and lightly flour two 8" layer pans. Measure flour, baking powder, soda, salt on waxed paper, blend well. Cream shortening till fluffy, gradually add sugar, mixing till creamy. Add vanilla. Add eggs, beating well after each. Blend in chocolate, add dry ingredients, alternately with milk, blending well after each addition (begin and end with dry ingredients).

Turn batter evenly into pans. Bake 30 - 35 minutes at 350°F. Remove. Let stand 5 minutes; turn out on rack to cool. Frost as desired.

Mrs. F. Bruce Trask

Speckle Cake

1 cup sugar
½ cup butter
2 cups sifted flour
3 tsp. baking powder
1½ tsp. vanilla
3 egg whites beaten with ½ cup

sugar (sugar optional)
½ tsp. salt
1 cup Superior milk
2 sqs. Bakers bitter chocolate
(grated)

Cream butter and add sugar gradually. Add sifted flour, salt and baking powder, alternately with milk. Add vanilla and grated chocolate. Fold in beaten egg whites. Bake in moderate oven 45 minutes in 8 x 8 x 2 pan.

Mrs. Nate Bain

Tri-Marble Delight Cake

½ cup shortening
1 cup granulated sugar
2 eggs
1½ cups pastry flour

2 tsp. baking powder
½ tsp. salt
½ cup Superior milk
½ tsp. vanilla

Blend shortening and sugar. Add eggs and beat until creamy. Sift dry ingredients together twice. Then add alternately with milk to sugar mixture. Add vanilla. Divide batter into three portions.

LIGHT PORTION — Use ⅓ of batter.

SPICE PORTION — Add ⅛ tsp. cinnamon, ⅛ tsp cloves to ⅓ of batter.

CHOCOLATE PORTION — Add ½ square melted Bakers chocolate. Mix with ⅛ tsp. soda, 1 tsp. hot water and 1 tsp. granulated sugar. Add to remaining ⅓ batter.

Drop above batters alternately in greased angel cake tin. Bake 350°F. 45 minutes.

Frosting: white 7 minute boiled frosting.

Mrs. J. D. Cohen

Two-Layer Dark Chocolate Cake

1 cup white sugar
1 cup brown sugar
½ cup butter or margarine
Cream above ingredients:
2 egg yolks (reserve whites for boiled icing)
OR 1 full egg
1 cup Superior milk in which is dissolved

1 tsp. soda
½ cup Bakers cocoa, dissolved in ½ cup warm water, and put another tsp. soda in cocoa
2 cups all purpose flour
1 tsp. cream of tartar
1 tsp. salt, sifted together. Add:
1 tsp. vanilla last

Divide mixture and bake in two layer pans in moderate oven for approximately 25 minutes.

This cake is especially good when put together with chocolate or mocha filling, and topped with boiled icing.

Helen Brezet

Chocolate Cake

1 cup sugar	1 tsp. soda
1 lg. tsp. shortening	3 lg. tbsp. Bakers cocoa
1 egg	salt
½ cup Superior milk	vanilla
1 cup flour	½ cup hot water
1 tsp. baking powder	

Mix in order given. Batter will be thin but will make a perfect cake. Bake in moderate oven.

Doris Forbes

Sour Cream Chocolate Cake

⅓ cup butter	1 tsp. soda
1¼ cups sugar	vanilla
1 egg	¾ cup sweet Superior milk
3 sqs. Bakers chocolate	2 cups sifted pastry flour
½ cup thick sour Superior cream	

Cream sugar and butter, add 1 unbeaten egg, then melted chocolate, sour cream and fold in flour, (in which soda and salt have been sifted) alternately with milk. Flavor. Bake in 9 x 9 pan at 350°, at least 50 minutes.

Mrs. Harold Guest

Chocolate Intrigue

3 cups all purpose flour	1 cup Superior milk
2 tsp. double action baking powder	1½ tsp. vanilla
½ tsp. salt	¾ cup chocolate syrup
1 cup butter or margarine	¼ tsp. soda
2 cups sugar	¼ tsp. peppermint extract (optional)
3 unbeaten eggs	

Sift flour, baking powder and salt. Cream butter, add sugar till light. Blend in eggs, one at a time. Combine milk and vanilla. Add alternately with dry ingredients. Pour 2/3 of batter into 10 in. tube pan greased on bottom.

Blend into remaining batter, chocolate syrup, soda and peppermint extract. Pour chocolate batter over white batter. DO NOT MIX. Bake in 350 deg. oven 45 mins. Place sheet of foil over top of pan and bake 20 to 25 minutes longer. Cool completely in pan. Sprinkle icing sugar or thin icing on top of cake.

(Use recipe for chocolate syrup or sauce from Nestles Quick box.)

Mrs. Herman Shapiro

Chocolate Custard Cake

1 cup brown sugar
½ cup cocoa or 4 sqs. Bakers chocolate

½ cup Superior milk

Put on stove, heat slowly to a custard. Cool before adding to cake part.

CAKE PART

½ cup butter or margarine
1 cup brown sugar
2 egg yolks
½ cup Superior milk and 2 cups flour, added alternately
salt

Add cooled custard, vanilla,
2 beaten egg whites
Lastly, 1 tsp. soda dissolved in little hot water

Bake in oven temp. 350° for 35 - 40 minutes.

Dorothy Robbins

Cookie Sheet Chocolate Cake

Heat 1 cup Superior milk, 2 tbsp. Bakers cocoa. Stir until mixture begins to thicken. Remove from heat. Add and beat ½ cup shortening (or butter) and 1 egg. Add 1 cup brown sugar, well packed, ¼ tsp. salt, 1 tsp. vanilla, 1 cup all-purpose flour, ½ tsp. baking powder. Mix 1 tsp. baking soda in 1 tbsp. Superior milk. Add soda mixture to cocoa-flour mixture, beat well. Use shallow cake pan or cookie sheet 15" x 10½". Bake 12 to 15 minutes in moderate oven (350° F.).

Ice with Fudge Icing.

Mrs. George Ellis

Limelight Fudge Cake

2 cups boiling water
4 sqs. Bakers bitter chocolate
3 cups sifted all purpose flour
1 tsp. baking powder
1½ tsp. soda

1 tsp. salt
2 cups sugar
2/3 cup butter or shortening
2 eggs
1 tsp. vanilla

Pour water on bitter chocolate in bowl, cool until lukewarm without stirring. Sift dry ingredients. Cream butter and sugar, add eggs and vanilla, cream well. Pour off water from chocolate and save. Blend chocolate into first mixture. Add dry ingredients alternately with water, blending after each addition. Pour into a 10 inch tube pan, well greased and floured on the bottom only.

Bake at 350 degs. for one hour. This is a nice moist cake that keeps well.

Mrs. Wilmot Dean

Marble Layer Cake

2 cups sifted cake flour
2½ tsp. baking powder
¼ tsp. salt
½ cup shortening
1 cup sugar

1 tsp. vanilla
2 eggs, separated
¾ cup Superior milk
1 sq. Bakers unsweetened chocolate

Grease and flour 2 8" or 9" cake pans (round). Heat oven to 375°F. Sift together flour, baking powder and salt. Cream shortening and sugar together until fluffy. Add vanilla. Beat egg whites until stiff, but not dry. Add beaten egg yolks to the shortening mixture, and beat well. Add dry ingredients alternately with the milk. Beat until smooth after each addition. Fold in egg whites. Divide batter in two equal portions. Add melted chocolate to one portion. Spoon batter into prepared pans, alternating light and dark batter. Bake 25 to 30 minutes or until top of cake springs back when gently touched with the finger. Cool in pans 10 minutes on rack, then remove from pans and cool completely. Put layers together and frost with your favorite butter (chocolate) frosting.

Clara Harris

Burnt Sugar Cake

BURNT SUGAR SYRUP
½ cup sugar

⅓ cup boiling water

Heat sugar in a small heavy skillet, stirring as it melts. When it is dark colored, slowly add boiling water, and stir until dissolved.

CAKE
3 cups sifted cake flour
3 tsp. baking powder
¾ tsp. salt
¾ cup butter

1 cup sugar
3 eggs, separated
1 cup Superior milk
1 tsp. vanilla

Measure flour, add baking powder, salt and sift together twice. Cream butter, add sugar gradually and beat until light and fluffy. Add egg yolks one at a time, beating well after each. Add 3 tbsp. burnt sugar syrup and blend. Add flour mixture alternately with milk. Add vanilla. Beat egg whites until stiff, but not dry. Fold quickly into batter. Turn into 2 prepared pans and bake in moderate oven of 350° for 30 minutes. Let cool before removing from pans. Frost with butter icing to which 1 tbsp. burnt sugar syrup has been added. Boil remaining syrup until thick and dribble over frosting on cake.

Mrs. Irving Pink

Lazy Daisy Cake or Squares

1 cup dates, cut small
1 cup boiling water poured over
dates and let stand until cool
Cream together:
¼ cup butter
1 cup white sugar
1 well beaten egg

1 tsp. vanilla
Sift together:
1½ cup flour
1 tsp. baking powder
1 tsp. soda
¾ tsp. salt

Add alternately with date mixture to creamed mixture. Bake 40 minutes in 350° oven.

TOPPING

After cake is cooled, make the following:

5 tbsp. brown sugar
3 tbsp. butter

2 tbsp. Superior cream

Boil above mixture 2 minutes. Remove from stove and add:

½ cup coconut

¼ cup chopped nuts

Spread on cooled cake and bake until brown. Use 8 x 8" pan.

Pubnico Women's Institute

Prize Orange Cake

½ cup butter
1 cup granulated sugar
1 egg
2 eggs, separated
½ cup sour Superior milk
1 fairly large orange

1 cup seedless raisins
2 cups flour
1½ tsp. baking powder
⅛ tsp. salt
½ tsp. soda, dissolved in
1 tsp. hot water

Squeeze juice of orange and add to milk. Put remainder of orange through food chopper, together with raisins, and add stiffly beaten egg whites to the batter made same as butter cake. Add minced rind and bake in moderate oven 350°, for 45 minutes.

Mildred Hayes

Kiss Me Cake

2 cups all purpose flour
1 tsp. soda
1 tsp. salt
½ cup butter
1 cup sugar

2 eggs
1 lg. orange (reserve juice)
grind rind with 1 cup raisins
1 cup Superior milk

Sift dry ingredients. Cream sugar and butter. Blend eggs, one at a time. Add ground oranges and raisins. Add milk and dry ingredients. Blend. Bake in 8x8 pan in 350 oven 45 minutes. Cool 15 minutes. Pour orange juice over warm cake. Add topping!

TOPPING
¼ cup sugar

1 tsp. cinnamon
¼ cup chopped walnuts

Mrs. Laurie Mushkat

Butterscotch Pudding Cake

2 cups sifted pastry flour or
  1¾ cups sifted all purpose
  flour
2½ tsp. baking powder
½ tsp. salt

1 pkg. butterscotch pudding
10 tbsp. butter or margarine
1 cup sugar
1 egg & 1 tsp. vanilla
2 egg yolks
¾ cup Superior milk

Preheat oven to 350° (moderate). Sift flour, baking powder, salt, and butterscotch pudding powder together 3 times. Cream butter or margarine, gradually blend in sugar. Beat the egg and egg yolks together until thick and light. Add to creamed mixture, part at a time, beat well after each addition. Measure milk, add vanilla. Add flour mixture to creamed mixture, a quarter at a time, alternating with 3 additions of milk. Combine lightly after each addition. Turn into prepared pan. Bake 25 to 30 minutes or until done. Ice with Fluffy Vanilla Frosting. Sprinkle top with cocoa.

FLUFFY VANILLA FROSTING

In top of double boiler, combine 2 egg whites, 2 cups sugar, ½ cup cold water. Place over boiling water and cook, beating constantly with rotary beater until frosting stands in peaks, about twelve minutes. Remove from heat. Beat in 2 tsp. vanilla, 1 tsp. baking powder. Spread immediately.

Mrs. George Ellis

Apple Sauce Cake

½ cup butter or shortening
1 cup white sugar
1 egg well beaten
1¾ cups flour (all purpose)
¼ tsp. salt
1 level tsp. soda
1 level tsp. baking powder

1 cup cooked thick apple sauce
  (unsweetened)
1 cup seedless raisins
½ cup chopped walnuts
½ cup dates
1 level tsp. cinnamon
½ tsp. cloves

Sift together flour, spice and baking powder. Stir soda into apple sauce. Cream shortening, sugar and egg until light and fluffy. Add dry ingredients. Bake in slow oven 325° for about 1 hour or more.

Mrs. Leo Muise

Honey Cake

4 eggs
1 cup white sugar
1 lb. honey, melted
¾ cup of coffee
½ cup Mazola oil

½ tsp. soda
3 tsp. baking powder
4 cups flour
rind and juice of one orange

Beat the whites with sugar, add egg yolks, honey with soda, coffee, oil and rind. Add flour and baking powder, alternately with orange juice. Bake in 8 x 12 pan in 350° oven for 1 hour.

Alice Garson

Apricot Nectar Cake

2 cups sifted pastry flour
3½ tsp. baking powder
½ tsp. salt
4 tbsp. instant skim-milk powder
½ cup butter
1 cup granulated sugar
2 eggs
1 cup canned apricot nectar
½ tsp. vanilla

¼ tsp. almond extract
FROSTING
¼ cup butter
2½ cups sifted icing sugar
1 egg yolk
½ tsp. salt
3 tbsp. apricot nectar
¼ tsp. almond extract
10 toasted almonds

Grease and line bottoms of two 8-inch layer cake pans with greased, waxed paper. Heat oven to 375 degrees.

Sift together flour, baking powder and salt. Add instant skim-milk powder and sift again.

Blend butter and sugar thoroughly. Add eggs one at a time. Beat well after each addition.

Combine apricot nectar, vanilla and almond extract. Add to butter mixture ⅓ at a time alternately with flour mixture, combining lightly after each addition.

Turn batter into prepared pans and bake for 25 minutes in moderately hot oven.

Let cake remain in pans for 10 minutes before removing to cake rack to cool completely. When cool, frost cake with Apricot Nectar Frosting and decorate with almonds.

To Make Frosting: Beat butter until soft. Add about half of sugar, beating well. Add egg yolk, apricot nectar, almond extract, salt and remaining sugar. Beat until smooth.

Tested

Jack and Jerry Cake

1 cup butter
2 cups sugar
3 eggs
1 cup Superior milk
1½ cups all purpose flour

1½ cups cake flour
1 tsp. baking powder
¼ tsp. salt
1 tsp. vanilla

Cream butter and sugar and add beaten eggs. Sift dry ingredients together. Add alternately with the milk. Add vanilla. Divide batter into two parts. To one part add:
1 tsp. cinnamon
2 tbsp. Silver Lasses molasses
¼ cup raisins
¼ cup walnuts

Place dark part in bottom of pan (9 x 9), and the light part on top. Bake in 350° oven until done (45 - 50 minutes). Don't overbake.

Mrs. Bruce Raymond

Crumb Date Cake

1 cup white sugar   2 cups sifted flour
¾ cup butter

Mix together and keep out ½ cup for topping. Sprinkle this over cake before putting in the oven.

Add:
1 cup sour Superior milk   1 tbsp. vanilla
  or buttermilk   1 egg
1 tsp. baking soda   1 cup dates, cut fine

Dissolve soda in milk. Add egg, flavoring and dates. Bake in 8 x 8 pan in moderate oven (375°).

Hospital Auxiliary

Lemon Molasses Cup Cakes

2 cups flour   ½ cup sugar
2 tsp. baking powder   1 egg
½ tsp. soda   ½ cup Silver Lasses molasses
1½ tsp. cinnamon   ½ cup Superior milk
¼ tsp. salt   1 tsp. lemon flavoring
½ cup butter

Sift flour, measure and add baking powder, soda, cinnamon and salt. Cream butter, add sugar gradually and cream until light and fluffy. Add well beaten egg and Silver Lasses molasses. Then add dry ingredients alternately with Superior milk. Add lemon. Beat well. Bake 350° oven for 25 minutes. Makes 16.

Tested Y Auxiliary

Batter For Small Cakes

¾ cup butter   ⅛ tsp. salt
1 cup sugar   ½ tsp. baking powder
4 eggs   2 tbsp. Superior milk
1½ cups flour   1 tsp. vanilla

Cream butter well. Add sugar gradually. Beat very light and add eggs. Sift flour, salt, baking powder together. Add milk and vanilla. Put in small cupcake tins or bake in a shallow pan and cut in fancy shapes. Bake in slow oven, 350°.

H. G. Clarke

Never Fail Cream Puffs

½ cup boiling water   ¼ tsp. salt
¼ cup butter or margarine

Put in saucepan and bring to a boil. Quickly add ½ cup flour while still on stove. Stir hard.

Remove from stove and add 2 eggs (unbeaten), one at a time. Beat until smooth. Drop from teaspoon on pan and bake for about 40 - 45 minutes in a 400° oven. Open and fill with whipped cream when cool.

Mrs. George Nickerson

Lemon Pound Cake

2/3 cup shortening (part butter   Mix together. Then add:
  may be used)   2¼ cups cake flour
1¼ cups sugar   1¼ tsp. salt
1 tsp. grated lemon peel   1 tsp. baking powder
1 tbsp. lemon juice   Mix and add:
2/3 cup Superior milk   3 eggs, one at a time, beating
                        well after each egg

Bake in loaf pan for 1 hour 20 minutes, at 300°. When cool, sift icing sugar over.

Mrs. Milledge Nickerson
Tusket Women's Institute

Orange Pound Cake

¾ cup seedless raisins   ½ cup soft shortening
2 cups flour   grated peel and juice of small
1¼ cups sugar   orange, plus water to make
1½ tsp. baking powder   ½ cup
1 tsp. salt   2 eggs unbeaten
½ tsp. cream of tartar

Coarsely chop raisins. Sift together the next five ingredients. Add shortening and liquid and peel. Beat 2 minutes (very dry texture). Add the eggs, beat two minutes. Fold in raisins by hand. Greased loaf pan, 9 x 5 x 3, lined with foil and greased again. Bake 350 oven about one hour. Remove from pan and pour over warm cake: ¼ cup sugar, dissolved in ¼ cup orange juice (or Tang mixture) and 2 tsp. rum flavoring. Gently prick with fork.

Mrs. C. Fry

Mac's Pound Cake

½ lb. Crisco (use Crisco only)
1½ cups white sugar
4 eggs
2 cups flour (pastry)
1 tsp. baking powder

1 tsp. salt
½ cup Superior milk
1 tsp. each of lemon, almond and
  vanilla
½ tsp. mace

Cream Crisco well. Add white sugar and continue beating until well blended. Add eggs one at a time beating after each. Add dry ingredients alternately with milk. Add flavoring. Bake at 350° for 15 minutes, then turn oven down to 325° and bake 1½ hours.

Mrs. D. J. Urquhart

Coconut Cake

1 cup fine coconut
1 cup Superior milk
Soak coconut and milk for 15
  minutes
¾ cup butter
2 cups white sugar

3 eggs
1 tsp. baking powder
1 tsp. vanilla
½ tsp. salt (or more)
2½ cups all purpose flour

Cream butter and sugar. Add eggs, one at a time, beating slowly after each addition. Add flour mixture, alternately with milk and coconut. Bake 1 hour in moderate oven in a large loaf pan, or in two small loaf pans.

Mrs. Milton Summerville

White Fruit Cake

3 sqs. butter
2 cups white sugar
6 eggs (beaten)
4 cups flour (all purpose)
1 lb. (white) raisins
¼ lb. citron
¼ lb. almonds (blanched)
¼ lb. candied pineapple

2 small bottles green maraschino
  cherries
1 lg. bottle red maraschino
  cherries
2 tsp. baking powder
½ cup Superior milk
½ cup brandy
1 tsp. almond extract

Cream butter and sugar. Add beaten eggs. Add dry ingredients alternately with Superior milk and brandy. Add fruit which has been slightly dredged with a small amount of flour. (The cherries should be well drained and left to dry out on a clean towel with the rest of the fruit, overnight.) Bake at 300° for about ten minutes, then turn oven down to 275° and bake about 2¼ hours in a tube pan which has been lined both bottom and sides with 2 thicknesses of brown paper. Cover loosely with brown paper during baking time. (The almonds and citron may be omitted and more pineapple added instead.)

Ruth Urquhart

Crushed Pineapple Fruit Cake

¾ cup butter (1½ sq.)
2/3 cup white sugar
2¼ cups bread flour
3 eggs
2 tsp. baking powder
salt

Let stand overnight:
1 16-oz. can crushed pineapple
1 lb. sultana raisins
½ lb. red cherries
½ lb. green cherries
2/3 cup mixed peel

In the morning make batter, add fruit mixture. Bake 2½ to 3 hours, moderate oven.

**Hilda A. Height and
Eileen Rhuda**

Cherry Pound Cake

1 cup butter
2 cups sugar
3 eggs
3 cups flour
1 tsp. salt
1 tsp. baking powder

¾ cup warm Superior milk
1 tsp. vanilla
1 tsp. lemon extract
2 cups cut cherries (maraschino
or glace)

Cream butter and sugar well, then add lemon flavoring. Add well beaten eggs. Sift together flour, salt and baking powder, then add alternately with the milk to the above mixture. Lastly add vanilla and cut cherries, well floured. Bake until done, about 2 hours and 20 minutes in a covered tin at 325 degrees.

(Use foil to cover pan.)

Mrs. Irving Pink

Sultana Cake

½ lb. butter
1 cup granulated sugar
3 eggs
2 cups all purpose flour
½ tsp. baking powder

3 tbsp. Superior milk
2 tsp. vanilla
1 tsp. lemon
1 lb. raisins (boiled, drained,
cooled)

Cream well the butter and sugar. Add beaten eggs. Sift together the flour and baking powder and combine with first mixture, together with the flavoring. Last add the raisins that have either been steamed or cooked for a few minutes with a little water, drained and cooled. It is a good idea to prepare the raisins the day before. Bake in a moderate over about 350° from 1 to 1½ hours.

Mrs. Vera Boudreau

Gum Drop Cake

1 cup white sugar
½ cup butter
2 eggs
¾ cup Superior milk
¾ lb. seedless raisins (or less)
1 cup gumdrops

2 cups flour
2 tsp. baking powder
¼ tsp. salt
1 tsp. vanilla
½ tsp lemon

Cream sugar and butter. Add eggs and beat well. Add milk and sifted dry ingredients alternately. Add seasoning and fruit. Bake in 9 x 9" pan in moderate oven for 1½ hours.

Phyllis Adams (Mrs. G. W.)

Sultana Cake

Cream:
1 cup butter or margarine
1 cup white sugar
Add:
2 eggs
½ cup orange juice
1 tsp. vanilla

Sift together and add:
2¾ cups flour (pastry)
1 full tsp. baking powder
½ tsp. salt
Add:
2 cups floured raisins

Cherries or other fruit may be used. Mix as given. Bake 350°F. about 1 hour.

Mrs. Hubert Morton

Dark Christmas Fruit Cake

½ lb. butter
1 cup white sugar
1 cup brown sugar
2½ cups flour
1 tsp. soda
¾ cup Silver Lasses molasses
2 tsp. cinnamon
1 tsp. each cloves and allspice
8 eggs

1 cup each shelled walnuts and
   almonds
1 lb. white raisins
1 lb. seeded raisins
1 lb. currants
½ lb. figs
½ lb. dates
1 cup grape juice

Soak raisins, currants, figs and dates in 1 cup grape juice overnight.

8 oz. glace or bottled cherries
1 cup crushed drained pineapple
   or rings

1 cup strawberry preserves
8 oz. mixed peel
2 oz. citron peel

Cream butter. Add sugar, cream well. Add eggs, 2 at a time beating well. Add molasses, flour sifted with soda and spices. Add all fruit. Mix well.

Steam 3 hours. Bake one hour in slow oven. Makes one large square cake 8x8x4" and loaf cake. I only staemed large one. Line pans well with tin foil.

Mary Sinclair

Old Fashioned Pork Cake

1 ½ lbs. fresh fat pork
1 pt. Silver Lasses molasses (hot)
1 cup sugar
1 pt. Superior buttermilk
1½ cups flour (enough to make like gingerbread, quite runny)

2 tsp. soda
1 tsp each cloves, allspice and cinnamon
1 lb. dates chopped
½ lb. walnuts chopped

Grind pork, pour on the hot molasses and let cool. Then add buttermilk. Sift sugar and spices with 1½ cups flour and add enough more flour to make thin batter. Add dates and nuts. Bake in slow oven 1 hour. Makes 2 loaves.

Kemptville Women's Institute

Christmas Nut Cake

Cream:
1 scant cup sugar
1 cup butter
Add:
2 eggs well beaten
¼ cup Superior milk, alternately with 1½ cup flour, sifted with 2 tbsp. baking powder
Add all fruit:

¼ lb. pecans
¼ lb. brazils
¼ lb. filberts
3 slices pineapple
2 cups white raisins
1 small pkg. each of red and green cherries
1 tbsp. glycerine
Flavoring

Mix in usual manner. Add floured fruit and nuts. Bake 2 hours, not over 250°.

Mrs. E. M. Woodward

SQUARES

By Cracky Bars

Sift together:
1¾ cups flour
1 tsp. salt
¼ tsp. soda
Blend and cream together well:
¾ cup shortening

1 cup sugar
Add 2 eggs, beat well
Combine:
⅓ cup Superior milk
1 tsp. vanilla

Add milk alternately with dry ingredients to cream mixture. Place ⅓ batter in second bowl and add:

1 sq. melted Bakers chocolate   ¾ cup chopped walnuts or
                                                      coconut

Spread in pan 13 x 9 x 2. Cover with:

graham crackers   Add:
                              ¾ cup Bakers Chocolate chips

to remaining batter and spread over graham crackers. Bake in 350° oven 25 to 30 minutes. Frost with your favorite icing.

M. MacDonald
Emily Harlow

Party Chews

BOTTOM:
½ cup butter

1 cup flour
½ cup brown sugar

Cream butter and sugar, blend in flour and press mixture in pan. Bake 15 minutes 350 degree oven.

TOP LAYER
2 eggs
1 cup brown sugar
½ tsp. vanilla

¼ tsp. salt
1 cup coconut
1 cup rice crispies
1 cup nuts

Beat eggs, add sugar, then add vanilla, salt, coconut, rice crispies and nuts, and mix well. Spread on botton crust. Bake again 20 to 25 minutes, 350 degree oven.

Eleanor Russell

"Food For The Gods"

16 graham wafers rolled fine
1 cup brown sugar
1 cup shredded coconut or dates
  (I use ½ cup of each)

1 cup walnuts chopped
1 tsp. baking powder
2 eggs well beaten

Mix all dry ingredients, fold in well beaten eggs. Mix well together, press mixture into 8 x 8 greased baking dish. Bake 30 minutes in a 325° oven. Let cool. Ice with butter icing and grated orange peel, or sprinkle with crumbs of 3 graham wafers.

Mrs. Raymond Amirault

Marshmallow Dreams

BASE:

1½ cup sifted flour
⅛ tsp. salt
1¼ tsp. baking powder
¼ cup shortening

½ cup sugar
1 egg beaten
½ tbsp. vanilla
1½ tbsp. Superior milk

Cream shortening and sugar together. Add egg and vanilla. Sift dry ingredients and add to creamed mixture alternately with milk. Pack in 9 x 9 greased pan. Bake 350° until light brown. Cool.

TOPPING:

Boil 1 cup sugar, 1 cup water, 2 envelopes unflavored gelatine for 5 minutes. Let cool. Beat in 1 cup icing sugar and beat until it thickens. Pour over base. Melt 2 sqs. Bakers semi-sweet chocolate and dribble over marshmallow.

Dot Brown

Peanut Butter Fingers

Bake at 350° for 20 to 25 minutes.

½ cup shortening
½ cup white sugar
½ cup firmly packed brown
  sugar
1 egg
⅓ cup peanut butter
½ tsp. soda
¼ tsp. salt

½ tsp. vanilla
1 cup all-purpose flour
1 cup quick cooking oats
1 cup Bakers semi-sweet
  chocolate bits
½ cup sifted icing sugar
¼ cup peanut butter
2 to 4 tbsp. Superior milk

Cream shortening. Gradually add sugar; cream well. Blend in egg, ⅓ cup peanut butter, soda, salt and vanilla. Add flour and rolled oats; mix well. Spread in greased 13 x 9 pan. Bake until lightly browned. Sprinkle with chocolate. Return to oven 1 minute. Spread melted chocolate over base. Combine icing sugar, ¼ cup peanut butter and milk; mix well. Spread over cooled chocolate. Cut in bars.

Mrs. John N. Nickerson

Mock Cheese Squares

Separate three eggs. Beat yolks and add one can of Eagle Brand Condensed milk. Add ⅓ cup lemon juice. Beat well. Add well beaten egg whites.

Roll out 24 Graham Cracker wafers very fine, add ¼ lb. melted butter to make crumb crust.

Put ½ cracker mixture on bottom of 8 x 8 pan, then your mixture of other ingredients and put rest of crumbs on top. Bake for one hour at 325° oven.

Mrs. Lou Fridhandler

Candy Pink Cheese Squares

20 Graham Crackers or more; ¼ lb. butter (melted).

Crush crackers and mix with melted butter and put in square pan (8" x 8") and pat down with spoon. Let stand.

1 pkg. Superior Cottage Cheese; few drops vanilla; ½ cup sugar, 2 eggs. Mix above well and put on top of graham butter mixture and bake 25 minutes in 350° oven.

While this is baking, mix ½ pint sour Superior cream, 2 large spoons sugar, few drops vanilla. Using red coloring, tint it a pale candy pink. As soon as you take cake out, pour the above topping over cake and put back in oven for 5 minutes. Take out. It still is liquidy but do not worry. When cool, put in refrigerator at least a day before serving.

Cut in squares and serve in coloured paper cups.

Mrs. George Beiner

Lemon Coconut Sponges

½ cup butter	2 tbsp. brown sugar
1 cup flour	salt

Cream butter, add sugar and flour and salt. Press into 8x8 pan.

Bake 12 - 15 minutes in 350° oven. While this is baking:

2 eggs	juice & rind of 1 lemon
1 cup white sugar	1½ cups coconut
2 tbsp. flour	salt

Beat eggs. Add sugar and continue beating. Add rest of ingredients. Pour over the first mixture and bake at 350° for 20 - 30 minutes. Ice with small dabs of icing if desired.

Ruth Urquhart

Lemon Moments

BOTTOM:

½ cup butter	1 egg & 2 egg yolks
½ cup white sugar	½ cup flour
	¼ tsp. baking powder

Mix like cake batter. Place in 9 x 9 pan. Bake 20 - 30 minutes.

FILLING:
Prepare while above is baking:

1 tin Eagle Brand milk	grated rind & juice of 2 lemons

Beat until thick (about 5 minutes.) Spread over cooled bottom.

TOP:

Beat 2 egg whites with	1 tbsp. lemon juice
½ cup sugar	Sprinkle ¼ cup coconut over top

Bake until brown in 350° oven.

Mrs. Tracy Goodwin

Lemon Meringue Squares

Mix well:	Add:
23 - 25 soda crackers crushed	½ cup sugar
¾ cup flour	½ cup coconut
1 tsp. baking powder	½ cup butter

Mix until crumbly. Put ¾ of this mixture in 9 inch greased pan. Bake 10 minutes. While this is baking, beat together:

1 can sweetened condensed milk   juice and rind 1 lemon
2 egg yolks

This should be thick and fluffy. Pour over baked crumbs. Top with meringue made with the 2 egg whites and 4 tbsp. sugar. Sprinkle reserved crumbs over this meringue. Bake 30 minutes longer or until light brown.

Mrs. Ainsley Smith

Lemon Squares

22 graham wafers   ½ cup butter
½ cup sugar

Roll out wafers. Cream butter and sugar. Add wafers and mix well together. Take out ½ cup of mixture. Put remainder in greased 8 inch cake pan. Bake 8 to 10 minutes. When cool spread with following:

3 egg yolks	3 tbsp. water
¾ cup sugar	juice of 1 lemon
⅓ cup flour	

Cook and cool and spread on above. Beat egg whites with 6 tbsp. white sugar, 1 tsp. baking powder. Spread on lemon mixture. Sprinkle with ½ cup of crumbs. Bake 20 minutes in slow oven. Cut in squares when cool.

Mrs. Doris Tufts

Delicious Ginger Bars

2 eggs beaten	2 pieces preserved ginger
1 cup sugar	(cut fine)
3 tbsp. butter	1 cup dates (cut fine)
1 tsp. vanilla	½ cup walnuts (chopped)
¼ tsp. salt	½ cup crushed pineapple
¾ cup all purpose flour	(drained)
1 tsp. baking powder	⅓ cup cherries (cut)
	1 tsp. of the syrup

Mix above ingredients together, bake in pan (7x11) or similar size for 25 minutes.

Ice with butter icing, almond flavoring.

Mrs. Ernest Sinclair

Austrian "Linzer" Bars

1½ cups sifted all-purpose flour	½ cup butter or margarine
¼ cup granulated sugar	1 slightly beaten egg
½ tsp. baking powder	⅓ cup blanched almonds, ground
½ tsp. salt	½ cup red-raspberry jam
½ tsp. cinnamon	1 slightly beaten egg yolk
½ cup brown sugar	1 tsp. water

Sift together flour, sugar, baking powder, salt and cinnamon; stir in brown sugar. Cut in butter till mixture is crumbly. Add egg and ground almonds; mix with fork. Reserve ½ cup mixture for lattice and into it mix 2 tbsp. additional flour; chill 1 hour. Meanwhile press remaining mixture evenly into 9x9x2 inch pan. Spread with raspberry jam. Roll out reserved mixture on well-floured surface to ¼ inch. Cut in strips a little less than ¼ inch wide. For lattice top, line up 11 strips across filling; then lay 11 strips diagonally across. Combine egg yolk and water; brush over lattice for glaze. Bake in moderate oven (375°) about 25 minutes or till done. Decorate with bits of red and green candied cherries. Cool. Cut in bars or squares.

Tested

Chocolate Pineapple Squares

BASE:	2 tsp. vanilla
½ lb. butter	2 cups sifted flour
1 egg	2 sqs. grated Bakers bitter
1 cup sugar	chocolate
1 cup walnuts, chopped	

Cream butter, add sugar and egg. Cream well. Add walnuts, vanilla, chocolate and sifted flour. This mixture should be quite stiff. Pat ¾ of this into bottom of large utility pyrex dish. Reserve ¼ for lattice work on top.

TOP:

1 tin crushed pineapple, drained	1 cup sugar
2½ tbsp. flour	2 eggs

Beat eggs, add sugar, flour and pineapple. Pour over base. Take remainder of base mixture and roll between floured palm of hands to thickness of ½ inch. Make lattice over pineapple. Bake in moderate oven 350°, for 45 minutes.

Mrs. Austin Churchill

Candid Fruit Squares

1 cup white sugar	1¾ cups all purpose flour
½ cup shortening and butter	½ cup walnuts
(mixed)	½ cup coconut
2 eggs	½ tsp. baking powder
½ cup orange juice	2 cups candied mixed fruit
½ tsp. salt	

Cream shortening and sugar. Add eggs and beat well. Add juice, then dry ingredients.

Bake ¾ of an hour 350° oven. Ice with Orange Icing.

Zelda Hansford, Arcadia

County Fair Date And Nut Squares

2/3 cup (small can) undiluted evaporated milk	1 tsp. vanilla
1 cup chopped dates	1 cup sifted flour
⅓ cup shortening	¼ tsp. baking powder
½ cup sugar	1 tsp. salt
1 egg	½ cup chopped walnuts (or less)

Heat evaporated milk and dates in saucepan over low heat, stirring occasionally until dates soften. Remove from heat and mix until thick paste forms. Cream shortening and sugar together in medium sized bowl. Add egg and vanilla; beat well. Sift flour, baking powder and salt together and add to shortening mixture; mix well. Add date mixture and walnuts; stir well. Turn into greased 8 inch square pan. Bake in 350 deg. (moderate) oven 30 minutes, or until cake tests done. Cool. Ice with your favorite butter icing flavored with vanilla. Cut in squares.

Mrs. Bernard Strong

Orange And Raisin Squares

1 cup sugar	2 cups flour
3 tbsp. butter	1 tsp. baking powder
1 egg	¼ tsp. salt
1 cup sour Superior milk	1 orange & rind
1 tsp. soda	1 cup raisins

Put orange, rind and raisins through food chopper. Cream butter, sugar and egg. Add the orange and raisin mixture. Sift the flour, baking powder and salt. Add to the creamed mixture alternately with the sour milk to which the soda has been added. Bake 45 minutes in a moderate oven.

Mrs. P. Thomas

Cherry Squares

1 cup flour	⅓ cup chopped cherries
1 tsp. baking powder	⅓ cup butter or shortening
½ tsp. salt	1 cup brown sugar (packed)
⅛ tsp. soda	1 egg
½ cup fine coconut	1 tsp. vanilla

Sift together flour, baking powder, salt and soda and set aside. Melt butter in saucepan and remove from heat, add sugar (1 tbsp. hot water if shortening is used). Cool and stir in egg, vanilla, cherries and coconut, then add flour mixture and mix well. Spread in greased 9x9 pan. Bake 20 - 25 minutes at 350 degrees.

Clara Harris

Pineapple Squares

Sift together:
1½ cup flour
½ tsp. salt
1 tsp. baking power
Cream:

¾ cup butter
1½ cups sugar
Add:
3 eggs
1 tsp. vanilla

Add dry ingredients. Mix well. Take 1 cup of batter and add 1 cup drained crushed pineapple. To remainder of batter add 2 sqs. melted chocolate. Divide dark batter, placing one layer in large pan 9x9. Add pineapple layer and top with remainder of dark batter. Bake 35 - 40 minutes in moderate oven.

Margaret (Mrs. F. A.) Nickerson

Rainbow Squares

2 cups flour
3 tbsp. brown sugar

1 cup margarine or butter

Mix together and press in pan 9 x 9. Bake 15 - 20 minutes in 350° oven. Cool. Cook until thick:

1 15-oz. can crushed pineapple
(do not drain)
½ cup sugar
yolks of 2 eggs beaten

3 tbsp. cornstarch
1 small bottle red cherries
(cut up, no juice)
1 tsp. almond extract

Pour over first mixture.

Beat 2 egg whites stiff   **Add 4 tbsp. sugar**
Spread over top, sprinkle with coconut and brown in oven.

Mrs. Raymond Dease
Mrs. Kenneth Blakney

Sour Cream Apple Squares

1½ cups sifted flour
½ cup white sugar
2 tsp. baking powder
salt
½ tsp. cinnamon
¼ cup Superior milk
½ cup butter

1 egg
1 cup apples, diced
½ cup Superior sour cream
1 egg
½ cup sugar
some nuts

Sift all dry ingredients. Add milk, butter (creamed), egg. Stir in apples lightly. Blend sour cream and egg. Spread batter in 10 x 10 pan. Spoon sour cream mixture over batter. Sprinkle with sugar and nuts. Bake 375 oven for 30 minutes. Will freeze well. Makes nice dessert, warmed. Serve with ice cream, or sauce.

Eve Fry

Apple Spice Squares

2½ cups sifted all purpose flour	1 cup sugar
2 tsp. baking soda	1 egg
1 tsp. cinnamon	1 tsp. vanilla
½ tsp. cloves	1½ cup applesauce (in cans)
½ tsp. nutmeg	1 cup cut up dates
½ cup soft butter	1 cup nuts (optional)

Sift together flour, baking soda and spices. Cream the butter and sugar, add egg and beat well. Add vanilla and ½ tsp. salt. Beat in flour mixture just until combined. Add applesauce and dates,, stir well. Spread batter in buttered 9x12 in. cake pan. Bake 35 to 40 minutes in 375 oven. Cool in pan and cut and frost as desired.

Mrs. Loran Crowell

Holly Cakes

BOTTOM:
Mix well:
1 cup flour

2 tbsp. sugar
1 sq. butter (¼ lb.)

Sift flour and sugar; add butter; mix well and crumble. Press mixture firmly into well greased sq. pan.

CENTER:
1 box red or green glace cherries
  cut, or half of each

TOP:
1 cup white sugar	
1 cup fine coconut	2 tsp. flour
1 cup cut walnuts	1 tsp. vanilla
2 tsp. butter	2 beaten eggs

Mix well: Spread on top of cut cherries and smooth evenly. Bake at 375° oven 20 - 30 minutes. Cool. Cut in squares.

Mrs. E. K. Ford

Strawberry Squares

1½ cups flour (scant)	½ cup butter
2 tbsp. white sugar	

Bake for 10 minutes in medium oven.

1 pkg. frozen strawberries	½ cup sugar
1 pkg. strawberry jello powder	1 pkg. gelatin

Boil on stove about 20 minutes. Cool about 1 hour in refrigerator.

Beat 1 pt. cream with   1 pkg. Dream Whip

Take mixture out of frig and add ¼ of the cream mixture till fluffy. Pour over short bread bottom. Put rest of cream over the top Keep in refrigerator. Use pan about 11 x 7.

Nancy Gardner Richards

Jewel Bars

½ cup butter
1 cup brown sugar
3 eggs
2 cups flour
½ tsp. salt
3 tbsp. Superior milk
1¼ cups nuts
(brazils, filberts, pecans or
peanuts)

¾ cup glazed pineapple
¾ cup red cherries
½ cup raisins (optional)
1 tsp. vanilla
1 tbsp. Sherry or brandy
¼ cup sugar

Cream butter, add sugar. Add 1 egg. Sift flour and salt together. Add alternately with milk to butter mixture. Blend well. Spread in a 15 x 10 x 1 inch buttered pan. Bake in a moderate oven 350° for about 10 minutes.

Mix nuts, fruit, vanilla and flavoring. Beat the remaining 2 eggs very slightly and stir in the sugar. Add to the fruit mixture and spread over the top layer. Bake 20 minutes longer in 350° oven. Cut in strips while still warm.

Mrs. Charles Robbins

Apricot Dream Squares

1 cup crushed graham wafers
1 cup sifted flour
1 cup shredded coconut

1 cup brown sugar
½ cup melted butter
½ tsp. salt

Combine dry ingredients, add melted butter and mix well. Reserve 1 cup for topping. Pack remainder in 9 x 9 cake pan. Bake for 10 minutes at 350°.

1 cup dried apricots

Simmer until tender, drain and chop.

2 eggs
1 cup brown sugar
1 tbsp. lemon juice

⅓ cup flour
½ tsp. baking powder
1 tsp. salt

Beat eggs until light. Add brown sugar and lemon juice. Stir in sifted dry ingredients and apricots. Spread over crust. Sprinkle with topping. Bake 30 - 35 minutes at 350°. Cool and cut in squares.

Barb Robbins

Almond Sponge Squares

½ lb. almonds (ground)
1 cup sugar

yolks of five eggs
½ tsp. almond flavoring

Beat egg yolks until light; slowly add sugar and keep beating until thick. Fold ground almonds into well beaten egg whites and add. Bake 45 minutes in 300° oven in 8 x 12 pyrex pan which has been lined with wax paper. Remove from pan and put carefully on wire cake rack to cool. Frost.

Mrs. J. S. Robertson (Halifax)

Valley Apple Squares

BASE:
⅓ cup butter

2 tbsp. brown sugar
1 cup flour

Make up like pastry and spread in bottom of 8 x 8 pan.

FILLING:
½ cup sugar
1 lg. apple sliced thin

1 egg
juice and rind 1 lemon
1 tsp. butter

Mix all together and cook over low heat until soft. Cool. Spread on base.

TOP:
¾ cup sugar
1 tbsp. butter

1 egg
1¼ cups coconut

Mix in order given and spread on filling. Bake in one operation in moderate oven (350°) or until a golden brown, about 30 minutes.

Helen Clarke

Raspberry Bars

BASE:
1½ cups pre-sifted all-purpose
   flour
1 tsp. baking soda
¼ cup brown sugar
¼ cup white sugar
½ cup butter
1 egg
1 tbsp. Superior milk

½ cup raspberry jam
TOPPING:
2 tbsp. butter
1 cup sugar
2 eggs separated
¼ tsp. salt
1 tsp. vanilla
1 cup chopped walnuts

BASE:— Preheat oven to 375°F. (moderate). Measure flour, soda and sugars into a bowl. Stir thoroughly to blend. Cut in butter. Beat egg and milk together. Make a well in dry ingredients. Pour in liquid and mix into a dough. Press dough evenly into greased 9 inch square pan. Bake at 375°F for 12 to 15 minutes. When cool spread with jam, cover with topping.

TOPPING:— Cream butter and sugar together. Beat in egg yolks Add salt, vanilla and chopped nuts. Beat egg whites until stiff. Fold into creamed mixture. Spread mixture evenly over jam and pastry. Bake at 350° for 25 to 30 minutes, or until golden brown. Cool and cut in bars.

Doris MacKinnon

Never Fail Brownies

½ cup butter
1 cup white sugar
2 eggs
¼ tsp. salt
vanilla
Blend well. Add:

¼ cup all purpose flour
½ cup Bakers cocoa, dissolved in
   enough warm water to moisten
   or 2 sqs. Bakers melted chocolate
½ cup nuts

Spread in 8 x 8 pan and bake 25 minutes at 350°.

Marge DeViller

Calypso Bars

2½ sqs. Bakers unsweetened
   chocolate
2/3 cup hot water
1⅓ cups granulated sugar
1⅓ cups chopped dates
1 cup butter or margarine
1 tsp. vanilla

1¼ cups packed brown sugar
1½ cups sifted flour
½ tsp. salt
½ tsp. soda
1 cup chopped nuts
1½ cups quick cooking rolled
   oats

Melt chocolate in hot water and add sugar. Stir well, add dates, cook until thickened, about 5 minutes. Blend in ¼ cup butter. Add vanilla. Cool.

Cream ¾ cup butter and brown sugar until fluffy. Sift flour, salt and soda, add to creamed mixture. Blend well. Add nuts and oats. Press ½ into bottom of pan 13 x 9. Add date mixture, top with rest of mixture. Bake 350° 40 minutes.

Maude Churchill

Butterscotch Brownies

Melt over hot (not boiling) water:
1 6-oz. pkg. Bakers butterscotch
   chippits
¼ cup butter
Remove from heat: Stir in:
1 cup light brown sugar (packed)
Cool five mins. Blend in:
2 unbeaten eggs
½ tsp. vanilla

Sift together:
1 cup sifted pastry flour
1 tsp. baking powder
¾ tsp. salt
Stir in:
½ cup broken walnut meats

Spread in greased, lightly floured pan 13 x 9 x 2". Bake at 350° for 25 minutes. Cool. Cut in squares.

Norma Crowell

Banana Fudgies

1 pkg. Bakers semi-sweet
   chocolate
½ cups sifted flour
½ tsp. baking powder
¼ tsp. salt
2 eggs

½ cup sugar
1 cup mashed bananas (3 med.
   size)
1 tsp. vanilla
1 cup chopped walnuts

Melt chocolate in top of small double boiler over simmering water; remove from heat. Sift flour, baking powder, salt onto waxed paper or foil. Beat eggs well in a medium-sized bowl. Beat in sugar gradually. Stir in melted chocolate and mashed banana. Sift in dry ingredients, blending well. Stir in vanilla and walnuts. Pour into greased baking pan, 8x8x2. Bake in moderate oven (350°) 40 minutes or until firm on top. Cool completely in pan and cut.

Ruth Urquhart

Swiss Chocolate Fingers

1 cup sifted flour	2 eggs
¼ cup sugar	2/3 cup sugar
¼ tsp. salt	2 tsp. flour
⅓ cup butter	¼ tsp. salt
½ cup flaked coconut	¾ cup Superior coffee cream
1 8-oz. pkg. cream cheese	1 tsp. vanilla
2 sqs. melted Bakers chocolate	½ tsp. cinnamon

Sift flour, sugar and salt together and cut in butter until particles are fine. Add coconut. Press into greased 8 inch pan.

Beat cheese, chocolate and eggs together until fluffy. Stir in sugar, flour and salt. Beat well. Add cream, vanilla and cinnamon. Pour into prepared pan. Bake 350° oven 45 minutes. Chill and cut into thin fingers. These squares are very rich. They freeze well.

Ruth Pink

Chocolate Date Squares

¾ cup butter or margarine	½ tsp. baking powder
6 oz. pkg. Bakers semi sweet chocolate bits	2 eggs
1⅓ cup sifted flour	¾ cup peanut butter
¼ cup sugar	¾ cup chopped dates
¾ cup confectionery sugar	¾ cup finely chopped walnuts
	1 tbsp. water

Melt ½ cup butter and ½ cup chocolate bits. Blend well and add flour and sugar. Press in bottom of pan (10 x 10) and bake 10 minutes in 350° oven. Cool. Combine confectionery sugar and baking powder in mixing bowl. Add eggs, ¼ cup melted butter or margarine, peanut butter. Mix well. Add dates, walnuts and water. Mix well. Spread over crust and bake 15 minutes or till lightly brown. Cool and spread with thin icing.

Mrs. F. R. Currier

Ruggles Squares

½ cup butter	2/3 cup white sugar
2 tbsp. icing sugar	Add: 2 eggs
1 cup flour	one at a time, beating well
Bake 15 minutes	after each
Cream:	2 sqs. melted Bakers chocolate
½ cup butter	Vanilla

Pour on baked base. Top with whipped cream. Keep refrigerated until served. This makes a wonderful filling for a pie.

Pauline Crowell

Tweed Squares

2/3 cup butter
2/3 cup white sugar
1½ cups pastry flour
1 tsp. baking powder
1 tsp. vanilla

½ cup Superior milk
2 egg whites, beaten stiff
2 tbsp. sugar
2 sqs. Bakers semi-sweet
   chocolate, chipped

Cream butter and sugar. Sift flour, baking powder together and add to first mixture. Add milk gradually and then the vanilla. Beat egg whites stiff, add the 2 tbsp. sugar and semi-sweet chocolate, chipped. Fold into mixture. Turn into greased 9 x 9 inch pan. Bake 350° oven 30 minutes.

ICING:

¼ cup butter, 1 cup icing sugar, 2 egg yolks, 3 sq. semi-sweet chocolate melted

Cream butter, add icing sugar gradually and then add egg yolks. Spread over squares. Dribble melted chocolate over top.

Mrs. Archie d'Entremont

Saucepan Brownies

Melt and cool slightly:
½ cup butter
2 sqs. Bakers chocolate
Add:
1 cup brown sugar
2 eggs unbeaten
Blend well and add:

½ cup flour
¼ tsp. salt
1 tsp. vanilla
1 cup chopped nuts
¼ tsp. soda in 2 tbsp. warm
   water

Place in greased 9 x 9 pan. Bake 30 minutes. Ice with Butter Chocolate **Icing.**

Mrs. Gertrude Wathen
Tusket Women's Institute

Congo Squares

Cream:
1 cup brown sugar
½ cup butter
Add:
2 eggs
1 tsp. vanilla
½ cup Bakers Chipits

½ cup nuts
¼ cup coconut
Sift together:
1⅓ cups all purpose flour
1 tsp. baking powder
½ tsp. salt

Bake about 25 minutes in moderate oven and cut in squares while still warm.

Pubnico Womens Institute

Half-Way Squares

½ cup butter
¼ cup sugar
¼ cup brown sugar (firmly packed)
1 egg separated
½ tsp. vanilla
1 cup sifted all purpose flour

⅛ tsp. salt
¾ tsp. baking powder
½ 6-oz. pkg. Bakers semi-sweet chocolate pieces
2 tbsp. water
½ cup brown sugar (firmly packed)

Cream butter, gradually add granulated and brown sugar, creaming well. Add egg yolk and vanilla. Mix thoroughly. Mix in well the dry ingredients which have been sifted together. Spread in 8x8 inch pan. Add water to chocolate. Melt over hot water. Spread over first mixture. Beat egg white until stiff. Add brown sugar gradually and place on top of chocolate. Bake 325° for 30 minutes. When cool cut in squares.

For a variation add 1 cup coconut to meringue.

Mrs. J. D. Cohen
Mrs. Ave Vanderjonk

Black And Whites

1 cup butter
1 cup white sugar
3 tbsp. Bakers cocoa

1 cup flour (pastry)
3 eggs beaten

Cream butter and sugar. Add beaten eggs. Add flour and cocoa and beat well. Put in 8 x 12 pan and bake at 325° for 20 minutes. Cool slightly. Spread with mixture of 1 tin sweetened condensed milk and 6 to 8 oz. coconut. Return to oven and continue baking at 325° until nicely browned. Frost with icing made from 1 sq. semi-sweet chocolate melted, 1 cup icing sugar and 1 tbsp. butter.

Mrs. D. J. Urquhart

Marble Squares

Beat 2 eggs well; add:
1 cup brown sugar
¼ cup white sugar
¾ cup flour

½ tsp. salt
1 tsp. vanilla
½ cup coconut

Mix well, then pour ½ of this batter into 8x8 greased pan.

To the remainder add 1 square Bakers chocolate melted with 1 tbsp. butter. Add ½ cup walnuts, drop over the first batter with spoon. Bake 30 minutes at 375°F. Frost with chocolate icing.

Mrs. Clifton Brayne
Tusket Women's Institute

Day And Night Squares

DOUGH:
3 egg yolks
3 tbsp. oil
3 tbsp. sugar
1 tsp. baking powder
1 cup flour
¼ tsp. salt

¼ cup sugar
¼ cup almonds chopped
1 heaping tbsp. Bakers cocoa
3 egg whites beaten stiff
  to which ¾ cup sugar has been
  added slowly

FILLING:
¼ lb. walnuts chopped

Cream sugar, oil and egg yolks. Add flour, baking powder and salt. Mix well. Divide into 3 portions. Roll out to fit size of pan 8x8 or 9x9. On top of first layer in pan place nut mixture, made by mixing together the chopped walnuts, ¼ cup sugar, cocoa and 4 tbsp. of the egg white mixture and 1 tbsp. water. Cover with 2nd layer of dough; then 2nd filling made of chopped almonds and rest of egg white mixture. Cover with 3rd layer of dough. Bake 1 hour 325°. Cut in small squares decorated with a rosette of any desired icing.

Ruth Pink

Hoosier Peanut Bars

2 cups sifted all purpose flour
1 tsp. soda
½ tsp. salt
½ cup butter
½ cup sugar (white)
1½ cups firmly packed brown
  sugar

2 egg yolks
1 tsp. vanilla
1 cup (6 oz. pkg. Bakers semi-
  sweet chocolate bits
¾ cup salted peanuts, chopped
2 egg whites

Sift together flour, soda and salt. Cream butter; gradually add white sugar and ½ cup brown sugar, creaming well. Blend in unbeaten egg yolks and vanilla. Stir in dry ingredients gradually to form a crumb mixture. Press into greased 13x9x2 or two 8x8x2 pans.

Sprinkle semi-sweet chocolate pieces and ½ cup chopped peanuts over dough. Pat in gently. Beat egg whites until slight mounds form. Gradually add remaining 1 cup brown sugar. Beat until stiff, straight peaks form. Spread over chocolate pieces.

Sprinkle with ¼ cup chopped peanuts. Press into meringue slightly. Bake at 325° for 40 to 45 minutes. While warm cut into bars. Makes about 2½ doz. More if you cut in squares.

Joyce (Mrs. E. R.) Syvertsen

Chocolate Coconut Squares

BASE:

2 tbsp. melted butter
2 egg yolks
½ cup Bakers cocoa
½ cup Superior milk

1 cup brown sugar
1 cup flour
1 tsp. baking powder
1 tsp. salt

Blend butter, sugar and egg yolks. Add dry ingredients and milk. Place in 8 x 8 pan. Bake in 350° oven 20 minutes.

TOP:

2 egg whites beaten stiff with

½ cup white sugar
2 cups fine coconut

Place this on baked base while hot and put it back in oven until brown.

Cover with Frosting while hot.

2 sqs. melted Bakers unsweetened
   chocolate

2 tbsp. butter (melted)

enough icing sugar to spread evenly.

Mrs. Abe Star

Congo Squares

(Large Amount Recipe)

2¾ cups sifted flour
2½ tsp. baking powder
½ tsp. salt
2/3 cup shortening
2¼ cup brown sugar

3 eggs
1 cup nut meats
1 pkg. Bakers semi-sweet chocolate bits

Mix and sift flour, baking powder and salt. Melt shortening and add brown sugar. Stir until mixed. Allow to cool slightly. Add eggs one at a time, beating well after each addition. Add dry ingredients, then nut meats and chocolate bits. Pour into greased pan 15x10. Bake at 350° 25 - 30 minutes.

**Mrs. Harold Hopkins,
Plainfield, Conn.**

Chocolate Brownies

(Large Amount Recipe)

2 cups white sugar
1 cup butter
4 eggs
4 sqs. Bakers unsweetened
   chocolate melted
2 tbsp. sour Superior milk

1½ cups flour
½ tsp. soda
1 tsp. cream of tartar
1 tsp. salt
2 tsp. vanilla
1 cup chopped walnuts

Cream butter and sugar. Add beaten eggs and then melted chocolate and sour milk. Sift dry ingredients and add to above. Lastly fold in nuts and vanilla.

Bake in 2 pans each 8x8 approximately 30 minutes in 350° oven, then turned down 300°. Cut in diamonds.

Lois Sweeny

Marble Fudge Squares

(Large Amount Recipe)

Melt:
2 sqs. Bakers chocolate
2 tsp. butter
Beat 4 eggs with mixer

Add:
2 cups brown sugar
½ cup white sugar

Continue beating with mixer, until sugar is well mixed. Fold in:

1½ cups flour which has been
   sifted with 1 tsp. salt.
Add:

1 cup nuts
coconut if desired
vanilla

Spoon half this mixture into two 7x7 pans or one 7x14. Add remaining mixture to the chocolate (melted) and pour over first part. Bake at 350° for 20 - 25 minutes. Squares are cooked when a toothpick comes out clean.

Helen Filliter

Easy Ice Cream Squares

24 graham wafers crushed   ½ cup butter
½ cup white sugar

Mix and pat in 7x11" pan. Bake at 350° for 15 minutes. Cool. Meanwhile:

Dissolve 1 pkg. lemon jello in
1 cup hot water and juice of
   ½ lemon

Add:
1 brick Superior vanilla ice
   cream

Place jello and ice cream mixture over first mixture and sprinkle with a few graham cracker crumbs. Refrigerate.

Any other flavor jello can be used for contrast in color. Filling is also suitable to fill a baked pie crust.

Myrtle Caldwell

Uncooked Cherry Squares

½ cup shortening
1½ cups icing sugar
salt
1 egg

½ cup chopped cherries
1 cup marshmallows
¾ cup coconut
almond or vanilla

Line 8" square pan with graham crackers. Top with filling made by creaming the shortening, icing sugar, salt and yolk of egg and flavoring until light and fluffy. Beat egg white until stiff and fold into first mixture. Add coconut, cherries and marshmallows. Spread evenly over crackers. Sprinkle top with cracker crumbs or more cherries. Put in refrigerator. You may substitute walnuts for the cherries for variety.

Mrs. Doris Tufts
Mrs. George Nickerson

Peanut Butter Squares

4 cups crushed corn flakes
½ cup peanut butter

2 pkgs. Bakers butterscotch chips
1 pkg. Bakers chocolate chips

Melt butterscotch chips and peanut butter in double boiler. Mix with corn flakes. Spread in greased utility pan. Melt chocolate chips and pour over top. Cool in fridge 10 minutes, then cut in squares.

Mrs. Abe Star

Mrs. Bruce Raymond

Chocolate Butterscotch Bars (Unbaked)

2 6-oz. pkgs. Bakers butterscotch
pieces
1 cup chopped walnuts
1½ cups miniature marsh-

mallows
2 6-oz. pkgs. Bakers semi-sweet
chocolate pieces
about 20 walnuts (optional)

Grease 8x8x2" pan. In double boiler, over hot (not boiling) water melt butterscotch pieces with 1 tbsp. shortening. Remove from heat. Spread in greased pan, arrange marshmallows evenly over surface, pressing gently. In double boiler melt chocolate pieces with 1 tbsp. shortening. Proceed in same manner as butterscotch pieces. Stir till smooth. Spread this mixture evenly over marshmallow layer. Lay walnuts on soft chocolate. Cool, then refrigerate. Cut into small bars.

Mrs. Herman Shapiro

Marshmallow Squares

½ cup butter
1 cup white sugar
2 eggs beaten

4 tbsp. coconut (dessicated)
1 tsp. maple flavoring

Cream butter and add sugar, eggs. Add coconut and flavoring. Cook mixture for half hour in double boiler.

Let cool 20 minutes. Put in larger bowl.

Add:
34 graham crackers crushed
24 marshmallows cut fine or

192 sm. marshmallows (not cut)
½ cup chopped walnuts

Put in pan and chill in fridge. Ice with thin coating of white icing as they are quite sweet.

Ruth Elderkin

Joyce Williams

Alice Garson

Unbaked Chocolate Squares

Melt together over low heat. Cook until thick. Cool.

3 sqs. Bakers bitter chocolate
1 tbsp. butter
½ cup white sugar
1 small tin evaporated milk
Add:
24 cut marshmallows

½ cup chopped nuts
½ cup maraschino cherries
¼ tsp. salt
vanilla
2¼ cups crushed graham
   crackers

Reserve ¼ cup to place in bottom of pan. Mix fruit and chocolate mixture well. Place in crumb-lined pan. Chill well. Frost with chocolate icing.

Kathryn Ladd

Noodle Chipit Squares

In top of double boiler, melt:

1 pkg. Bakers caramel or butterscotch chipits

½ cup peanut butter
small amt. margarine or butter

Remove from heat, then add:

1 cup small marshmallows
½ cup fine coconut (optional)

¼ cup cut walnuts (optional))
1 can chow-mein noodles, broken

Place all ingredients that have been well mixed into a greased pyrex square pan; place in frig until ready to serve. Cut in squares. Keep refrigerated. (Or these may be dropped by teaspoon on waxed paper, to use as cookies).

Mrs. E. K. Ford

Banana Unbaked Squares

Line 9″ x 9″ pan with graham
  wafers
Cream:
½ cup butter
½ cup sugar

Add:
1 lg. mashed banana
1 cup coconut
1 tsp. vanilla
few chopped nuts and cherries

Spread filling on wafers and cover with another layer of wafers. Spread with chocolate frosting or whipped Superior cream and place in refrigerator.

Mrs. Walter Sweeny

COOKIES

Coffee Butter Bits

½ cup cornstarch
½ cup confectioners sugar (or
   icing sugar)

1 cup sifted enriched flour
1 cup butter
2 tbsp. instant coffee

Mix and sift dry ingredients. Have butter at room temperature, then blend it into dry ingredients with a spoon, until a soft dough is formed. Shape into one-inch balls; place on ungreased cookie sheet about 1½ inches apart. Flatten with lightly floured fork. Bake in slow oven 300 degrees, 20 - 25 minutes. About 3 dozen cookies.

Grace S. Lewis

Almond Balls

1 cup butter
¼ cup icing sugar
2 cups sifted flour

candied cherries
1 cup ground almonds
1 tsp. vanilla

Cream butter with sugar until fluffy. Add other ingredients except cherries; mix well. Take a teaspoon of dough and start to form a ball. Push in half a cherry and roll again in hands to make a perfect ball. Bake on greased baking sheet in 325 degrees oven, 35 minutes. While hot, roll in tinted icing sugar.

Mrs. Karl Harris

Thimble Cookies

Cream:
1 cup shortening
1 cup brown sugar
Add:
2 eggs beaten
Sift together:

1½ tsp. baking powder
3 cups flour
salt
Add:
vanilla

Shape in small balls. Roll in fine coconut. Top with a cherry half. Bake in moderate oven. Ideal for special occasions.

Eloise Forbes

Cheese Crescents

½ lb. butter
1 pkg. cottage cheese

2 cups all purpose flour

Cream butter and cheese well. Add flour and form into balls. Place in fridge overnight. Roll out, spread jam and roll up. Bake 350° about 20 minutes or until brown. These should be kept in fridge after baked and warmed up before serving.

Mrs. Jerry Star

Orange Nut Cookies

½ cup butter
¼ cup sugar
1 egg yolk
½ tsp. vanilla

1 tbsp. lemon juice
1 tbsp. grated orange rind
1 cup flour
salt

Mix ingredients, then chill. Form in small balls and dip in beaten egg white, then roll in crushed nuts. Decorate with cherry and bake in 325 degrees oven for 10 or 15 minutes.

Mrs. Lawrence Cosman

Pecan Rolls

½ cup butter
2 tbsp. icing sugar
1 tbsp. cold water
pinch salt

1 tsp. vanilla
1 cup pastry flour, possibly a bit
more to make fairly firm
1 cup chopped pecans or almonds

Cream butter, add sugar, water and salt. Mix in rest of ingredients and form in shape of date. Bake in 325° oven until light brown. While still warm roll in granulated or icing sugar.

Mrs. W. D. King

Hazelnut Cookies

2 eggs
1¼ cups brown sugar
½ tsp. vanilla

¼ tsp. salt
¾ lb. chopped hazelnuts, not
blanched, or filberts

Beat eggs, add sugar, nuts, salt and vanilla. Drop on greased pan, bake in moderate oven 375 degrees until light brown. This should be a very stiff batter.

Glad MacDonald

Fudge Cookies

Blend in bowl:
1½ cups flour
½ tsp. salt
2 oz. melted Bakers chocolate or
4 tbsp. Bakers cocoa

1½ cups rolled oats
1 cup white sugar
¾ cup shortening
¼ cup cold instant coffee

When well mixed roll in finger length cookies. Roll in crushed peanuts. Bake 12 minutes.

Mrs. Wm. Woodward

Cinnamon Disks

½ cup margarine
1 cup white sugar
Cream well and add:
1 beaten egg
1 tsp. vanilla
    Roll in balls and roll in mixture of:
½ cup white sugar

Add:
1¼ cup all purpose flour
¼ tsp. salt
1 tsp. baking powder
½ cup chopped nuts

1 tsp. cinnamon

Press flat on greased cookie sheet with fork. Bake 350° - 375° approximately 10 minutes. Remove from sheet while hot, and put on cooling rack.

Gloria Beckingham

Swiss Chews

1 cup Bakers semi-sweet chocolate morsels
1 egg
½ cup brown sugar

¼ tsp. salt
1 tsp. vanilla
½ cup chopped almonds
(no flour)

Melt chocolate over hot water. Cool 5 minutes. Beat egg until thick. Beat in sugar gradually until very thick. Add remaining ingredients. Drop on greased pan. Bake 325° 10 minutes. (2 dozen).

Margaret (Mrs. F. A.) Nickerson

Scotch Cookies

½ lb. butter
5 tbsp. icing sugar
2 tbsp. corn starch

2 cups all purpose flour
½ tsp. vanilla
pinch of salt

Cream butter well. Add icing sugar and corn starch. Mix well. Add salt to flour, add gradually mixing well after each addition. Add vanilla.

Place on floured board, roll or pat to about ½ inch thickness. Cut round or square. Place on a greased and floured cookie sheet. Bake in a 350° oven till edges turn golden.

When cold, put a dab of butter icing on center of cookie. Add a piece of walnut or cherry.

Mrs. Raymond Amirault

Scotch Cakes

1 lb. butter
1 cup icing sugar (sifted before
  measuring)

4 cups bread flour
1 tsp. salt

Cream sugar and butter. Add flour and salt, with exception of one-half cup which may be used for kneading batter. Roll out to desired thickness and cut. Bake in 300 deg. oven till very lightly browned.

Mrs. J. T. Balmanno

Commandos

½ cup butter
1 egg yolk
1 tsp. baking powder
¼ cup brown sugar

1 cup cake flour or ⅞ cup sifted
hard wheat flour
⅓ tsp. salt
jam or jelly

Cream butter and sugar, add egg yolk. Mix in flour sifted with baking powder and salt. Roll small pieces of dough in balls and place on greased baking sheet. Make deep impression in each with thimble or finger tips. Bake in rather slow oven of 325°, 10 minutes. Deepen impressions and fill with jam or jelly. Beat egg white but not dry, and gradually beat in 4 tablespoons icing sugar. Add a few drops of almond flavoring. Drop spoonfuls of meringue on jam. Bake at 300° until meringue is brown.

Mrs. Eugene Saunders

Melting Moments

½ cup melted butter
½ cup shortening
¾ cup brown sugar
1 egg

1¾ cups pastry flour
½ tsp. cream of tartar
½ tsp. baking soda
1 tsp. vanilla

Combine brown sugar and fats, add egg and beat well. Mix and sift dry ingredients, and add to first mixture. Add vanilla and chill thoroughly. Drop by small spoonful on ungreased baking sheet 1½ inches apart. Place a piece of maraschino cherry in center of each and bake in moderate oven (350°) about 6 minutes.

Pubnico Women's Institute

Thumb Print Cookies

1½ cup sifted flour
½ tsp. salt
½ cup butter
½ cup brown sugar, firmly
packed

1 tsp. vanilla
2 tbsp. Superior milk
¼ cup chocolate bits, chopped
¾ cup sifted confectioners' sugar

Sift flour and salt. Blend butter, sugar, and vanilla. Add flour mixture, milk, semi-sweet bits. Form in 1 inch balls. Place on ungreased cookie sheet. With thumb, make depression in centre of balls. Bake at 375° F. 10 - 12 minutes. Roll several times while warm in confectioners sugar. Cool.

FILLING:
Melt ¾ cup Bakers chocolate
bits with
1 tbsp. shortening

Add:
2 tbsp. corn syrup
1 tbsp. water
1 tsp. vanilla

Stir until smooth. Cool. Fill cookies.

Mrs. George Biener

Chocolate Crackle Tops

2 eggs	¼ cup dry bread crumbs
1 cup sugar	2 tbsp. all purpose flour
3 sqs. Bakers unsweetened chocolate (finely grated)	½ tsp. cinnamon
2 cups shelled pecans (finely ground)	½ tsp. cloves
	icing sugar

Beat eggs and sugar till blended, with wooden spoon stir in chocolate, pecans, bread crumbs, flour, cinnamon, cloves. Mix well. Refrigerate 15 minutes. Heat oven 325 degrees.

Shape dough into small balls. Roll each on all sides with icing sugar. Arrange 1" apart on greased cookie sheet.

Keep rest of dough chilled when baking first sheet of cookies. Bake 12 to 15 minutes. They'll be soft and crackled on top. Remove to wire racks to cool. Store cookies tightly covered.

Mrs. Herman Shapiro

Strudelettes

1¼ cups sifted flour	1 tbsp. lemon juice
½ cup butter	3 egg whites
3 egg yolks beaten	½ cup sugar
1 tsp. lemon rind	1 cup ground walnuts

Sift flour into a medium size bowl; cut in butter until mixture is crumbly; stir in mixture of egg yolks, rind and juice. Blend to form a small ball. Chill for 30 minutes.

Beat egg whites until foamy in medium sized bowl; beat in sugar 1 tbsp. at a time, until mixture stands in stiff peaks. Fold in nuts. Divide dough into 5 - 6 parts. Roll out on a lightly floured board, until quite thin. Spread with nut mixture. Roll up jelly roll fashion, using a spatula or broad knife to help. Place seam side down on ungreased cookie sheet. Bake in moderate oven 15 - 20 minutes, or until light brown. When cooled, slice diagonally and sprinkle with icing sugar.

Mrs. David Goldberg

Almond Strips

½ lb. almonds	whites of 2 eggs
½ lb. icing sugar	salt and flavoring

Beat egg whites and sugar until foamy. Reserve 2 tbsp. in saucer adding 1 tbsp. more icing sugar to it. Put almonds through chopper and add to egg white mixture. Roll or pat flat on board using icing sugar to prevent from sticking. Cut in strips. Frost with sugar mixture from saucer. Bake in 300 degree oven until light brown. These keep well.

Mrs. Marguerite Eagles

Chipit Oatmeal Cookies

1 cup shortening — part butter
1 cup brown sugar
1 tsp. vanilla
½ cup coconut
¼ cup boiling water

2 cups sifted flour
1 tsp. baking soda
2 cups rolled oats
1 pkg. Bakers Chipits
½ tsp. salt

Cream shortening and sugar. Dissolve soda in hot water and add with vanilla. Add flour mixture part at a time. Stir in chipits.

Drop by small spoonfuls, flatten with fork. Bake in moderate oven 12 minutes.

For a plain oatmeal cookie omit chipits and coconut.

Mrs. John Robbins
Mrs. H. B. Stackhouse

Double Crunchie Cookies

1 cup all purpose flour
½ tsp. soda
¼ tsp. salt
½ cup shortening
½ cup white sugar
½ cup brown sugar

1 egg
½ tsp. vanilla
1 cup crushed corn flakes
1 cup oatmeal
½ cup coconut

Cream shortening, sugars, egg and vanilla. Add dry ingredients. Drop by spoonfuls on greased cookie sheet. Bake 8 - 10 minutes in 350° oven. When cool put together with chocolate icing.

VARIATION: Use a frosted flake cereal, and add ½ pkg. Bakers butterscotch chipits. Then proceed as for a drop cookie, and use singly.

Mrs. G. A. Patterson

Spice Oatmeal Drop Cookies

1 cup sugar
½ cup shortening
1 egg
3 tbsp. Silver Lasses Molasses
1½ cups sifted flour
¼ tsp. salt

½ tsp. cinnamon
½ tsp. nutmeg and ½ tsp. cloves
½ tsp. soda
½ tsp. baking powder
½ cup Superior milk
1½ cups oatmeal

Combine sugar, shortening and egg and molasses in large bowl. Beat until light and fluffy. Add dry ingredients with milk. Drop by teaspoonsful onto a greased baking sheet (about 2 inches apart as they spread). Bake in 350°, or moderate, oven 10 to 15 minutes, or until lightly browned.

Glenna (Mrs. Victor) King

Crisp Oatmeal Cookies

Cream:
1 cup butter (half Crisco)
1½ cups brown sugar
Add:
1 egg
Add these dry ingredients well
  mixed:

1½ cups oatmeal
1 cup coconut
1½ cups flour
½ tsp. soda
1 tsp. cream tartar
salt
vanilla

Drop from spoon. Half this recipe makes a nice batch.

Mrs. Harry Drew

Scratch-Me-Back Cookies

1 cup rolled oats
1 cup flour
2 cups fine coconut
1 cup brown sugar
1 cup shortening (butter &
  Crisco)

1 egg
½ tsp. soda
½ tsp. baking powder
¼ tsp. salt

Mix dry ingredients, work in shortening, add beaten egg. Drop by teaspoons on baking sheet, and flatten with fork. Bake 375° 8 - 10 minutes.

Hope Langille

Fruited Oatmeal Drop Cookies

2 cups oatmeal
3 cups flour
2 cups brown sugar
1 cup melted butter
1 cup walnuts chopped
1 cup chopped and seeded raisins

½ cup sour Superior milk
2 eggs well beaten
1 tsp. soda dissolved in the sour
  Superior milk
1 tsp. cinnamon

Mix dry ingredients together, then add other ingredients. Drop by teaspoon on greased pans. Bake in moderate oven.

Mrs. P. G. Boutilier

Chocolate Oatmeal Cookies

½ cup brown sugar
¼ cup white sugar
½ cup butter
1 egg
2 tbsp. coffee

2 sqs. Bakers melted chocolate,
  added last
2 handsful oatmeal (good ½ cup)
1 scant cup flour
1 tsp. baking powder
1 tsp. vanilla

Cream butter and sugar, add egg and beat well. Add coffee, beat. Add: oatmeal, the dry ingredients, the vanilla. Lastly add chocolate. Drop by spoonfuls on greased pan, a bit apart, as they spread. Bake in a hot oven.

Mrs. Wm. Muir

Coated Cookies

Cream:
1 cup brown sugar
2/3 cup shortening
Add:
2 eggs
Sift and add alternately with:
4 tbsp. Superior milk

2 cups flour
1 tbsp. baking powder
½ tsp. soda
salt
Add:
½ cup dates and nuts cut fine

Form into balls and roll in 2 cups crushed corn flakes. Bake in moderate oven.

Eloise Forbes

Caramel Nut Drops

(Makes about 3 dozen cookies)

Sift together:
2 cups sifted flour (pastry)
2 tsp. double acting baking
powder
½ tsp. salt

Cream:
¾ cup shortening with
½ cup brown sugar
Blend in:
1 egg yolk
½ tsp. vanilla

Add dry ingredients to creamed mixture. Mix until well blended. Shape dough into small balls about the size of a walnut. Dip into 1 egg white, unbeaten, then in ½ cup finely chopped nuts. Place on greased cookie sheet. Bake in moderate oven 15 - 20 minutes.

Corinne Pink

Slice O' Spice

3 cups sifted all-purpose flour
1 tsp. baking soda
1 tsp. cream of tartar
½ tsp. salt
½ cup butter or margarine
½ cup shortening

2 cups brown sugar
2 eggs unbeaten
1 tsp. vanilla extract
1 cup quick cooking rolled oats
½ cup granulated sugar
4 tsp. cinnamon

Sift together flour, soda, cream of tartar, and salt. Set aside. Cream together butter and shortening. Gradually add brown sugar, creaming well. Blend in eggs and vanilla. Beat well. Gradually stir in sifted dry ingredients; mix thoroughly. Stir in rolled oats. Chill dough about 1 hour for easier handling.

Divide dough into three parts; place each part on aluminum foil, shape into 12 inches long rolls, then wrap up in the foil and refrigerate at least five hours, or until firm enough to slice.

Mix sugar and cinnamon. Cut chilled rolls into ¼" slices and dip each slice into cinnamon-sugar. Place on greased baking sheets. Bake in 350°F. oven 9 to 12 minutes until golden brown. (Makes 9 dozen).

Mrs. Joseph Martin

Chocolate Drop Cookies

1½ cups flour
¼ tsp. salt
1 tsp. baking powder
2 oz. Bakers chocolate
½ cup shortening melted

1 cup brown sugar
1 egg
½ cup Superior milk
1 tsp. vanilla

Sift flour, salt, baking powder together. Melt shortening and chocolate. Add sugar, egg, milk and vanilla, then add sifted ingredients. Let stand 10 minutes. Drop from teaspoon onto greased baking sheet. Bake 375° 12 - 15 minutes. Makes 36.

Betty Ruth Stairs

Ginger Balls

¾ cup Crisco
½ cup sugar
3 tbsp. Silver Lasses Molasses
1 egg
2 cups bread flour

2 tsp. soda
2 tsp. ginger
1 tsp. each of salt, cinnamon
and nutmeg

Mix ingredients in order given, roll in balls, then roll in sugar. Place on greased pan and flatten slightly. Bake 12 minutes in quick oven.

Mrs. Seymour Kenney

Fruit Cookies

½ cup butter
¾ cup brown sugar
3 egg yolks
1¼ cups flour
¼ cup chopped nuts

½ cup chopped dates
⅓ cup chopped cherries
1 tsp. baking powder
1 tsp. vanilla
¼ tsp. salt

Cream butter and sugar. Add beaten egg yolks. Fold in rest of ingredients. Then fold in stiffly beaten egg whites until well blended. Drop on baking sheet and bake 10 minutes in 375° oven.

Myrtle Prosser

Silver 'Lasses Drop Cookies

1 cup Silver Lasses molasses
½ cup sugar
½ cup shortening
½ cup warm water containing
 1 tsp. soda
1 tsp. cinnamon

1 tsp. cloves
1 egg
1 tsp. salt
3 cups bread flour, scant
1 cup seedless raisins
⅓ cup walnuts chopped

Combine molasses, sugar, shortening and egg, and beat well. Add spice to flour and add to first mixture alternately with water. Add raisins and nuts and drop by teaspoons on greased baking sheet. Bake in moderate oven.

Bernice Trask

Ginger Cookies (Refrigerate)

½ cup butter
½ cup Crisco
¾ cup Silver Lasses molasses
2 tsp. baking soda
⅓ cup brown sugar

3 tsp. ginger
½ tsp. cloves
½ tsp. cinnamon
½ tsp. mace (optional)
3 cups flour

Cream shortening and sugar. Dissolve baking soda in molasses and allow to stand a few minutes. Add and stir well. Add dry ingredients. Form into two rolls. Wrap in waxed paper or foil and refrigerate. When desired, slice thin, flatten down as thin as possible with fork dipped in water, and bake at 350°. These improve in flavor the longer they are refrigerated.

Tested

Ice Box Cookies

1 cup butter or shortening
1 cup white sugar
1 cup brown sugar
2 eggs
1 tsp. vanilla

1 tsp. baking soda
3½ cups all-purpose flour
⅛ tsp. salt
1 cup nuts or 1 tbsp. caraway
  seeds

Cream butter, add sugar gradually and cream until light and fluffy. Add well beaten eggs, vanilla, beat well. Mix and sift flour, soda and salt and add to first mixture. Add chopped nuts and mix well. Form long rolls and leave in refrigerator overnight. Slice thin for cookies and bake in greased baking sheet in hot oven (400°) for 10 - 12 minutes or until light brown.

Mrs. G. M. MacDonald

Hawaiian Filled Cookies

2/3 cup shortening
2/3 cup sugar
2 eggs
1 tsp. vanilla
1 tsp. grated lemon peel

2 cups sifted flour
1½ tsp. baking powder
½ tsp. salt
1 cup pineapple filling

Cream shortening, sugar. Add eggs, beat well. Stir in vanilla, lemon peel. Sift flour, baking powder, salt together. Stir into creamed mixture. Chill.

Roll out lightly on floured board, ⅛ inch thick. Cut dough with 2½ inch cutter. Place half the circles on an ungreased baking sheet. Spread 1 tsp. filling almost to edges. Cut slits in remaining circles. Place over filling. Seal with fork.

Makes 30 cookies. Bake 400° 8 - 10 minutes.

FILLING:
¼ cup sugar
  Cook until thick. Cool.

1 tbsp. cornstarch
1 cup crushed pineapple

Mrs. J. D. Cohen

Perfect Raisin Cookies

2 cup raisins	4 cups flour
1 cup water	2 tsp. baking powder
1 tsp. soda	1 tsp. cinnamon
1 cup shortening	¼ tsp. nutmeg
2 cups white sugar	1 tsp. salt
3 eggs beaten	

Boil raisins and water together 5 minutes. Add soda and let cool. Cream shortening, add sugar and beaten eggs and blend well. Add sifted ingredients (flour, baking powder, cinnamon, nutmeg and salt). Lastly add raisin mixture. Drop on greased baking sheet. Bake 350° oven 15 - 20 minutes.

Mrs. P. Thomas

Date Pinwheels

Cook until thick and smooth:	1 tsp. cinnamon
1 lb. dates	1 tsp. baking soda
1 cup brown sugar	1 tsp. salt
1 cup water	1 cup shortening
Cool	2 cups brown sugar
DOUGH:	2 eggs well beaten
4 cups flour	

Cream shortening and sugar. Add eggs. Stir in sifted dry ingredients. Chill dough. Then divide into 4 portions. Roll between two layers of wax paper to ¼" thick. Remove top paper. Spread with date mixture, then by lifting edge of bottom paper roll dough as for jelly roll. Chill rolls overnight. When ready, slice and bake in moderate oven. This makes a large amount.

Mrs. Anna Shane (Halifax)

Double Chocolate Nuggets

Cream:	Add:
½ cup butter or margarirne	2 cups flour
1 cup brown sugar packed	½ tsp. baking powder
Add:	¼ tsp. salt
1 egg	alternately with:
1 tsp. vanilla	¾ cup Miracle Whip
2 sqs. Bakers chocolate, melted	1 cup Chipits
and cooled	Add lastly:
	½ cup nuts

Drop by teaspoon on buttered cookie sheet 2" apart Bake 10 minutes, moderate oven.

Mrs. F. A. Nickerson

Swedish Cookies

1 lb. butter	4 cups cake flour
1 cup sugar (add gradually)	1 tsp. vanilla
1 well beaten egg	

Put through cookie press on ungreased sheet. Cook in hot oven (400°) 4 - 5 minutes. If no cookie press, roll 2½" in diameter and chill overnight, then slice thinly and bake.

Joyce (Mrs. E. R.) Syvertsen

Oatmeal — Banana Macaroons

½ cup white sugar	½ tsp. soda
½ cup brown sugar	1 cup flour
½ cup shortening	1 cup oatmeal
1 egg	½ cup coconut
1 banana, mashed	1 tsp. vanilla
½ tsp. salt	

Cream together sugar and shortening. Add the mashed banana and then the remaining ingredients.

Bake as drop cookies in hot oven 10 to 15 minutes.

Mrs. W. N. Tinkham

Surprise Meringues

2 egg whites beaten stiff	1 tsp. vanilla
¾ cup white sugar	6 oz. pkg. Bakers chocolate chipits
¼ tsp. cream tartar	⅓ cup chopped walnuts
⅛ tsp. salt	

Mix dry ingredients. Add slowly to beaten egg whites. Add vanilla, chipits and nuts. Drop by teaspoonfuls on brown paper placed on cookie sheets. Bake at 300° 25 minutes.

Gwen Rand

Coconut Kisses

3 egg whites, beaten stiff	cornstarch (mix together)
1 cup white sugar and 1 tbsp.	1 tsp. vanilla

Fold into egg whites, cook in double boiler for 10 minutes. Take from heat and add:
2 cups coconut (1 cup shredded
   and 1 cup dessicated)

Drop on buttered sheet, top with small piece of cherry. Bake in slow oven until brown.

Mrs. Arnold Moses

Aunt Pat's Cookies

1 cup shortening (or butter)
1 egg
1 cup sticky raisins cut fine
3 or 4 cherries cut fine

¾ cup brown sugar
2 cups flour
1 tsp. vanilla

Cream butter and brown sugar well. Add egg, mix and add sifted dry ingredients. Lastly add fruit and mix. Drop from spoon on buttered cookie sheet and bake until brown in moderate oven. This is like a shortbread.

Mrs. Keith Cann

Date or Fig Filled Cookies

DOUGH:
½ cup butter

1 cup sugar

Cream with hands until runny.

Add:
1 egg
2 cups cake flour sifted with

1 tsp. baking powder and salt
vanilla

Form dough into roll 2" in diameter. Wrap and place in refrigerator overnight.

FILLING:
1 cup dates or figs

¼ cup brown sugar
½ cup water

Cook in double boiler, stirring until it is smooth and thick. Cool. Cut dough in slices. Place dab of filling on each slice. Then either cover with 2nd slice, or fold over to make crescents. Seal edges. Bake in moderate oven 10 - 12 minutes.

Nell Morton

Cherry Macaroon Cookies

1 egg
¾ cup sugar
2/3 cup butter
1¾ cups sifted flour
¼ tsp. salt
1 tsp. baking powder

½ tsp. soda
¾ tsp. almond extract
½ tsp. lemon rind
½ cup chopped cherries
¾ cup coconut

Beat egg until light and fluffy, add sugar, blend in shortening then dry ingredients, lastly add flavoring, lemon rind, cherries and coconut. Drop on cookie sheet and bake 350° for about 10 minutes.

Mrs. Lionel Purdy, Arcadia

Maple Praline Cookies

2/3 cup shortening (½ butter, ½ Crisco)
2/3 cup brown sugar
1 egg
½ tsp. maple flavoring

1¾ cups sifted all purpose flour
¼ tsp. salt
¼ tsp. soda
2 cups rice crispies

Cream shortening and sugar till fluffy; beat in egg and flavoring. Sift together flour, salt, and soda; add to creamed mixture; mix well. Stir in cereal. Drop from teaspoon 2" apart on greased cookie sheet Flatten with bottom of glass. Bake in 350° until brown. Makes about 3 dozen.

Ruth Urquhart

Tutti-Frutti Drops

1 tbsp. grated orange rind
¼ cup orange juice
1 cup finely grated apple
1 cup seeded raisins cut up
1 cup dessicated or flaked coconut
½ cup Superior milk
1 tsp. vanilla

1 tsp. salt
3 cups all purpose flour
2 tsp. baking powder
¼ tsp. soda
1 cup soft shortening
2 cups brown sugar packed
1 egg

Heat oven to 375°.
Combine orange rind, orange juice, apple, raisins and coconut in small bowl. Add milk and vanilla. Sift dry ingredients together.

Cream sugar, shortening and egg together, until fluffy. Add sifted dry ingredients to creamed mixture alternately with fruit mixture, mixing well after each addition. Drop by teaspoonfuls on cookie sheet, bake about 15 minutes.

Mrs. Loran Crowell

Peanut Cookies

2 cups sifted flour
3 tsp. baking powder
2 tsp. cinnamon
½ tsp. salt
½ cup butter

½ cup maple syrup
½ cup sugar
2 eggs beaten
1 cup salted peanuts

Heat oven to 350°. Sift flour with baking powder, cinnamon and salt. Set aside. In large bowl, at medium speed, beat butter until light. Gradually add syrup and sugar. Beat until very light and fluffy. Add eggs. Beat until well combined. At low speed add flour mixture until just blended. Stir in peanuts. Drop by teaspoon. Bake 12 minutes.

Mrs. Charles Robbins

Peanut Butter Cookies

½ cup butter
¼ cup peanut butter
½ cup white sugar
½ cup brown sugar
1 egg unbeaten

½ tsp. vanilla
1 cup flour (pastry)
½ tsp. salt
½ tsp. soda

Cream butter, peanut butter, and sugar. Add egg and mix well. Add vanilla, then dry ingredients. Roll in balls, flatten slightly and if desired peanut may be pressed on top. Bake at 350° until lightly browned.

Mrs. Munroe Gardner

English Tea Cakes

Cream:
1 cup white sugar
1 cup margarine
Add:
3 cups flour (all purpose)
1 tsp. salt
1 tsp. soda

2 tsp. cream of tartar
1 cup dates
Mix well and add:
2 beaten eggs
⅛ cup Superior milk
1 tsp. vanilla

Form in balls, dip in sugar. Bake 350°F. 15 to 20 minutes.

Mrs. Hubert Morton

Sugar Cookies

1 cup white sugar
¾ cup shortening (½ butter and
  ½ Crisco)
1 well beaten egg
2 cups all purpose flour
1 tsp. soda

1 tsp. cream tartar
salt
1 heaping tsp. ginger
½ tsp. nutmeg
¼ tsp. mace

Cream butter and sugar. Add well beaten egg. Add dry ingredients and spices. Roll in balls. Flatten very thinly with fork dipped in water and sprinkle with sugar. Bake in 350° oven about ten or twelve minutes.

Ruth Urquhart

Greek Cookies

2 eggs separated
2/3 cup sugar
½ cup salad oil
2 tbsp. orange juice
1 tsp. vanilla
3½ cups sifted flour

1½ tbsp. baking powder
½ tsp. salt
¼ cup Superior milk
1 egg, beaten
½ cup sesame seed (optional)

Beat 2 egg yolks thick and lemon-coloured. Add sugar gradually and beat till light. Add salad oil alternately with orange juice, beating constantly. Add vanilla. Sift dry ingredients together. Add 1½ cup dry mixture alternately with milk to first mixture. Beat 2 egg whites till stiff, but not dry. Fold into mixture. Fold in remaining dry ingredients. Knead lightly for about 2 minutes, on lightly floured board. Roll out ¼ inch. Cut into desired shapes. Beat whole egg and water, and brush on cookies. Sprinkle with sesame seeds. Place on greased baking sheet. Bake in moderate oven 350°F. about 20 minutes.

Grace S. Lewis

Fancy Almond Tea Tartlets

Line 2 doz. small tart pans with rolled out pie crust. Spread in bottom of each pan **1 tsp. of thick tart jam.**

TOP:
Put through food chopper:
¼ lb. washed and dried almonds
Beat until stiff:
1 egg white

Add:
¼ cup white sugar
½ tsp. almond extract
minced almonds

Drop a small spoonful of this almond mixture over jam. Bake 400° oven about 8 - 10 minutes.

Before removing from oven place ¼ of a marshmallow on top of each tart, return to cooler oven for 7 - 10 minutes or until marshmallow melts and is a light brown.

Mrs. Myra Sutherland

Pork Pies (Date)

1 sq. butter
3 tbsp. icing sugar
1 cup flour
1 cup dates
1 cup water

1 tsp. vanilla
1 cup brown sugar
¼ cup Superior cream (coffee or blend)
1 tbsp. butter

Press small amount of pastry into small tart pans. Shape to fit and bake at 325° until nicely brown.

FILLING: Cook dates and water. Add vanilla, allow to cool.

ICING: Boil brown sugar and cream for 2½ minutes. Add butter and cool in cold water. Beat and add a tsp. or two of icing sugar. As tart shells soften if kept filled, both filling and icing can be stored in fridge and filled and iced as desired.

Ruth Urquhart

Lena Myrtle's

Boil:	Add:
1 cup raisins	1 egg
1 cup water	Add raisin mixture:
Cool:	Sift and add:
Cream:	1½ cups flour
¾ cup brown sugar	1 tsp. baking powder
½ cup shortening	1 tsp. soda
	½ tsp. salt

Cook in paper cups approximately 20 minutes in 350° - 375° oven.

Joan Nickerson Johnston

Butter Tarts

Line tart pans with uncooked pastry. Place 1 tsp. filling in each. Bake in hot oven 400° till brown.

FILLING:

1 cup raisins or currants (scalded for 5 minutes). Drain and while still warm add 1 cup brown sugar and 2 tbsp. butter. Stir until butter melts and sugar dissolves. Add 1 beaten egg and 1 tsp. vanilla.

Mrs. Earl Churchill

Raised Doughnuts

1½ cups Superior milk	½ cup very warm water
¼ cup sugar	(110 - 115 degrees)
2 tsp. salt	2 pkg. active dry yeast
½ tsp. nutmeg	3 eggs beaten
2 tbsp. butter	6 cups sifted flour (about)

Scald milk. Stir in sugar, salt, nutmeg and butter; cool to lukewarm. Measure very warm water into bowl. Sprinkle with yeast; stir until dissolved. Add lukewarm milk mixture. Stir in well beaten eggs and ½ the flour; beat until smooth. Cover and let rise in a warm place, free from draft, until double in bulk (about 30 minutes). Stir down; beat in remaining flour. Turn dough out on lightly floured board; knead lightly to shape into smooth ball. Divide dough in half. Roll each half into circle ½ inch thick. Cut with doughnut cutter; place doughnuts on baking sheets. Cover with clean towel; let rise in warm spot free from draft until double in bulk (about 30 min.). Fry in 350° hot fat until golden brown, turn once. Do not prick with fork. Drain. Sprinkle with granulated sugar. Serve hot or cold. Makes 3 dozen

Hilda Zellers, Tusket Branch
Women's Institute of Nova Scotia

Refrigerator Doughnuts

1 cup white sugar	2 tsp. cream of tartar
3 tbsp. butter	1 tsp. baking powder
2 eggs well beaten	1 tsp. salt
To 4 cups sifted bread flour add:	1 tsp. nutmeg
1 tsp. soda	½ tsp. ginger

Beat eggs very well, and add sugar and melted butter. Then add dry ingredients alternately with 1 cup Superior milk. Chill overnight and fry the following day.

Alice (Mrs. James) Robbins

Fried Boats — Steiktir Partar (Icelandic)

2 eggs	2 tbsp. milk
2 tbsp. sugar	1 tsp. vanilla
¼ tsp. salt	Flour to make stiff dough

Beat eggs and add milk, sugar, vanilla and salt and then enough flour to make a stiff dough. Roll out as thin as possible and cut in oblongs 2 x 3 inches. Fry quickly in deep fat at 350°. These may be served plain or sprinkled with icing sugar. Others prefer them filled with whipped cream.

Eleanor Russell

Ginger Delights (Unbaked)

1 cup white sugar	2 tbsp. butter
½ small bottle preserved ginger	1 tsp. vanilla
(cut in fine pieces) and juice	pinch salt
½ cup chopped dates	

Cook these ingredients together 10 minutes or three minutes after it starts to boil. Cool a little then add.

1½ cups broken arrowroot biscuits	½ cup chopped nuts

Make in small balls and roll in dessicated coconut. Put in refrigerator to set. Makes 30 small balls.

Mrs. Douglas King

Brazil Logs

1 tin condensed milk	28 (single) graham wafers, rolled fine
2 sqs. Bakers unsweetened chocolate, melted	vanilla

Mix and chill until easy to handle, then roll small portion around whole brazil nuts to form log. Roll in coconut.

Mrs. Donald Chipman

Cherry Balls (Chocolate)

1 pkg. icing sugar
¼ cup butter

2 small bottles cherries
8 oz. coconut (fine)

Blend sugar, butter, coconut, make into balls placing well-drained cherry inside. Place in refrigerator to set.

Melt together:
1 pkg. Bakers semi-sweet
  chocolate

½ bar parawax
1 tsp. butter

Dip each cherry ball in this mixture to coat well. Place on wax paper to cool.

Mrs. John D. Corning

Cherry Balls

1 cup soft butter
1 cup icing sugar
1 tsp. vanilla

½ cup cherries (chopped)
¾ cup coconut
2 cups rolled oats

Cream butter and sugar. Add cherries, coconut, rolled oats and vanilla. Shape into balls. Roll in chopped nuts. Keep in fridge. Will keep for several weeks. Bring out several hours before serving as butter will be hard.

Mrs. C. L. Brown, Amherst

Peanut Butter Balls

1½ cups peanut butter
1½ cups icing sugar
1 cup dates (chopped)
1 cup walnuts (chopped)

6 tbsp. milk
6 sqs. Bakers semi-sweet
  chocolate
2 tbsp. parowax

Mix first five ingredients together and form into balls. Dip balls into the melted chocolate and parowax. Place on waxed paper until chocolate is set.

Mrs. Lyman Jackson

Date Balls

1½ cups dates cut fine
2 eggs

1 cup sugar

Cook above for 15 minutes or until fairly thick. Add:
¼ tsp. salt

1 tsp. vanilla

When above mixture is cool add 1 cup coconut and 1 cup rice crispies. Form in balls and roll in coconut. Keep in refrigerator.

Pubnico Women's Institute

Chocolate Dreams

6 oz. pkg. Bakers chocolate chips	8 oz. pkg. mixed candied fruit
6 oz. pkg. Bakers butterscotch chips	4 oz. pkg. marshmallows finely cut, or 2 cups miniatures
8 oz. pkg. cream sheese softened	2 cups dessicated coconut

Melt chipits in a 2½ qt. bowl over hot water. Stir in cream cheese, fruit and marshmallows. Mix well. Shape into balls, logs or patties. Roll in coconut. Place on wax paper. Chill until firm.

For variety: use 1 cup nuts or maraschino cherries in place of mixed fruit.

Claudia Swift

Rum Balls

½ lb. vanilla wafers	½ cup corn syrup
1 cup icing sugar	¼ cup rum
2 tbsp. Bakers cocoa	pecan halves
1 cup chopped pecans	

Roll wafers into fine crumbs. Mix with icing sugar and cocoa, nuts, syrup and rum. Stir well until all is blended. Shape into 1" balls. Let stand 1 hour. Roll in icing sugar and stick a nut in top of each. Store in tight container. Makes 5 dozen. Need to age several days before using.

Mrs. Boyd Ellis

Chocolate Snowballs

½ lb. marshmallows (quartered or miniature)	⅓ can condensed milk
½ cup chopped almonds or walnuts	18 graham wafers
	1 pkg. Bakers semi-sweet chocolate
¼ cup red or green cherries	1 cup desiccated coconut

Mix marshmallows, nuts and cherries with just enough Superior milk to hold together. Shape into round balls and roll in crushed wafers. Melt chocolate in double boiler. Dip each ball into chocolate, then roll in desiccated coconut. Place on waxed paper and let harden for a few minutes in refrigerator.

Olive Penney

Marshmallow Brownie Balls

1st PART:
1 cup icing sugar
1 egg well beaten
1 tsp. vanilla
¼ tsp. salt
2 sqs. Bakers unsweetened
chocolate (melted)

2nd PART:
½ cup chopped nuts
3 cups midget marshmallows
(plain or colored)

Mix first part together and add 2nd part. Form in small balls and roll in coconut. This will keep several weeks in fridge.

Mrs. J. M. MacDonald, Hebron

Fruit Balls

¼ lb. candied cherries
½ lb. almonds

1 cup coconut
1 unbeaten egg white

Put cherries, almonds and coconut through chopper, and mix with egg. Form into small balls and roll in sugar, or shape as strawberries. Roll in strawberry jello. Make stems of green citron or icing sugar. Keep in fridge.

Claudia Swift

Chocolate Chip Drops

1 6-oz. pkg. Bakers chocolate
chips
3 tbsp. soft peanut butter
Melt over hot water and add:
½ tsp. salt

1 tsp. vanilla
2 cups of crisp crumbled corn
flakes or
2 cups rice krispies

Mix well and drop from spoon on waxed paper-lined cookie sheet, and refrigerate.

Peg Cann

Golf Balls

1 cup Superior cream

2 small pkg. marshmallows (cut
in small pieces)

Whip cream stiff, add marshmallows. Let stand in refrigerator 4 - 5 hours. Add:
1 cup chopped dates

1 cup chopped walnuts

Let stand until stiff enough to handle. Form in balls and roll in graham wafer crumbs.

Mrs. G. A. Patterson

Chocolate Bon-Bons

1 cup peanut butter	½ cup chopped nuts
1 cup icing sugar	½ cup coconut
4 tbsp. butter	1 cup rice krispies

Mix well together, form into small balls the size of a walnut. Dip in the following:

1 6-oz. pks. Bakers chocolate chipits melted over hot water
add 2 tbsp. melted parafin

Dip the balls in the chocolate mixture a few at a time, using a fork to help remove them from pan. Allow to drip along the side of the pan before removing entirely. Place on waxed paper, chill, and when the coating has set, place in can and keep in a cool place.

Mrs. Leland Trask

FROSTINGS

Fluffy White Frosting

2 egg whites, unbeaten
¾ cup white sugar
⅓ cup corn syrup

2 tbsp. water
¼ tsp. cream of tartar
¼ tsp. salt

METHOD: Combine all ingredients. Cook over rapidly boiling water until mixture stands in stiff peaks, beating constantly. Remove from heat and add 1 teaspoon vanilla. Continue beating until thick enough to spread.

Mrs. Flo (Bill) MacConnell

Pineapple Parfait Frosting

Mix in double boiler:
2 unbeaten egg whites
1½ cups sugar

3 tbsp. canned pineapple juice
⅛ tsp. salt
⅛ tsp. cream of tartar

Mix well. Place over rapidly boiling water, beat constantly with rotary egg beater until mixture holds a peak (takes about 7 minutes). Remove from fire, add ⅓ tsp. grated lemon rind. Beat until thick enough to spread.

Virginia Ross

Fluffy No-Cook Icing

¾ cup sugar
1 tsp. vanilla
¼ cup boiling water

food coloring
¼ tsp. cream tartar
1 egg white, unbeaten

Place sugar, cream of tartar, vanilla and egg white in small deep bowl. Mix well. Add boiling water. Beat at high speed electric beater until mixture will stand in stiff peaks, about 4 or 5 minutes. Add few drops of coloring to tint desired shade. Sprinkle with coconut.

Mrs. Shenton Nickerson, Arcadia

Fudge Icing

Boil slowly until soft ball is formed in cold water:
1⅓ cups white sugar
2 tbsp. Bakers cocoa
1 scant ½ cup Superior milk
pinch salt

1 tsp. butter
½ tsp. vanilla

Remove from heat, beat until thick, but still soft. Spread on cake.

Mrs. George Ellis

Chocolate Fudge Icing

1 cup brown sugar
¼ cup Superior cream
2 sqs. Bakers chocolate

Boil 2½ minutes. Add:
2 tbsp. butter

Cool in pan of cold water and beat until quite thick, adding a few tsps. icing sugar just before putting on cake. Do not overbeat.

For plain fudge frosting omit chocolate.

Tested

Judy Icing

1 cup icing sugar
1 egg
1 sq. Bakers chocolate

4 tbsp. light Superior cream
2 tbsp. butter
½ tsp. vanilla

Melt chocolate and butter, add remainder of ingredients. Beat over ice water until light and thick, like mocha.

Mrs. Dave Goldberg

White Icing

Mix:
2 tbsp. flour into
½ cup Superior milk
and cook until thickened. Cool.

Mix until fluffy:
½ cup butter
½ cup white sugar
½ tsp. vanilla

Add cooled flour and milk mixture and beat until fluffy. Sufficient to cover 8 x 8 cake.

Y Auxiliary

Grandmother's Layer Cake Filling

(Lemon Honey)

Mix grated rind and juice of
1 lemon
1 cup sugar (white or brown)

2 tbsp. butter
1 well beaten egg

Cook over hot water until thickened, stirring constantly. Make in larger quantities and keep in refrigerator. Nice for hot biscuits or waffles.

Ethel Norris

Instant Topping

Mix ½ cup instant dry milk with ½ cup cold water in bowl, beat to soft peak stage (about 3-4 minutes.) Add 2 tbsp. lemon juice, beat until stiff. Add ¼ cup sugar, fold in well. Serve at once. Makes about 3 cups.

Joyce (Mrs. E. R.) Syvertsen

Butterscotch Frosting

⅓ cup butter   1 tbsp. Superior cream
½ cup brown sugar   ¼ tsp. vanilla

Beat butter until light and fluffy. Beat in sugar at high speed, then add cream and vanilla and mix well.

Tested

Never Fail Icing

1 egg white   ¼ tsp. vinegar
¾ cup white sugar   salt
2 tbsp. cold water   ¾ tsp. vanilla

Put unbeaten egg white, sugar, water, salt and vinegar in top part of double boiler. Place over heat and beat with egg beater for 5 minutes.) (3 minutes with electric beater). Have water boiling hard in bottom part of pot. Remove from heat. Add vanilla and beat for 2 minutes.

Mrs. Leland Trask

Soft Icing For Dark Cakes

Strain the juice of 1 lemon and mix with 2 tbsp. water. Boil in enamelled pan and pour it over about 1 lb. of icing sugar. Mix thoroughly with a wooden spoon. Add chopped almonds if desired.

Spread on cake while it is hot. Frosts large cake.

Mrs. C. C. McKay

Peanut Butter Frosting

2 tbsp. peanut butter   ⅛ tsp. salt
1½ tbsp. butter   2 tsp. lemon juice

Cream above ingredients together well, then cream in 2 tsp. orange juice, 2 tbsp. icing sugar, then 1 cup icing sugar.

Mrs. Ernest Syvertsen

Maple Syrup Icing

¾ cup maple syrup   1 egg white
¼ cup white sugar

Place in double boiler over boiling water. Beat until it forms peaks. Cool and beat two minutes.

Mrs. Harold Wilson

Almond Paste

½ lb. almonds   rose water OR lemon juice
pulverized sugar

Blanche and put almonds thru food chopper. Use equal weight of sugar and mix well, enough rose water OR lemon juice to moisten. Will cover one cake.

Dot (Mrs. E. L.) Brown

PIES, PASTRY AND FILLING

Vinegar Egg Pastry

1 lb. shortening
5 cups flour
1 tsp. baking powder

2 tsp. salt
3 tbsp. brown sugar

METHOD: Sift dry ingredients and blend well with shortening. Combine one egg with 1 tbsp. white vinegar. Beat with a fork. Add water to make ¾ cup liquid. Combine with dry ingredients mixing well. Store in refrigerator until ready to use.

Mrs. Flo (Bill) MacConnell

Pie Shell Mix

1 cup flour
¼ cup brown sugar
¼ lb. butter

½ cup coconut or walnuts
½ tsp. salt

Make crumble of above ingredients. Put in pie plate, cook 15 minutes, stirring once. Remove from oven. Save ¼ mixture for top. Pack remainder in pie plate, let cool. Fill with your favourite filling.

Gwen Rand

Bride's Pastry

½ lb. shortening (1 cup)
¼ lb. margarine or butter
3 cups flour

1 tsp. salt
½ cup cold water

METHOD — Cream shortening and butter or margarine, thoroughly. Add flour and salt, creaming in after each addition. Add water and mix well. Mixture will be a little sticky, so use plenty of flour on the board or cloth when rolling. This pastry will never be tough and will keep in the refrigerator for a week.

Mrs. Hayward Matthews
Corner Brook, Nfld.

Delicious Pastry For Tarts Or Cream Pie

2 cups flour
4 tsp. baking powder
1 cup butter or shortening
1 tsp. vanilla

½ tsp. salt
2 tbsp. sugar
1 egg
¼ cup Superior milk

Mix these in order given, roll out little thicker than usual.

Mrs. Clyde Churchill

Meringue Pie Crust

2 egg whites	¼ tsp. salt
¼ tsp. cream of tartar	½ cup sugar

Beat whites until frothy. Add salt and cream of tartar, beat until stiff but not dry. Add sugar gradually and beat until peaks form. Spread on bottom and sides of well greased 9" pie plate. Bake in slow oven 250° one hour or until light brown. Fill with berries or ice cream just before serving.

Mrs. Frank Rogers

Cottage Cheese Tartlets

Plain Pastry	3 tbsp. flour
⅓ cup orange marmalade	¼ tsp. salt
1½ cup cottage cheese	¼ cup Superior cream
2 eggs	1 tbsp. lemon juice
½ cup sugar	

Prepare pastry. Cut into 3½ inch rounds. Fit into small muffin pans. Spoon a little marmalade or jelly into each. Beat cheese with egg beater until smooth. Beat eggs until thick. Add sugar gradually, beating well after each addition. Add flour, salt, cream, lemon juice, and cheese. Mix lightly but thoroughly. Pour into pastry-lined muffin pans, filling to top. Bake in slow oven of 300° for 1 hour. These tartlets are delicious served warm.

Mrs. A. B. Anthony

Lakelawn Tarts

New Pastry for Tarts	Mix these in order given.
2 cups sifted flour	Filling:
½ tsp. salt	Juice of 2 oranges, rind of 1
¼ cup icing sugar	orange
1 tsp. baking powder	½ tsp. lemon flavoring
1 cup Crisco	¾ cup sugar
1 egg	2 tbsp. butter
1 tbsp. Superior milk	2 eggs

Mix and then fill unbaked shells half full. Bake in hot oven 400° for 10 minutes. Then reduce heat to 350° until filling is firm.

Mrs. Clyde Churchill

Pineapple Cottage Cheese Pie

An elegant two-layer pie

This makes a 9" pie.

Pineapple Filling:
1½ cups crushed pineapple
¼ cup sugar
1 tbsp. cornstarch
1 tbsp. water

Cottage Cheese Filling:
(Creamed cheese may be
    substituted)
½ cup sugar
1 tbsp. butter
¼ tsp. salt
3 tbsp. flour
½ cup creamed cottage cheese
OR 1 4 oz. pkg. creamed cheese
2 eggs
1 cup Superior milk
½ tsp. vanilla

Method:

Start oven at 450° F.. Adjust rack 5 or 6 inches above bottom of oven. Make unbaked pastry shell with high fluted edge.

Pineapple Filling:

Measure pineapple and sugar into a 3 qt. saucepan, and heat to boiling, stirring constantly. Remove from heat. Blend cornstarch and water to a smooth paste and stir thoroughly into pineapple mixture. Cook until thick and clear. Remove from heat and chill until cold. Meanwhile make

Cheese Filling:

Measure sugar and butter into mixing bowl. Mix thoroughly either with electric mixer or rotary beater. Then add salt, flour and cottage cheese or softened creamed cheese, and beat until thick and smooth. Beat eggs with a fork, and add them very slowly to cottage cheese mixture. Do not add any faster than mixture will take up the eggs. In same way, add milk very slowly, turning mixer (if used) to lowest speed. Stir in vanilla. Spread pineapple mixture over bottom of pastry-lined pan; place on stove. With cup, dip up cheese mixture and pour gently over pineapple mixture, so as not to disturb fruit. Carefully place in oven and bake 15 minutes at 450° F.; reduce heat to moderately slow (325° F.) and bake 30 to 35 minutes longer. Remove to cake rack and cool 2 or 3 hours before cutting. Different and delicious.

Clara Harris

Date Pie

First Part:
1 cup dates
2 cups Superior milk
⅛ tsp. salt

Second Part:
1 cup Superior milk
2 eggs
1 tsp. vanilla

Allow dates, salt and 2 cups milk to simmer on stove till mushy. Then add the 1 cup milk, vanilla and two well beaten eggs. Pour in unbaked pie shell. Bake in hot oven 450° for 10 minutes. Reduce heat to 325° and bake 30 - 40 minutes longer or until knife inserted comes out clean.

Mrs. Bernard Strong

Rhubarb Meringue Pie

3 cups rhubarb cut in ½" pieces
boiling water
1½ cups sugar
2 tbsp. flour

salt
¼ tsp. cinnamon
1 tbsp. melted butter
3 egg yolks, beaten

Pour boiling water over rhubarb and let stand for 5 minutes, drain, mix other ingredients and add to drained rhubarb. Spread mixture in unbaked pie shell. Bake 10 minutes in 425° oven. Reduce heat to 350° for 35 minutes. Top with meringue and brown.

Meringue:

Beat 3 egg whites with ¼ tsp. cream of tartar to soft peaks. Add 6 tbsp. sugar gradually, and beat to soft peaks.

Doris Cox

Rhubarb Creamed Pie

2½ cups rhubarb
1 cup sugar
2 eggs
2 tbsp. butter

3 tbsp. flour
½ cup orange juice
rind of 1 orange

Pour boiling water over Rhubarb and let stand for 10 minutes. Then pour off. Arrange rhubarb in pie shell. Mix sugar, flour, beaten eggs, juice, rind and butter and pour over the rhubarb. Roll out pie pastry, cut into ½ inch strips length of pie, and arrange them on top to suit your taste. Bake in hot oven until golden brown. Reduce heat, until cooked. About 1 hour. Good with whipped cream.

Mrs. Clyde Churchill

Custard Pie

4 eggs, beaten slightly   **Pinch salt**
½ cup sugar
3 cups scalded Superior milk, added gradually to the above mixture.
Then add ¼ tsp. vanilla or nutmeg.

Pour into unbaked pie shell and bake 10 minutes in hot oven, then 20 - 25 minutes in moderate to slow oven.

NOTE:—1.   Chill pastry after it is rolled.
        2.   Brush pastry with egg white.
        3.   Hot oven; then cool to moderate.
        4.   A cup of cooked pitted prunes cut up are a delicious addition to a custard pie.

These rules apply to all filled pies in unbaked shells.

Mrs. Wilfred Kinsman

Coconut Cream Pie

2 cups Superior milk   butter size of a walnut
½ cup coconut   ¼ tsp. salt
2 egg yolks   2 tbsp. cornstarch
¾ cup sugar

Mix coconut and milk in top of double boiler. When hot stir in sugar, beaten egg yolks, and cornstarch dissolved in milk. Add salt and butter. When thick pour into cooked pie shell. Use whites of eggs for meringue, and brown in medium oven.

Mrs. Odessa Ellis

Butterscotch Cream Pie

1 cup brown sugar   1½ cups Superior milk
3 tbsp. flour (level)   ¼ tsp. salt
3 tbsp. butter   1 tsp. vanilla
3 eggs

Scald milk in top of double boiler over boiling water. Make a paste of flour, salt, brown sugar, and ¼ cup cold milk (this amount is not taken from 1½ cups as mentioned above). Add to hot milk, stirring until smooth and thick. Cover, continue cooking for 10 minutes, stirring occasionally. Pour a little of the hot mixture over the slightly beaten egg yolks. Stir into the hot mixture, continue cooking 3 minutes. Remove from heat, add butter and vanilla. Pour into baked shell, cover with meringue and bake in moderate oven, 350°, until delicately brown.

Eloise Forbes

Lemon Meringue Pie

Add juice and rind of one lemon to 1¼ cup water and bring to a boil.

Mix together:	Salt
1 cup sugar	3 egg yolks, beaten
⅓ cup flour	1 tbsp. melted butter

Pour hot lemon and water over egg mixture and cook in top of double boiler until thick and smooth.

Pour into baked pie shell and cover with meringue made with the 3 egg whites beaten stiff with 3 tbsp. sugar, ½ tsp. baking powder added gradually. Bake in 275 degrees oven for 20 - 30 minutes.

Mrs. C. F. MacMullen

Apple Pie

1 unbaked 9" pastry shell	½ tsp. nutmeg
3 or 4 large baking apples	½ cup sugar (for topping)
½ cup sugar (for filling)	¼ cup butter (for topping)
2 tbsp. flour (for filling)	½ cup flour (for topping)

Method:

Quarter apples and halve crosswise (approximately 7 cups) and place in large bowl. Make filling: Combine sugar, flour and nutmeg in cup. Sprinkle over apples and toss to coat well. Spoon into pastry shell. Drizzle with lemon juice. Combine sugar, flour for topping in a small bowl. Cut in butter. Sprinkle over apples to cover top. Slide pie into a heavy brown paper bag large enough to cover pie loosely. Fold open end of bag twice and fasten with paper clips. Place on large cookie sheet for easy handling. Bake one hour 425°.

Mrs. Flo (Bill) MacConnell

Grapefruit Pie

1 cup sugar	¼ tsp. salt
5 tbsp. cornstarch	2 egg yolks
¾ cup grapefruit pulp and juice	½ cup orange rind
1½ cup boiling water	½ cup pecans, chopped

Mix sugar, cornstarch and part of grapefruit and juice. Add boiling water and salt. Stir until thick. Cook 10 minutes more in double boiler, then add remaining grapefruit. Beat egg yolks with orange rind and add to cooked mixture. Cook 2 minutes, add pecans. Remove from heat and pour into baked pie shell. Cover with meringue made from 2 egg whites. Brown in oven.

If canned grapefruit is used, reduce amount of orange rind.

Mrs. Omer Milestone

Mock Cherry Pie

1 cup cranberries	1 cup sugar
½ cup raisins	1½ tbsp. flour
½ tsp. vanilla	1 cup water
pinch of salt	

Cook all together until thick. Bake between two crusts in 400° oven until brown.

Mrs. Gordon Hughes

Pineapple Pie

1 recipe pastry	¼ cup sugar
1 can crushed pineapple	1 tbsp. butter
2 tbsp. cornstarch	1 tbsp. lemon juice
¼ tsp. salt	

Line 8" plate with pastry, cook undrained pineapple, cornstarch, salt and sugar over low heat until thick. Add butter and lemon juice and pour into pastry lined plate. Cover with lattice top. Bake at 425° until light brown (35 - 40 minutes).

Mrs. Frank Rogers

Raisin Pie

2 cups raisins	2/3 cup sugar
3 tbsp. lemon juice	2 tbsp. cornstarch
1½ cups boiling water	¼ tsp. salt
1 tsp. grated lemon rind	

Wash raisins if necessary, cover with boiling water, simmer over low heat until raisins are plump. Mix sugar and cornstarch and stir into raisins. Cook, stir constantly until mixture begins to thicken. Remove from heat, cool slightly, add juice and rind of lemon. Bake between two pastry crusts.

Tested

Eggnog Chiffon Pie

9" pastry shell (baked & cooled)	2 tsp. rum extract
2 tsp. plain gelatin	¾ cup Superior whipping cream
3 tbsp. cold water	3 egg whites
1 cup Superior milk	¼ cup plus 3 tbsp. sugar
3 egg yolks, beaten	¼ tsp. nutmeg or
½ cup sugar	2 tbsp. chopped pecans or
¼ tsp. salt, scant	pistachios

Method:

Sprinkle gelatin over cold water for 5 minutes to soften. Blend next 4 ingredients thoroughly in top of double boiler. Place over boiling water and cook and stir with wooden spoon until mixture just thickens. Remove from heat, add gelatin, stir to dissolve; add extract.

Chill until thick like syrup. Beat cream until thick, but still smooth. Remove mixture from frig and fold in with rubber scraper. Quickly beat egg whi·es to stiff foam; gradually beat in remaining sugar until stiff and shiny. Fold meringue quickly but thoroughly into gelatin mixture; quickly pour into pastry shell. When filling settles, sprinkle with nutmeg or nuts. If both are desired, fold nutmeg into filling with rum extract. Chill 2 to 3 hours.

Clara Harris

White Chiffon Pie

Make a 9" pie shell with high fluted edge.
Soften 1 envelope of unflavored gelatin in ¼ cup cold water

Mix together in saucepan:
½ cup sugar
4 tbsp. flour
⅛ tsp. salt
Stir in gradually 1½ cups Superior milk

Cook over low heat, stirring constantly until it boils. Boil 1 minute. Remove from heat, stir in softened gelatin until dissolved. Cool. When mixture is partially set beat with rotary beater until smooth. Blend in ¾ tsp. vanilla and ¼ tsp. almond extract. Gently fold in ½ cup Superior heavy cream, whipped until stiff. Carefully fold in meringue (recipe below), fold in 1 cup moist shredded coconut. Pile into cooled pie shell. Sprinkle over top ¼ - ½ cup shredded coconut. Chill until set, about 2 hours. Take pie from fridge 10 minutes before serving, to remove chill from crust.

Meringue:
Beat until frothy 3 egg whites and ¼ tsp. cream of tartar. Gradually beat in ½ cup sugar, continue beating until mixture is stiff and glossy.

Joyce (Mrs. E. R.) Syvertsen

Pumpkin Chiffon Pie

1½ tbsp. gelatin
¼ cup cold water
1½ cups of pumpkin
½ cup Superior milk
¼ tsp. ginger

½ tsp. nutmeg
½ tsp. salt
1 cup sugar
3 eggs, separated

To beaten egg yolk add pumpkin, ¾ cup sugar, milk, salt and spices. Cook until thick (double boiler). Soak gelatin (cold water). Add to hot mixture. Stir well. Cool.

Beat egg whites stiffly. Add sugar slowly. Fold egg whites into mixture. Put in pie shell which has been cooked, or graham cracker shell.

Mrs. G. E. Littlefield

Strawberry-Rhubarb Chiffon Pie

1 pkg. (1 lb.) frozen rhubarb
¼ cup water
½ cup sugar
1 reg. size pkg. (3 ozs.) Straw-

berry Jello
1 pkg. frozen strawberries
½ cup Superior whipping cream
1 baked 9" pie shell, cooled

Place rhubarb, water and sugar in saucepan. Simmer 5 - 10 minutes or until large pieces rhubarb can be broken with a fork. Remove from heat. Add jello, stirring until it is dissolved. Add frozen strawberries, stirring until separated. Then chill until thickened. Whip cream until stiff. Fold into fruit mix. Pour into shell. Chill 3 hours. Garnish with whipped cream. Serves 8.

Mrs. Tracy Goodwin

Lemon or Lime Chiffon Pie

1 baked pie shell
1 envelope (1 tbsp.) gelatin
½ cup cold water
4 egg yolks
⅛ cup sugar
⅛ tsp. salt

⅓ cup lemon or lime juice
1 tsp. rind
food coloring (green if desired)
4 egg whites
½ cup sugar

Bake pie shell and cool. Sprinkle gelatin on cold water in top of double boiler. Beat egg yolks slightly with beater. Add ½ cup sugar, salt and juice. Mix well. Add to softened gelatin. Cook over boiling water until gelatin is dissolved and mixture slightly thickened (3 minutes). Remove from hot water. Add fruit rinds and coloring. Chill, stirring occasionally until mixture mounds slightly when dropped from spoon. Beat egg whites until they will hold a soft peak. Gradually add ½ cup sugar, beating well after addition. Fold into partially set gelatin mixture. Fill pie shell. Chill in refrigerator.

Tested Y Auxiliary

Heavenly Pie

4 egg whites
1 cup white sugar
¾ tsp. cream of tartar

½ tsp. vanilla
1 tsp. vinegar

Beat egg whites, sugar and cream of tartar together until stiff, but not too dry, add vanilla and vinegar. Spread in buttered 9" pie plate. Cook for one hour in a 275° oven.

Filling:
4 egg yolks

½ cup white sugar
juice of one lemon

Put in double boiler, add 3 tbsp. water and cook until thick. Whip ½ pint of Superior whipping cream. Put ½ of cream on top of meringue, then put in filling (which has been cooled) and rest of cream. Dot with cherries and walnuts.

Mrs. Lyman Jackson

Magic Pie

Mix 1 heaping cup of cornflakes, measured after being crushed, with ¼ cup melted butter and ¼ cup sugar. Pat down in a square pan or pie plate.

Filling:

1 can sweetened condensed milk
¼ cup lemon juice

1 small can crushed pineapple
10 - 12 marshmallows cut in pieces

Fold into the above ½ cup cream, whipped. Pour filling into pan. Chill in refrigerator. Garnish with cherries. Serves 9.

Mrs. Gertrude Baker

Peach and Ice Cream Pie

16 marshmallows
2 tbsp. crushed peaches
2 egg whites
¼ cup granulated sugar
¼ tsp. salt

1 brick Superior vanilla ice cream
Sliced fresh or canned peaches for garnish
3 tbsp. lemon juice

Heat marshmallows with crushed peaches slowly folding over and over until marshmallows are half melted. Remove from heat and continue folding until mixture is smooth and fluffy. Cool. Beat egg whites until they hold a peak. Add sugar slowly, beating constantly. Add salt. Fold into marshmallow mixture. Slice ice cream and place in baked pastry shell. Cover with sliced peaches, mixed with lemon juice and top with marshmallow meringue swirled attractively.

Brown quickly in broiler or very hot oven (450 F.) for ½ minute. Tuck peach slices on top in swirls and serve immediately.

Mrs. Joseph Martin

Strawberry Pie

1 quart fresh strawberries

1 baked pie shell

Take 1 cup of the berries cut in half, add ¾ cup of water. Heat and simmer for 4 minutes.

Add:
1 cup sugar, mixed with
3 tbsp. cornstarch

Cook until thick and transparent.
Add:
1 tbsp. lemon juice

Take remaining whole strawberries, cover pie shell bottom evenly, pour cooked mixutre over. Serve with Superior whipped cream.

Mrs. Arnold Moses

Strawberry Glamour Pie

2 egg whites
½ tsp. vinegar
¼ tsp. salt
⅓ cup sugar
1 9" baked pastry shell

Filling:
2 cups sliced fresh strawberries
¼ cup sugar
1 tbsp. cornstarch
½ cup water
½ cup Superior whipping cream

Beat egg whites with vinegar and salt to soft peaks. Gradually add ⅓ cup sugar beating to stiff peaks. Spread on bottom and sides of pastry shell. Bake in 325° oven 12 minutes. Cool. Mash ½ cup of berries with ¼ cup sugar. Combine cornstarch and water; stir in mashed berries. Cook and stir until mixture boils. Cook 2 minutes. Stir in few drops red food coloring and rest of berries. Cool slightly. Spread over meringue, chill. Whip cream. Spread over all.

Mrs. D. J. Urquhart

Pink Cloud Pie

1 9" baked pastry shell
Meringue:
3 egg whites
¾ tsp. lemon juice
6 tbsp. fine fruit sugar
Topping:

1 egg white
½ - 1 cup sugar
1 tsp. lemon juice
1 cup drained, sliced or crushed
    fresh or frozen strawberries
⅛ tsp. salt

Make a pastry shell. cool.

Make meringue by beating egg whites until they hold a soft peak. Gradually beat in the sugar, adding the lemon juice when half the sugar has been added. Continue to add sugar, beating until egg whites will hold a stiff peak.

Spread meringue in cooled pie shell and bake in a slow oven 300 - 325 degrees until meringue is set, but not brown, about 15 minutes. Remove from oven and cool slowly.

Topping. Beat egg white until it is foamy. Add sugar, lemon juice, strawberries and salt. Beat vigorously with electric beater. until fluffy and stiff. Pile on meringue filled shell just before serving.

Ruth Pink

Pecan Pie

½ cup white sugar
¼ cup butter
1 cup light corn syrup

1 tbsp. vanilla
3 eggs

Beat all together, well. Place in unbaked 9" pie shell. Pour pecans over top to completely cover pie. Bake 375° - 40 minutes.

Maude Churchill

Chocolate Marvel Pie

Melt and blend 1 pkg. Bakers
  semi-sweet chocolate
3 tbsp. Superior milk
2 tbsp. sugar
Cool, and add:

4 egg yolks, one at a time, beaten
  well after each addition
Beat egg whites and fold in chocolate mixture

Put in 9" pie shell which has been baked. This is a very rich pie. For a lighter, more chiffon-like pie, use a 6 oz. pkg. Bakers chocolate chips.

Mrs. G. E. Littlefield

Chocolate Cheese Pie

1¼ cup chocolate wafers

¼ cup margarine, melted

Roll wafers and add melted margarine and press into pie plate. Save a few for top.

In double boiler combine:
8 oz. Philadelphia Brand cream
  cheese
½ cup sugar

Blend well:
Add:
3 beaten egg yolks
¼ cup Superior milk

Cook 10 minutes, stirring. Remove from heat and add:

1 envelope gelatin, softened in
¼ cup water and ¼ cup lemon
  juice

Beat 3 egg whites to soft peaks
add ¼ cup sugar

Fold into cheese mixture. Pour into chocolate crust. Add rest of chocolate wafer mix. Chill until ready to serve, then garnish with Superior whipped cream and maraschino cherries.

Mrs. D. F. Macdonald

Lemon Cake Pie

1 cup sugar
¼ cup flour
¼ cup butter, melted
⅛ tsp. salt
2 eggs, separated

2 lemons, juice and grated peel
  (about ¼ cup)
1 cup Superior milk
1 9" baked pie shell

Combine sugar, flour, melted butter, salt and egg yolks. Beat until smooth. Beat in lemon juice and peel. Add milk, beating slowly. Beat egg whites stiff but not dry, fold in mixture. Bake pie shell in a moderate oven, 350 degrees for 5 minutes. Pour filling into pie shell. Bake 40 minutes or until filling is firm. When cut there will be a delicate cake layer on top of pie filling.

Hilda Zellers, Tusket Branch
Women's Institutes Nova Scotia

Funny Cake Pie

1 unbaked pie shell	¼ cup shortening
1¼ cups cake flour	½ cup milk
1½ tsp. baking powder	1 egg, unbeaten
½ tsp. salt	3 tbsp. chopped nuts or coconut
¾ cup sugar	½ tsp. vanilla

Method:

Measure shortening into bowl. Sift in dry ingredients, add milk and vanilla. Beat two minutes on low speed with mixer. Add egg and beat one minute more. Pour batter into uncooked pie shell. Pour luke warm chocolate sauce gently over batter. Sprinkle with nuts or coconut. Bake 50 - 55 minutes, 350°.

Mrs. Flo (Bill) MacConnell

Mock Apple Pie

Pastry for 1 crust pie	1 tsp. grated lemon peel
30 Ritz crackers	½ cup butter
2 cups water	½ cup brown sugar
2 cups sugar	⅓ cup flour
2 tsp. cream of tartar	¼ tsp. cinnamon
2 tbsp. lemon juice	

Roll out pastry and fit into 9" pie plate. Combine water, sugar and cream of tartar in sauce pan. Boil and add crackers. Boil gently 10 minutes. Add lemon juice and peel. Cool, then pour in pie shell. Bake at 425° for 10 minutes. Meantime combine brown sugar, flour, butter and cinnamon, with blender until size of peas. Sprinkle over top of pie and return to oven for 15 minutes.

Shirley Kempton

Spicy Apple Twists

Peel 3 large apples. Cut into 15 or 16 wedges.
Sift: 1½ cups flour (approx.)   1 tsp. salt
Cut in: ¼ cup shortening

Sprinkle 4 to 5 tbsp. water. Toss lightly. Form into a ball. Flatten to ½" thick. Smooth edges. Spread on 2 tbsp. butter. Fold and roll out to 16 x 10 rectangle. Cut into 1" strips. Wrap around apple slices and arrange in 13 x 9 pan, sides not touching. Brush with ⅓ cup melted butter. Sprinkle with mixture of ½ cup sugar and 1½ tsp. cinnamon.

Pour: ¾ cup water in pan. Bake 20 to 30 minutes in 450° oven.

Serve warm with whipped cream.

Gloria Beckingham

STEAMED AND BAKED PUDDINGS

English Plum Pudding

1¼ cups white sugar	1½ tsp. salt
6 eggs, well beaten	1 lb. seeded raisins
½ cup Silver Lasses molasses	½ lb. currants
½ cup corn syrup	¼ lb. glaced cherries, quartered
1½ cups dry bread crumbs	¼ lb. candied orange peel
1¾ cups pastry flour	¾ lb. shredded suet
1 tsp. nutmeg	(add nuts if desired)

Combine sugar and eggs, beat well and add the molasses and corn syrup. Add the dry bread crumbs and other dry ingredients. Now mix in the chopped fruit and suet. Turn into well greased moulds and steam until done. (Twenty or twenty-eight oz. cans may be used, covered with waxed paper and tied tight with a piece of twine. These should steam for three hours.)

Mrs. J. T. Balmanno

Prize Plum Pudding

1¼ cups flour	¾ cup seeded raisins
½ tsp. cinnamon	1 cup currants
½ tsp. nutmeg	1 cup chopped figs
¼ tsp. mace	1 cup cut mixed fruit
¼ tsp. cloves	1 cup halved cherries
½ tsp. salt	½ cup honey
1½ cups stale crumbs	4 eggs, well beaten
1½ cups shredded suet	½ cup fruit juice or brandy
1½ cups brown sugar	½ - ¾ cup Superior milk
1 cup sultana raisins	½ tsp. soda, dissolved in
1 cup muscatel raisins	1 tbsp. warm water

This pudding is delicious. The amount of milk will depend on staleness of crumbs.

Mix ingredients in order given. Fill well-buttered bowls 2/3 full, cover with several layers of wax paper, tie down, then cover with foil or cloth, and tie. Steam 5 hours. Before using steam 2 hours more.

This pudding best if made at least 4 - 6 weeks before using to allow the flavour to mellow and mature.

Mary Sperry

Carrot Pudding

1 cup sugar	1 cup currants
½ cup butter	1 cup raisins
1 cup grated carrots	1 egg
1 cup grated potatoes	salt
2 cups flour	1 tsp. soda

Cream butter and sugar — add beaten egg, grated vegetables, mix well. Add sifted dry ingredients and fruit. A few cut dates and mixed peel may be added. Steam 3 hours.

Mrs. J. K. Taylor

Steamed Cranberry Pudding

½ cup Silver Lasses molasses	1 tsp. baking powder
½ cup boiling water	½ tsp. salt
2 tsp. soda	1 cup whole fresh cranberries
1½ cups flour (all-purpose)	

Combine molasses, boiling water and soda. Stir to blend. Cool to lukewarm. Sift flour, baking powder and salt together into cooled mixture. Stir in cranberries. Put in 1 quart casserole mold. Cover lightly with foil. Steam 1½ hours. (Serves 6 - 8)

BUTTER SAUCE
(FOR PUDDING)

½ cup sugar	½ cup light Superior cream
¼ cup butter	

Combine in small saucepan. Simmer for 15 minutes. Serve hot over Cranberry Pudding. Delicious!!

Marion Gardner

Cherry Dessert

Combine:

1st — 2 cups graham wafer crumbs, ⅓ cup butter

2nd — 2 cups miniature marshmallows, mixed with ½ pint Supperior whipped cream.

1 tin E. D. Smith's Cherry Pie Filling
Grease 8" pan. Arrange as follows:
1st layer is ½ crumb mixture
2nd layer is ½ marshmallow mixture
3rd layer is tin of Cherry Pie Filling
4th layer is rest of marshmallow mixture
5th layer is rest of crumb mixture
Chill in refrigerator overnight. Cut in squares to serve.

Marjorie Strong

Cranberry Crunch

Mix together:—
1 cup uncooked rolled oats

½ cup flour
1 cup brown sugar

Cut in ½ cup butter until crumbly. Place half this mixture in 8 x 8 greased pan. Cover with 2 cups (or little less) cranberry sauce (or canned cranberries). Spread rest of oatmeal mixture over sauce. Bake 45 minutes at 350° Cut in squares. Serve topped with vanilla ice cream.

Maude Churchill

Apple Tapioca

½ cup sugar
½ tsp. salt
½ cup quick cooking tapioca
2½ cups boiling water

¼ tsp. nutmeg
3 cups sliced, pared and cored
apples

Combine sugar, salt, tapioca in top of double boiler.

Add boiling water, gradually while stirring. Add apples and nutmeg, when mixture is transparent. Pour in baking dish and bake at 350° for 1¼ hours, or until apples are tender. Serve hot or cold with cream.

Mrs. Nathan Eaton

Raspberry Crunch

1 pkg. frozen rhubarb
1 pkg. frozen raspberries
½ cup sugar
3 tbsp. cornstarch
1½ cups flour

1 cup brown sugar
1 cup oatmeal
1 tsp. cinnamon
½ cup melted butter

Thaw and drain fruits. (Cut rhubarb in small pieces). Measure juice, add water, if necessary, to make 1 cup. Combine ½ cup sugar and corn starch. Blend in liquid. Cook, stirring constantly until thick and clear. Remove from heat and cover.

Mix flour, brown sugar, oats, cinnamon and butter to make coarse crumbs. Press 2/3 into 9 x 9 pan. Cover with fruit and thickened juice. Sprinkle with remaining crumbs. Bake in slow oven 325° for 55 to 60 minutes. Cool slightly; cut into squares. Serve warm or cold with whipped cream.

Mrs. Lloyd Crosby

Crepe Flambe

Crepes:
Ingredients:
3 eggs
1 cup Superior milk

¾ cup flour
1 tbsp. sugar
1 tsp. salt
2 tbsp. butter (melted)

Beat eggs and milk. Sift flour, sugar and salt. Mix both together with electric mixer or by hand and add melted butter. Let stand in a cool place, preferably in the refrigerator, for ¾ of an hour. Cook in an app. 8" omelet pan. Put a tiny amount of oil in bottom of pan and while frying butter sides. Crepes are to be paper thin.

Flambe:
Ingredients:
½ cup butter
2/3 cup of sugar

1 tsp. orange peel
1 tsp. lemon peel
3 oz. brandy
8 or 10 crepes

In a chafing dish put the butter, sugar and add the orange and lemon peel. Warm crepes in sauce and fold in triangles with fork and spoon. Place to the side while doing others. Put on centre, add brandy, ignite. Serve immediately when brandy has burned off.

Mrs. Laurie Mushkat

Baked Fudge Dessert

1 cup sifted cake flour
2 tsp. baking powder
½ tsp. salt
¾ cup white sugar
2½ tbsp. Bakers cocoa

½ cup nuts chopped
½ cup Superior milk
1 tsp. vanilla
2 tbsp. melted shortening

Sift flour, baking powder and salt; add sugar, cocoa, and nuts. Make a well in centre, add milk, vanilla and melted shortening. Stir lightly and rapidly. Pour batter into oiled 1½ qt. casserole.

TOPPING

4 tbsp. Bakers cocoa
1½ cup brown sugar

1¾ cups hot water

Measure cocoa, brown sugar, and hot water into a bowl. Beat rapidly for 3 minutes. Pour over uncooked batter. Bake at 350° until done. As this dessert bakes, the batter will rise through the rich chocolate sauce. Serve it hot with whipped cream.

Mrs. Eldon Eagles

Orange Pudding

3 egg yolks beaten
1 tbsp. cornstarch
1 cup Superior milk

½ cup granulated sugar
3 or 4 oranges
3 egg whites

Mix the first four ingredients together and cook until thick. When perfectly cold pour over oranges which have been cut in slices and placed in bottom of casserole. Beat egg whites until stiff but not dry and add 6 tablespoons sugar gradually and beat until whites hold shape. Pile meringue on top of pudding and cook in 350 degree oven for 10 - 12 minutes. Let cool at room temperature.

Mrs. Roy Carroll

Pineapple Cream Dessert

1st Part:
1 sq. melted butter

2½ cups plain cookies rolled to
    fine crumbs

Mix, pat in pan and bake 10 min. in 350 degree oven. Cool.

2nd Part:
1 sq. butter

1½ cups icing sugar
2 eggs well beaten

Cream together and spread on first mixture. (This part will be quite thin.)

3rd Part:
½ pt. Superior cream

1 16 oz. tin crushed pineapple
    thoroughly drained

Whip cream, add pineapple and spread on top of other mixture. Chill in refrigerator about 24 hours.

Cut in squares and serve on a chilled plate or use as tea squares.

Mrs. Douglas MacLeod

Maple Cream

6 servings

1 tbsp. gelatin
¼ cup cold water
½ cup scalded Superior milk
2/3 cup maple syrup

⅛ tsp. salt
½ pt. Superior cream béaten
    until stiff

Soak gelatin in cold water. Dissolve in scalded milk. Add maple syrup and salt. Chill and before it begins to thicken fold in cream and beat slightly to blend. Chill until firm.

Hazel Williamson

Pineapple Cream

1 cup crushed pineapple
1 cup sugar
1 cup water

1 envelope gelatin
1 cup Superior cream

Cook pineapple, sugar and water ten minutes, and while hot add 1 envelope of gelatine and stir until dissolved. Cool. When beginning to jell, add 1 cup of cream (whipped).

Glenna King

Oreo Chocolate Dessert

18 Oreo chocolate cookies (or   2 cups icing sugar
   plain chocolate wafers)   3 eggs (separated)
1 cup butter   ½ cup Superior cream (whipped)

Crush cookies with rolling pin. Combine butter, sugar and egg yolks. Beat until smooth and thick. Fold in well beaten egg whites. Put half of cookie mixture in bottom of 8 x 8" pan. Spread butter, sugar and egg mixture on top. Then whipped cream mixture. Put remaining cookie crumbs on top. Leave in fridge to set.

Dot Brown (Mrs. E. L.)

Ginger Cream

¼ box gelatin or   1 tbsp. wine
   1 tbsp. granulated gelatin   ½ tbsp. brandy
¼ cup cold water   2 tbsp. ginger syrup
1 cup Superior milk   ¼ cup ginger, cut in pieces
2 egg yolks   2½ cups Superior whipped cream
¼ cup sugar   (or 1 cup whipped cream plus
few grains salt   beaten egg whites)

Soak gelatine, and add to custard, made of milk, eggs, sugar and salt.

Chill, strain, and add flavourings. When it begins to thicken, fold in whipped cream (and egg whites if used).

This keeps well in a freezer.

Mrs. Aaron Churchill

Lemon Pudding Cheesecake (Or Pie)

1 pkg. (8 oz.) cream cheese   1 8-inch graham cracker crust
2 cups Superior milk
1 pkg. Jello Lemon instant
   pudding

Soften cream cheese, blend with ½ cup milk. Add 1½ cups milk and pudding mix. Beat slowly just until well mixed. (Do not overbeat.) Pour at once into graham cracker crust. Sprinkle cracker crumbs lightly over top. Chill about 1 hour. Keep refridgerated.

Mrs. Russell Cleveland

Cheesecake

Crust:

20 graham wafers (rolled)   ¼ lb. butter

Mix well and spread in 8 x 8 greased pan.

Filling:

Beat together until smooth: 2 eggs

(16 oz.) 2 lg. pkgs. Philadelphia   ½ cups sugar

cream cheese   ¼ tsp. vanilla

Pour into crust and bake 20 minutes at 375°. Cool.

Then mix and add: 6 tbsp. sugar

1 pt. sour Superior cream   ¼ tsp. vanilla

Pour on top of cake and bake 5 minutes at 475°. Chill several hours or overnight.

Audrey Kenney

Men's Cheesecake

1½ cups graham cracker crumbs 2 tbsp. sugar

3 tbsp. butter or margarine

Save ½ cup mixture for top of cake. Pat remainder of mixture in 9" spring bottom pan.

½ cup sugar   2 tsp. lemon juice

2 tbsp. flour   4 egg yolks

½ tsp. salt   1 cup cereal Superior cream

4 pkgs. (16 oz.) cream cheese 4 egg whites

1 tsp. vanilla

Sift sugar, flour, salt, into bowl. Blend in softened cheese. Add vanilla and lemon juice. Beat in egg yolks, one at a time. Stir in cream. Lastly, fold in stiffly beaten egg whites. Pour in pan, sprinkle ½ cup crumbs on top.

Bake in 325° oven 1 hour 20 minutes, or until set in center. Allow to cool in pan, at least 2 hours. Cake will shrink around edges. Top with a strawberry glaze or fresh strawberries, or raspberries.

Phyllis Churchill

Chocolate Marble Cheesecake

1 12 oz. box vanilla wafers,   1 8-oz. pkg. cream cheese, soft-

crushed (2½ cups)   ened

½ cup butter or margarine,   ½ cup sugar

melted   1½ tsp. vanilla

½ cup sugar   1 14 oz. can (1 2/3 cups) evapora-

1 envelope unflavoured gelatin   ted milk (chilled icy cold)

1 cup Superior milk   ¼ cup Bakers cocoa (dry)

Combine crumbs and butter, press on bottom and sides of 9" spring form pan or 13 x 9 x 9" baking pan. Chill.

Combine ½ cup sugar and gelatine, stir in milk. Heat and stir until gelatine and sugar dissolve. Cool till mixture begins to thicken. Beat together cream cheese, ½ cup sugar and vanilla. Blend in gelatine mixture. Beat evaporated milk to stiff peaks, fold into cream cheese. Place ⅓ mixture in small bowl, sift cocoa over gently, and fold in. Alternately spoon chocolate and vanilla mixture into crust. Swirl with spatula. Chill 8 hours or overnight.

Mrs. Herman Shapiro

Cherry Tart

16 graham crackers (crushed)   ½ cup butter
½ cup sugar

Mix together and spread in an oblong pan.

Beat: 2 eggs
8 ozs. Philadelphia cream cheese 1 tsp. vanilla
½ cup sugar

Spread over bottom mixture and bake 20 minutes in 325° oven.

When cold, spread with one can of Cherry Pie Filling. When ready to serve frost with whipped cream. Keep in fridge.

Mrs. Arthur Spears

Paradise Pudding

¼ lb. blanched almonds   1 doz. red cherries (cut fine)
1 doz. marshmallows (cut fine)

Dissolve 1 pkg. lemon jello in 1 pint boiling water. When partly set, whip, then fold in 1 cup whipped cream, fruit, ¼ cup sugar. Turn in square pan to cool. Cut in slices to serve. Delicious served with preserved strawberries.

Hilda A. Height

Lemon Pudding Cake

1 pkg. lemon Jello   juice and rind of 1 lemon
1 cup sugar   1 cup boiling water
    Pour water over all. Let stand until slightly jelled

2 small cans evaporated milk   (chilled)

Whip milk stiff. Whip jello until frothy. Fold together.

20 graham crackers crushed with ¼ cup butter

Spread part of crumbs in 8 x 8 pan, then mixture, patting remainder of crumbs on top.

Mrs. P. G. Boutilier

Hot Water Gingerbread

½ cup sugar	1 tsp. cinnamon
½ cup shortening	1 tsp. ginger
1 egg	½ tsp. cloves
1 cup Silver Lasses molasses	1 tsp. salt
2½ cups flour (all purpose)	1 cup hot water — last
1½ tsp. soda	

Cream sugar and shortening. Add egg and 1 cup molasses, then add flour, soda and spices, and blend. Add one cup hot water last, and mix well. Pour into greased pan and bake in medium oven for about 30 minutes, or until done.

Mrs. Ray Peverill
Aunt Maria Brown (Mrs. Charles)

Pineapple Upside-Down Cake

Butter a round pan about 8" in diameter and 3" deep. In it melt 1 cup brown sugar and 2 tbsp. butter. After melting, lay as many slices of drained canned pineapple as pan will hold. Pour over fruit a batter of:—

½ cup butter	2 cups pastry flour or
¾ cup sugar	1¾ cups all purpose flour
2 well beaten eggs	½ tsp. salt
½ tsp. vanilla	2 tsp. baking powder
¾ cup Superior milk	

Mix as any butter cake. Bake at 375° F. for 45 minutes, or until done. Turn at once on large round plate. Serve with Superior whipped cream.

Mrs. George Ellis

Blueberry Buckle

¼ cup shortening	1½ tsp. baking powder
½ cup sugar	⅓ cup Superior milk
1 egg	¼ tsp. salt
1 cup all purpose flour, sifted	

Cream shortening and sugar. Add beaten egg. Sift dry ingredients together and add alternately with milk. Spread into 8" x 8" pan. Cover with:—

1 pt. blueberries

Mix together:

¼ cup sugar	⅓ cup flour
¼ cup butter	½ tsp. cinnamon

Sprinkle this mixture over the blueberries. Bake in a moderate oven about 45 minutes. Serve with whipped cream, either hot or cold.

Lillian Amirault

Coconut Bread Pudding

1½ cups cubed dry bread
3 cups scalded Superior milk
2 eggs well beaten
½ cup sugar

¼ tsp. salt
½ tsp. ground cinnamon
½ cup shredded cocoanut

Put crumbs in buttered casserole. Pour on milk. Combine eggs, sugar, salt, cinnamon and cocoanut. Add to bread crumbs and stir until blended. Set casserole in large pan of hot water. Bake 40 - 45 minutes in 375° oven. Test with silver knife.

Pubnico Womens Institute

Chocolate Cream Roll (No Flour)

3 eggs
5 tbsp. sugar
3 tbsp. Bakers cocoa
1 tsp. vanilla

1 tsp. icing sugar
½ pt. Superior whipping cream
1 tsp. vanilla

METHOD:

Start oven at 350°. Grease 8 inch sq. cake pan and line with waxed paper. Separate egg yolks from whites. Beat yolks until light in color. Add sugar gradually and continue beating until mixture is very smooth. Mix in cocoa and 1 tsp. vanilla. Beat egg whites until they hold peaks, then fold into cocoa mixture.

Pour into square pan. Bake 25 minutes, or until cake pulls away from sides of pan. Cool 5 minutes. Remove from pan and peel off waxed paper.

Whip cream until it holds shape, add 1 tsp. vanilla and icing sugar. Spread cream over cake and gently bring two sides together to form roll. Chill before serving.

Add crushed walnuts to whipped cream for a change.

B. MacDonald

Chocolate Cake Roll

6 tbsp. flour
½ tsp. baking powder
¼ tsp. salt
¾ cup sugar

4 egg whites (beaten)
4 egg yolks (beaten)
1 tsp. vanilla
2 sqs. Bakers chocolate, melted

Sift flour, add baking powder and salt. (Sift 3 times). Fold sugar gradually into beaten egg whites, fold in beaten egg yolks and vanilla. Beat chocolate into egg mixture. Gradually add flour mixture. Turn into jelly roll pan. Bake in 375° oven for 12 minutes. Roll in towel sprinkled with icing sugar. Leave till cool. About 1½ hours before serving unroll and spread with whipped Superior cream. Roll up and leave in frig till serving time.

For variation in filling cook 1 pkg. vanilla pudding, using 1¾ cups Superior milk. When cool fold in 1 tbsp. shaved preserved ginger. Spread on jelly roll and reroll. Chill.

Mrs. G. M. MacDonald

Lemon Filled Jelly Roll

Lemon filling:

rind and juice of 1 lemon	1 egg
¼ cup white sugar	2 tbsp. cold water
1 tsp. butter	¾ tbsp. corn starch

Combine and cook over boiling water about 7 minutes, stirring. Set aside to cool.

Jelly roll:

Temp. 400	Time 13 minutes
2 eggs separated	2 tbsp. cold water
½ cup white sugar	¾ cup cake flour
1 tsp. baking powder	½ tsp. salt
¼ tsp. vanilla	¼ tsp. lemon flavoring

Beat egg yolks till light and add cold water and beat again. Gradually beat in sugar; and beat until very light. Sift dry ingredients four times and fold into the egg and sugar mixture; add the flavouring. Lastly fold in the stiffly beaten egg whites. Bake 13 minutes in 400 oven in paper lined cookie sheet (small). Take from oven and peel paper immediately and while cake is warm spread on the lemon mixture and roll and wrap in clean damp cloth for about 5 minutes.

This can be served with whipped cream as dessert, or is delicious served plain.

Peg Cann

Sacher Torte

(Princess Schwarzenberg's recipe)

6 oz. semi-sweet Bakers chocolate pieces	1½ cups sifted cake flour
¾ cup butter or margarine	raspberry or apricot jam
¾ cup sugar	¾ cup semi-sweet Bakers chocolate pieces
¼ tsp. salt	
6 eggs separated	½ cup butter or margarine

Melt 6 oz. chocolate over hot water. Cream the ¾ cup butter. Gradually add sugar and continue creaming until fluffy. Add salt and melted chocolate, blending well. Add egg yolks one at a time, beating well after each addition. Beat egg whites until stiff, but not dry, and fold into chocolate - yolk mixture. Fold in flour. Turn into a greased and floured 9 x 3⅓ inch spring form pan. Bake at 350° F. for 40 to 50 minutes. Cool; remove from pan. Spread raspberry jam over top and sides. Melt remaining chocolate over hot water. Add remaining butter and stir until blended. Cool until of spreading consistency. Spread over cake, serve with whipped cream if desired.

Magdi Ozvegy

Cherry Custard Cake

2 eggs
½ cup sugar
½ cup oil
1 tsp. vanilla or lemon
2½ cups flour

2 tsp. baking powder
pinch of salt
1 pkg. vanilla pudding
1 can pitted cherries

Cream sugar and eggs, add oil slowly, then the sifted dry ingredidents and flavouring. Take 2/3 of dough and put into a spring form pan, covering the bottom and halfway up the sides. Make one package vanilla pudding as directed. Pour it over the dough. Drain a can of pitted cherries, and place cherries over pudding. Roll balance of dough into long strips and make lattice work over cherries. To the juice drained from cherries add 1½ tsp. cornstarch and ½ cup sugar. Cook until it reaches the boil, then pour over cake. Bake cake in 350° oven 45 minutes.

Alice Garson

Cherry Dessert

Serves 8 or 9

1 can prepared pie cherries
½ pkg. yellow cake mix (2 cups)
½ cup melted butter or

margarine
½ cup chopped nuts

Spread cherries in greased 8 x 8 pan (or small Pyrex rectangular pan). Sprinkle dry mix over, then margarine and nuts. Bake at 325° 30 - 40 minutes, or until cake is done in center. Serve with vanilla ice cream.

Phyllis Churchill

Trifle In Jelly

Line a large glass dish with slices of Jelly Roll. Pour 1 tbsp. sherry or brandy over each slice, if desired. Drain one medium tin of fruit cocktail, and arrange in a layer to cover the slices of Jelly Roll. Spread a thin layer of strawberry jam over the fruit, and cover this with a layer of thin cooked custard. Now make up one package of strawberry or lime Jello powder, and pour this over the mixture in the dish. The Jello will soak down through the fruit, cake and custard. Allow to set in refrigerator. Top with whipped cream, decorate with grated nuts, and cherries with stems.

Janet Matthews

Glass Cake (Dessert)

1st Part:

Dissolve 3 packages of jello, all different colors in 1½ cups of water for each package, using 1 cup hot water and ½ cup cold water. Let each set until firm and then cut in cubes.

2nd Part:

Crush 2 dozen graham crackers, mix with ¼ lb. butter and ½ cup sugar. When mixed put in 9" x 12" baking dish, saving about ½ cup for topping.

3rd Part:

Dissolve 1 envelope plain gelatin in ¼ cup pineapple juice, then add 1 cup hot pineapple juice. Let stand for about 10 minutes in refrigerator to cool and thicken.

4th Part:

Whip 1 pint Superior cream, add ½ cup sugar, 1½ tsp. vanilla. Fold into pineapple gelatin mixture. Then add jello cubes. Top with graham crumb mixture. Let set overnight in refrigerator.

Mrs. Arthur Cottreau

Raspberry Bavarian Mold

1 10 oz. pkg. frozen red raspberries, thawed
1 pkg. red raspberry flavored gelatin
1 cup hot water
1 tbsp. lemon juice
dash salt
1 cup Superior whipping cream, whipped

Drain raspberries, reserve syrup. Dissolve gelatin in hot water; add syrup, lemon juice and salt. Chill till partially set. Whip cream. Whip gelatin till fluffy. Fold in whip cream and whip just enough to mix well. Fold in raspberries. Pour into 1 quart mold. Chill till firm. Decorate with whipped cream if desired.

Myra Sutherland

Chipped Almond Mold

½ lb. blanched almonds, finely ground
1 cup sugar
2 cups light Superior cream
1½ tbsp. unflavoured gelatin
¼ cup water
2 cups heavy Superior cream, whipped
pinch of salt
¼ tsp. almond flavouring
sweetened fresh or frozen mixed fruit or strawberries

Grind almonds, or chop very fine. In a saucepan combine almonds, sugar and light cream. Bring to a boiling point and simmer for 5 minutes. Soften gelatin in a ¼ cup water. Add gelatin to cream mixture and stir until gelatin has dissolved. Cool until mixture mounds. Add a pinch of salt and flavoring to whipped cream. Fold into cooled almond cream mixture. Spoon into 8 cup ring mold and allow to set. Invert on platter. Add fruit in centre. Serves 12.

Maude Churchill

Mont Blanc Of Chestnuts

Score 1 lb. chestnuts across rounded side with a sharp knife. Place in boiling water and simmer for 15 minutes. Drain, but keep warm. Slip off both skins. Return to pan, cover with boiling water and simmer for about 45 minutes, or until perfectly tender. Drain and mash with a little salt, a little sugar. Over a large serving dish (preferably silver) force chestnuts through a coarse sieve, a potato ricer (that's what I use), or a food mill with fairly large holes, into the shape of a mound. The chestnuts must be very light and fluffy.

Whip some cream and flavour with a little sugar and vanilla. Smooth cream over chestnut mound. Do not press down, or the mont blanc will lose its fluffiness. Chill for a short time and serve.

Magdi Ozvegy

Coffee-Raisin Pilau

1 5 oz. pkg. pre-cooked rice
regular strength coffee
⅛ cup golden raisins
½ cup chopped walnuts
⅛ tsp. salt
⅛ tsp. nutmeg

1 tsp. vanilla
½ cup brown sugar (firmly packed)
1 cup heavy Superior cream, whipped

Prepare pre-cooked rice according to directions, using coffee instead of water. Stir in remaining ingredients except cream, reserving enough for garnishing. Spoon into sherbet glasses. Top with remaining whipped cream and a few chopped walnut meats — or a piece of maraschino cherry. Makes 6 servings.

Clara Harris

Party Torte

TORTE — Bring 8 egg whites to room temperature. Add 1½ tsp. vanilla and 1 tsp. vinegar. Beat until mixture forms peaks. Add 2 cups sifted sugar, a tbsp. at a time. Beat until stiff and all sugar is dissolved. Divide into 2 9" round cake pans, lined with brown paper. Bake 1 hour and 15 minutes in 300 oven. Cool 15 minutes in pans These meringues will be delicately brown and crusty on outside and tender and moist inside.

FILLING — Whip 2 cups cream. Add 1 tin crushed pineapple well drained and 1 cup chopped cherries. Turn one meringue on large serving dish, spread with cream mixture. Top with second meringue. Frost top and sides with remainder of cream. Chill at least 12 hours, or overnight.

Mrs. Herman Slade

Fiesta Banana Cake

Measure into sifter:
2 cups sifted cake flour
1 tsp. baking powder
1 tsp. soda
¾ tsp. salt
1⅓ cups sugar
In mixing bowl stir to soften:

½ cup butter
Have ready: :
½ cup less 2 tbsp. sour milk
1 tsp. vanilla
1 cup mashed bananas
½ cup chopped nuts
2 eggs

Stir dry ingredients into soft butter. Add ¼ cup milk, mashed bananas. Mix well until flour is dampened. Beat 2 minutes. Add eggs, nuts, rest of milk. Beat 1 minute. Turn into 2 lined greased pans and bake 25 minutes in 375° oven. Cool 5 minutes before turning on racks.

TOPPING — Whip 1 cup cream. Fold ½ cup chopped cherries into ⅓ of whipped cream. Spread on one layer of cake with 2 sliced bananas. Cover with 2nd layer. Spread with remaining cream. Arrange sliced bananas and cherries halves around edge of cake. Chill until ready to serve.

Mrs. Herman Slade

Frozen Apricot Shortcake

1 cup dried apricots
2½ cups water
⅓ cup sugar
1 tsp. gelatine
1 tbsp. cold water

1 beaten egg
¼ cup powdered sugar
1 tsp. vanilla
1 cup Superior whipping cream
1 small sponge cake

Cook one cup of dried apricots (previously soaked) in 2½ cups water until tender, about 20 minutes. Add ⅓ cup granulated sugar and bring to a boil. Remove from fire and put through coarse sieve. Sprinkle 1 tsp. gelatine over 1 tbsp. of cold water and allow to stand until softened. Add to apricot pulp and return to heat until gelatine is dissolved, about 5 minutes, stirring constantly. Remove from heat and cool.

To one well beaten egg, add ¼ cup powdered sugar and 1 tsp. vanilla and blend well. Whip 1 cup cream until it begins to thicken and hold its shape, then fold into egg mixture.

Cut 1 small sponge cake so that it is about ¼ inch thick and arrange in bottom of refrigerator tray. Spread over this the apricot pulp and cover with the cream mixture. Freeze about 2 hours in refrigerator with temperature control set at highest point. Cut in squares to serve. This recipe will make 8 portions.

Mrs. A. B. Anthony.

Toll House Ice Box Cake

Make any white cake. Bake in angel cake pan with slanting sides. Split into three layers.

FILLING: 1 pkg. red Jello. Pour over this 1¾ cups of boiling water. Fruit Juice can be substituted for water if you have any left over from canned fruits. When this jello is ready to set add 1 cup of crushed pineapple, 1 cup of cream whipped stiff, sweetened and flavored, ½ cup chopped marshmallows and ½ cup chopped maraschino cherries. Now put layer of this filling in angel cake pan then the smaller layer of cake, a layer of filling and a layer of cake until the top layer of cake. Then let rest of the filling run down the sides of pan. Set in refrigerator for 6 hours.

To unmould dip for a few seconds in a pan of hot water and turn out quickly. Garnish with cherries. This makes a very pretty cake for parties.

Mrs. Harold Langille

Individual Baked Alaska

(Not difficult to make — but very effective)

For 6 to 8 servings:	**6 or 8 sponge cake cups or**
5 egg whites	**sliced fresh made jelly roll**
2/3 cup white sugar	**6 or 8 scoops very hard ice cream**
dash of salt	

Make meringue by beating egg whites and salt until stiff. Gradually beat in sugar, 2 tbsp. at a time, beating well after each addition. Prepare wooden board by covering with foil. On this put cake with ice cream and cover completely, individually, with meringue, making certain that each is sealed with meringue to aluminum foil. (These may be stored in freezer, set at coldest point, for an hour or two until needed). Bake in very hot oven (500° F.) for 3 to 4 minutes, or until meringue is golden brown. Serve at once.

Clara Harris

Chocolate Mint Bombe

1 quart chocolate ice cream	**½ tsp. peppermint extract**
2 egg whites	**1 cup heavy Superior cream,**
¼ cup granulated sugar	**whipped**

Line a quart mold with the ice cream, leaving centre hollow to hold mint filling. Place in freezer to harden.

Beat egg whites stiff, continue beating while adding sugar; beat until glossy. Fold in extract, whipped cream; tint pale green with 3 or 4 drops of food color. Place in centre of mold and return to freezer. When mint mixture is hard, cover top of mold with freezer wrap.

To serve: dip mold in cool water 5 or 10 seconds. Unmold and decorate top with blanched sliced almonds.

Bernice Trask

Fruit Sherbet

1 can evaporated milk
(chill well and beat until thick)
add ½ cup white sugar
juice of 1 orange
juice of 1 lemon

1 crushed banana (crush banana
in lemon juice to keep from
discoloring)
Freeze in refrigerator.

Mrs. John Green

Ice Cream - Jello Dessert

20 Graham Crackers
¼ cup butter or margarine
1 pkg. jello (any flavor)

1 pint or brick ice cream (any
flavor)
1 cup boiling water

Method:

Mix Graham cracker crumbs with melted butter or margarine and pat in a pan 7 x 10 or near that size. Dissolve jello in 1 cup boiling water and put ice cream in this and stir until melted. Pour on cracker crumb mixture and put in refrigerator and chill.

Mrs. Donald C. Richardson

Mrs. Douglas Porter

PUDDING SAUCES

Rich Chocolate Sauce

4 sqs. Bakers chocolate OR 1 cup   3 cups sugar
   Bakers cocoa   1 can evaporated milk
½ cup butter   1 tsp. vanilla

Melt the butter in a double boiler; add chocolate. When chocolate is melted stir in the sugar gradually, and continue to stir until sugar is dissolved. Slowly add the evaporated milk, stirring as you do so. It will begin to thicken immediately. When consistency desired; remove from heat, add vanilla. Makes a good pint. Can be stored and reheated.

Kemptville Women's Institute

Hard Sauce

¼ cup butter   1 tsp. brandy
½ cup icing sugar   ¼ tsp. nutmeg

Cream butter, add icing sugar, cream well and add nutmeg and brandy.

Keep in frig till hard.

Tested

New England Nutmeg Sauce

1 cup brown sugar; 1 tbsp. flour, salt, ½ tsp. nutmeg (scant).

Mix, add 2 cups boiling water. Stir, add 1 tbsp. butter. Cook 5 minutes.

Dot Kirk

Gold Sauce

½ cup butter   1 egg
1 cup icing sugar   1 tbsp. Superior cream
1 tsp. vanilla

Cream butter, add sugar gradually. Add beaten egg and cream. Mix well and add vanilla. Beat over hot water until thick, like a custard sauce.

Mrs. Ernest Syvertsen

Egg Sauce

3 eggs   vanilla
½ cup sugar   salt

Beat eggs until fluffy, then add other ingredients. Makes large quantity.

Mrs. D. F. Macdonald

Butterscotch Sauce For Apple Dumplings

¼ cup butter	¼ cup thin Superior cream
1½ cups brown sugar	2 tbsp. corn starch
¾ cup of hot water	pinch salt

This is to serve with Dumplings made with Pie crust type dough.

Melt butter in heavy saucepan. Add sugar and stir and cook over moderate heat until brown and bubbly. Slowly add the hot water, and cook until dissolved. Make a paste of cream and corn starch and salt. Stir this into hot mixture. Reduce heat and cook and stir until smooth. This makes a rich sauce and may be thinned with cream if desired.

Mrs. Keith Cann

Golden Sauce

1 cup pineapple juice	2 tbsp. water
1 cup orange juice	2 tbsp. cornstarch
juice of 1 lemon	1 cup crushed pineapple
¼ cup sugar	1 cup finely diced rhubarb

Heat pineapple and orange juice. Mix sugar and cornstarch, add lemon juice and water. Add hot juice. Return to stove and cook until thickened. Add pineapple and rhubarb, heat over low heat until rhubarb is soft. Excellent on cottage pudding or apple or cranberry dumplings.

Mrs. T. A. M. Kirk

Plum Pudding Sauce

1 egg	1 cup Superior whipping cream
1 cup white sugar	(beaten or unbeaten)
dash of salt	1 tsp. vanilla
butter size of egg	

Put egg, sugar, salt and butter in top of double boiler, and beat together wtih mixing spoon. Do not allow water to boil. Melt and stir. Add cream and vanilla shortly before ready to serve.

Mrs. J. T. Balmanno

Ice Cream Sauce For Puddings

Whip 1 cup Superior heavy cream: Mix together the following:

1 egg, well beaten	1 tsp. vanilla
⅓ cup melted butter	Salt
¾ cup sugar	

Fold into the cream and chill thoroughly.

Mrs. A. B. Anthony

Foamy Sauce

2 eggs, separated   1 tsp. vanilla
2 cups sugar

Beat yolks till thick and lemon coloured. Add sugar and vanilla. Fold in stiffly beaten egg whites. Mix well.

Miss Joan Gardner

Marshmallow Velvet Sauce

2 sqs. Bakers chocolate   ½ cup water
16 marshmallows

Melt in double boiler. Add ½ cup sugar, ¼ tsp. salt. Cook 5 minutes. Add vanilla, cool.

Lemon Sauce

¼ cup sugar   2 tbsp. butter
1 cup boiling water   Few gratings nutmeg or lemon
2 tbsp. lemon juice   rind
1 tbsp. cornstarch

Mix sugar and cornstarch, add liquids. Boil 5 minutes. Add remaining ingredients.

Joyce Syvertsen

SALADS AND DRESSING

Jellied Salad

(Salmon, Tuna or Chicken)

Dissolve:
1 envelope gelatine in
¼ cup cold water
⅓ cup Miracle Whip salad dressing
1 tin (7 oz.) salmon, chicken or

tuna (drained)
1 tbsp. lemon juice
½ cup thinly sliced celery
3 tbsp. sweet pickle relish and green pepper cut small
1 cup whipped Lucky Whip

Soften gelatine in cold water, dissolve over hot water. Blend into the satin smooth Miracle Whip. Add prepared fish or chicken, lemon juice, pickle relish, chopped green pepper and celery. Fold in whipped Lucky Whip.

Pour into 1½ qt. mold. Chill until firm. Unmold on bed lettuce. Garnish with ripe tomato wedges and parsley.

Mrs. Harold Langille

Tuna Salad

1 7 oz. tin of tuna
1 cup diced celery
1 cup Miracle Whip
1 cup Superior milk
1 envelope gelatine

¼ cup cold water
1½ tsp. horseradish
2 tbsp. lemon juice
1 tsp. salt
dash pepper

Dissolve gelatine in cold water. Blend milk and Miracle Whip, heat, add gelatine and stir until dissolved. Cool. Add flaked fish, celery, horseradish and lemon juice. Pour into individual moulds. Chill till firm. Serve on lettuce with Thousand Islands dressing. Serves 6 - 8.

Mrs. Hope Langille

Jellied Green Salad

1 tbsp. gelatine
¼ cup cold water
1 cup boiling water
¼ cup white sugar
¼ tsp. salt
¼ cup cider vinegar
1 tbsp. lemon juice

2 tsp. grated lemon rind
1 cup chopped celery
1 cup shredded cabbage
1 cup green peas
1 tsp. minced onion
6 chopped maraschino cherries

Soak the gelatine in the cold water for 5 minutes, dissolve in the boiling water. Add the sugar, salt, vinegar, lemon juice and rind. Cool. When the mixture begins to set, add the chopped vegetables and cherries. Pour into oiled ring mold and chill.

Mrs. T. A. M. Kirk

Cheese And Pineapple Salad

¾ cup sugar
½ cup syrup from canned
pineapple
1 tbsp. gelatine
¼ cup cold water

1 cup crushed pineapple,
drained
1 cup grated American cheese
OR 1 pkg. cream cheese
1 cup heavy Superior cream,
whipped

Dissolve sugar in pineapple syrup over low heat, add gelatine softened in cold water, chill until partially set, add pineapple, and cheese. Fold in whipped cream. Chill until firm. Serve with salad dressing. Serves 6 - 8.

Mrs. Furber Marshall

Party Fruit Salad

12 half pears (canned)
6 slices pineapple (canned)
1 tsp. grated orange peel
1 pkg. cream cheese
½ cup sour red cherries
(canned)

1½ cups cherry juice
1½ tbsp. vinegar
juice of 1 lemon
⅓ cup sugar
3 tbsp. corn starch

Drain pears and pineapple and chill. Mix orange peel with cheese. Drain cherries, chop very fine and add to cheese mixture. Put 2 pear halves together with ball of cheese mixture to make whole pear.

Heat to boiling point the cherry juice, vinegar and lemon juice. Mix sugar and cornstarch, add to hot liquid and cook, stirring constantly until transparent and as thick as heavy syrup; chill. When ready to serve, place one slice of pineapple in deep lettuce cup, arrange whole pear on this and place dressing on top. (Serves six.)

Mrs. Ernest Sinclair

Moulded Fish Salad

2 cups fish, either cooked or
canned
1 apple diced
1 tbsp. lemon juice
salt
1 cup diced celery

1 cup pineapple tidbits
¼ cup cut up olives, or whole
1½ tbsp. gelatine
¼ cup cold water
1 cup mayonnaise

METHOD: Sprinkle salt over fish, sprinkle lemon juice over apple. Combine fish, apple, celery, pineapple, olives. Sprinkle gelatine over cold water, place over hot water and dissolve. Blend mayonnaise and gelatine. Fold in fish and mix well. Place in oiled mould and set four hours. Serve on crisp lettuce cups.

Eve Fry

Spring Salad Souffle

1 small pkg. lime jello
½ cup water
1 can cream of asparagus soup
½ cup mayonnaise
1 tbsp. vinegar
1 tsp. grated onion

dash pepper
½ cup shredded unpared
  cucumber
¼ cup diced celery
1 tbsp. snipped parsley

In saucepan mix gelatin and water. Gradually blend in soup, heat and stir till gelatine dissolves. Add next 4 ingredients. Beat till smooth. Chill till partially set. Turn into chilled bowl and beat till thick and fluffy. Fold in vegetables. Spoon into 5-cup mould or 6 - 8 individual moulds. Chill till firm.

Mrs. Lloyd Crosby

Beet Jello Salad

1 can diced beets (15 oz.)
2 pkgs. lemon jello
4 heaping tbsp. horseradish

3 tbsp. vinegar
1 grated onion (medium)

Drain beets, add enough water to beet juice to make 3 cups. Boil this and add and dissolve jello powder. To this add remaining ingredients.

Cut in squares, or use jelly moulds.

Mrs. Eric H. Spinney

Salad

1 pkg. lemon jello
1 pkg. lime jello

1 cup crushed pineapple

Dissolve jello in 2 cups boiling water. Cool. Add pineapple. When it begins to thicken add:

½ cup chopped walnuts
1 lb. cottage cheese
onion powder

1½ cups celery, chopped fine
1 cup mayonnaise
1 cup light Superior cream

Mrs. (Capt.) William McMurtry
Margaretville, Nova Scotia

Basic Tomato Aspic

1 envelope gelatine
¼ cup cold water
1½ cup hot tomato juice
1 tbsp. lemon juice or vinegar

½ tsp. salt
1 tbsp. onion juice
1 tsp. horseradish if desired

Dissolve gelatine in cold water. Add to hot tomato juice and remaining ingredients. Pour into wet molds and chill. Minced fish, meat or shredded vegetables may be added. Serves 6.

Tested

Fruit Salad With Marshmallows

(Serves 20)

2 eggs	2 cups diced pineapple
4 tbsp. vinegar OR	2 oranges diced
3 tbsp. lemon juice + 1 tbsp.	2 cups white cherries
water	1 cup seedless grapes
4 tbsp. sugar	2 cups cut marshmallows
3 tbsp. butter	1 cup Superior cream, whipped

Beat eggs, stir in vinegar or lemon juice. Add sugar and stir over hot water until mixture thickens. Remove from heat. Add butter and cool. Fold in fruit and marshmallows and whipped cream. Turn into mould. Chill 12 hours or overnight. Any other fruit combination may be used in equal amounts.

Mrs. Ainsley Smith

Citrus Perfection Salad

1 3 oz. pkg. lemon jello	1 cup finely shredded cabbage
1 cup hot water	½ cup diced celery
1 tbsp. vinegar	2 tbsp. sliced stuffed olives
¼ tsp. salt	
1 1 lb. can (2 cups) grapefruit	sections

Dissolve gelatine in hot water; add vinegar and salt. Drain grapefruit, reserving syrup. Add water to syrup to make 1 cup; add to gelatine. Chill until partly set. Stir in grapefruit and remaining ingredients. Turn into a 1 quart mould. Chill until firm. Delicious with meat or fish.

Y. Auxiliary

Jellied Cranberry Salad

2 pkgs. raspberry jello	1 No. 2 can pineapple chunks or
1 cup boiling water	crushed pineapple (drained)
1½ cups cold water	1 lg. can whole cranberry sauce,
1 orange	slightly beaten
	½ cup chopped walnuts

Dissolve gelatine in boiling water, add cold water. chill until partially thickened. Peel orange, cut segments in thirds. If pineapple chunks used, cut in thirds. Fold fruit and nuts into gelatine. Pour into one large or 8 individual moulds. Chill until firm.

Serve with sour cream, mayonnaise or cottage cheese. Garnish with crisp greens.

(In place of orange, sometmies I use 1 small can Mandarin Oranges, drained.)

Mrs. Russell Cleveland

Waldorf Salad

2 cups cabbage, shredded
1 cup apples, cut

½ cup cut dates
¼ cup walnuts

Mix cabbage and apples with salad dressing. Put dates and walnuts on for garnish, after placing on lettuce leaf. Tomatoes and eggs may also be used for garnishing.

Mrs. Admanta Beauprie

Frosted Cheese Mould

1 cup Superior milk
2 envelopes unflavoured gelatine (2 tbsp.)
2 12 oz. cartons (3 cups) creamy style cottage cheese
¼ cup crumbled blue cheese
1 6 oz. can frozen limeade concentrate (thawed)

½ cup broken pecans (toasted & salted
6 drops green food coloring
1 cup Superior whipping cream (whipped)
(If limeade is not available, use lemonade concentrate).

Pour milk into large saucepan, sprinkle gelatine over milk and soften. Place over low heat and stir until gelatine is dissolved. Remove from heat. Beat cottage and blue cheese together till well blended. Stir into gelatine mixture.

Add limeade concentrate, pecans, and food colouring. Fold in whipped cream. Turn into 6 cup ring mould. Chill till firm, 4 to 6 hours. Unmould on serving plate. Fill center with melon balls and orange sections. Garnish with frosted grapes and mint sprigs.

NOTE: Frost grapes by brushing with slightly beaten egg white or fruit juice. Let dry on rack.

Mrs. Herman Shapiro

Fruit Salad Dressing

½ or ¾ cup canned pineapple juice
3 scant tbsp. flour
3 tbsp. sugar

1 tbsp. butter
1 egg
1 cup Superior cream

Mix flour and sugar and add enough juice to make a smooth paste. Heat remaining juice, add flour mixture. Cook until thickened, stirring constantly in double boiler. Add egg beaten, then butter. Cook about 10 minutes, stirring to prevent lumping. Cool until ready to serve. Then add 1 cup of cream whipped.

Mrs. Frank Hichens

Salad Dressing For Tossed Salad

½ cup mineral or salad oil
1 can tomato soup
¼ cup vinegar
1 tsp. Worchestershire sauce

⅛ tsp. mustard
salt and pepper
1 small onion cut up fine

Beat all together and keep in a cool place.

Mrs. Wendell Bain

Boiled Salad Dressing

¼ tsp. salt
1 tbsp. mustard or less
½ tbsp. sugar
1 egg
1½ tbsp. flour

¾ cup Superior milk
¼ cup vinegar
¼ tsp. pepper
1½ tbsp. butter

Mix dry ingredients, beat egg, milk, and vinegar. Add to the dry ingredients and cook in double boiler. Lastly add butter. If a thinner dressing is desired a bit of cream may be added.

Mrs. Roger Hall

Poppy Seed Dressing

½ cup sugar
¼ cup white vinegar
1 tsp. salt
1 tsp. dry mustard

Blend above ingredients. Slowly add:
1 cup vegetable oil
1 small onion, grated
⅛ cup poppy seeds

Mix well. A few drops of vegetable food coloring may be added, and makes a nice contrast to its salad.

Marjorie Phinney Dobson

Sweet Salad Dressing

1 cup prepared mustard
2 tsp. salt
paprika to taste
½ cup vinegar

1 lg. onion, grated
1 cup sugar
1 pt. vegetable oil
ketchup to taste

Mix first 6 ingredients. Add oil slowly, then ketchup. Makes 1 qt. Delicious on tossed salad or fruit salad.

Betty (Mrs. Victor) Cain

Mayonnaise or Potato Salad Dressing

1 cup sugar
2 eggs
¾ cup vinegar

1 tbsp. mustard
2 tbsp. flour
1 cup Superior milk

Bring vinegar to boil. Mix sugar, flour, eggs and milk into a paste. Add to vinegar with pinch of salt and small piece of butter. Boil until thick.

Marion Hammond

MEATS

Sweet & Sour Spare Ribs

2 tbsp. flour	2 cups water
1 cup brown sugar	½ cup ketchup
1 cup vinegar	1 tbsp. soya sauce

Mix flour and brown sugar together, add vinegar, water, ketchup and soya sauce. Pour over 4 lbs. spareribs. Put in covered roast pan and bake about 1½ hours at 350°. Keep checking, as you may need to add more water.

About ½ hour before ready add:

1 lg. onion, chopped fine	1 green pepper, chopped fine
4 celery stocks, chopped fine	½ cup sweet pickles

Dot Brown

Baked Stuffed Spare Ribs

2 lbs. spareribs

Place the spareribs in a pan. Sprinkle with salt. Make a stuffing as follows:

1½ cups bread crumbs	1 tbsp. poultry seasoning
1¾ cups rolled crackers	1 tsp. summer savory
2 cups scalded Superior milk	1 small onion (chopped fine)
1 tsp. salt	1 tbsp. butter or bacon fat
¼ tsp. pepper	

Spread stuffing over spareribs and roll up. Bake in oven 350° to 400°F. for 2 hours.

Eleanor Symonds

Chinese Spare Ribs (Sweet & Sour)

4 lbs. lamb ribs cut into 2" lengths	2 tbsp. shortening
1 lg. green pepper (finely chopped)	½ cup soya sauce
	3 or 4 cloves garlic (finely diced)
2 strips celery (diced)	juice of 1 lemon
1 lg. onion (diced)	½ cup brown sugar
¼ box mushrooms (diced)	¼ cup white vinegar

Melt fat in large skillet, saute until golden brown green pepper, celery, onion, mushrooms and garlic. Add washed and dried lamb ribs, and keep turning until meat is seared on all sides.

Prepare sauce: To the soya sauce add the juice of lemon, and the vinegar, and dissolve the sugar in this liquid. Pour sauce over meat and vegetables and place same in roast pan in 300° oven. Spread out the ribs very carefully, so that the meat does not fall off bones. Keep basting the ribs frequently. Cook 1½ hours. Serve hot with rice.

Mrs. J. D. Cohen

Beef Stroganoff

2 lbs. lean sirloin of beef	1 cup green pepper
4 tbsp. butter	⅛ tsp. pepper
1 can whole mushroom buttons	2 tsp. salt
½ cup tomato juice	1 can cream of mushroom soup
2 onions, diced	1 cup Superior sour cream
1 cup diced celery	

Trim and cut beef in strips. Saute onions, celery, peppers, button mushrooms, in butter; remove, add beef and cook until light brown, stirring constantly for 5 minutes. Add sauted vegetables, tomato juice. Steam over low heat for 30-40 minutes, until meat is tender. Add soup, seasonings, sour cream just before serving. Heat through. Serve with fluffy rice. Serves 6.

Phyllis Churchill

Continental Steak

2 lbs. round steak	½ cup dry red wine or juice of
¼ tsp. salt	1 lemon
¼ tsp. pepper	1 clove garlic, minced
⅛ cup onion, minced	2 tbsp. brown sugar
¼ cup celery, minced	2 tbsp. Worcestershire sauce
⅛ cup green pepper, minced	2 tsp. prepared mustard
3 tbsp. Mazola oil	dash of Tobasco or Accent
1 tin mushrooms (or ½ lb. fresh)	(optional)
1 tin condensed tomato soup	

Sprinkle steak with salt and pepper. Heat oil in dutch oven or saucepan, brown steak. Remove steak and brown vegetables lightly. Add remaining ingredients. Stir well, put back steak and cover. Cook over low flame for 1½ hours or until tender. (May be baked in 350 oven). Serve with rice or potatoes. Serves 6 - 8.

Mrs. Donald Chipman

Meat Curry

1 cup (or more) left-over meat, cubed (chicken, pork, beef) etc.	½ apple, chopped
2 or 3 cups gravy	¼ cup raisins
1 onion, sliced	dash sugar, pepper, ginger and cinnamon
1 tbsp. curry powder	salt
2 tbsp. margarine or fat	

Saute onion and curry in margarine or fat. Add gravy and when simmering add other ingredients, meat last. Simmer 10 minutes and serve over hot boiled rice. Pass mango chutney.

Ruth M. Rideout

Mushroom Pot Roast

3 to 4 pounds beef pot roast
2 onions, sliced
½ cup water
¼ cup catsup
⅓ cup cooking sherry
1 clove garlic, minced

¼ tsp. each dry mustard, marjoram, rosemary, thyme
1 bay leaf
1 6-ounce can broiled sliced mushrooms

Trim off excess fat. Dredge meat in flour. Brown slowly on all sides in a little hot fat. Season generously with salt and pepper. Add onions. Mix and add remaining ingredients except mushrooms. Cover; cook slowly 2½ hours or till done. Add mushrooms (and liquid); heat. Remove meat to warm platter. Skim fat from stock. Blend 1 tablespoon flour and ¼ cup cold water; gradually stir into stock. Cook and stir till sauce thickens; salt to taste. Serve over meat. Makes 6 to 8 servings.

Mrs. Irving Pink

Hamburgers Hawaiian

Combine:
2/3 cup **Carnation** evaporated milk
1½ lbs. ground beef

½ cup chopped onion
2/3 cup cracker crumbs
1 tsp. seasoned salt

Form six 4" individual patties by pressing each one between pieces of waxed paper. Brown patties in skillet in a little fat. Pour off fat. Cover hamburgers with sauce (below). Cover and simmer over low heat 15 minutes.

Sweet and Sour Sauce:

Drain can of pineapple chunks. Combine pineapple syrup and water to make 1 cup. Mix syrup with 2 tbsp. cornstarch, ¼ cup vinegar, ¼ cup brown sugar and 2 tbsp. soy sauce, in saucepan. Heat till thickened and clear. Add pineapple chunks and 1 cup coarsely chopped green pepper.

NOTE: Ordinary milk won't do when making hamburgers which won't fall apart, even when simmered. For a party, I put sauce in chafing dish, form hamburg into small balls, which I brown, then simmer in consomme, adding meat balls to sauce in chafing dish, as desired. Serves 6.

Mrs. R. M. Stoddart

Dinner In A Dish

2 tbsp. oil
¼ cup finely chopped onion
1 lg. green pepper
1 lb. lean minced beef
1 tsp. salt
⅛ tsp. pepper
⅛ tsp. oregano

¼ cup hot water
1 Oxo cube
2 eggs, beaten
4 medium tomatoes, sliced
2 cups whole kernel corn
½ cup buttered bread crumbs
Accent

In hot oil in fry pan, saute chopped onion, green pepper, and ground meat — about 8 minutes. Sprinkle this mixture well with Accent. Add seasonings, water and dissolved Oxo cube. Remove from heat, cool and add beaten eggs. In greased casserole, place layer of tomato slices, meat mixture, then corn. Repeat layers. Top with crumbs. Bake 35 min. in 375 oven.

Nancy Doty

Meat Loaf

1½ lbs. hamburg
¼ cup catsup
1 egg, beaten
1 cup water

1 cup oatmeal
1 tsp. mustard
2½ tsp. salt
½ tsp. pepper

Mix together well. Pack firmly in loaf pan. Bake at 375° for 1 hour.

Eloise Forbes

Hamburg Casserole

(Serves 20)

Fry in oil:
1 lb. sliced onions
1 can drained mushrooms
2 green peppers, chopped
1 head celery, chopped
2 lbs. hamburg
Add:
2 tsp. salt

½ tsp. pepper
⅛ tsp. curry powder
½ tsp. chili powder
2 cans tomato paste
1 can tomato soup
1 can mushroom soup
Cook in boiling water:
2 pkgs. wide noodles

Combine all ingredients, put in casserole. Cover with cheese slices. Bake ¾ to 1 hour in 350° oven. Serves approximately 20.

Ruth Boyd

Shipwreck Casserole

In bottom of large casserole put:
1 layer onions
1 layer thinly sliced potatoes

1 lb. hamburg
1 layer Minute rice
1 layer chopped celery

Season with salt and pepper and pour a tin of tomatoes or tin of tomato soup and 1 can boiling water over casserole. Bake 2 hours, uncovered in 350° oven.

Mrs. Hope Langille

"All In One" Main Dish

1½ lbs. chuck or round steak (1 inch thick)	butter
2 potatoes (quartered)	salt
4 carrots (sliced quite thick)	pepper
2 onions (small) sliced	½ pkg. Lipton onion soup

Place tinfoil on cookie sheet. (Take large piece of tinfoil to allow for wrapping and expansion.) Put steak on tinfoil, spread ½ pkg. Lipton soup on top. Next place potatoes and carrots, then onion on next layer. Dot with butter, salt and pepper. Seal edges of tinfoil. Leave room for expansion. Bake 425° for 1½ hours.

Dot Brown

Hamburger Pie

1 medium onion, chopped	drained, or ½ lb. green beans, cooked and drained
1 lb. ground beef	1 can condensed tomato soup
¾ tsp. salt	Potato Fluff Topper
dash pepper	
2 cups canned cut green beans,	

Cook onion in small amount hot fat till tender but not brown. Add meat and seasonings; brown lightly. Add drained beans and soup; pour into greased 1½ quart casserole.

Drop Potato Fluff Topper in mounds over meat. If desired sprinkle potatos with ½ cup shredded processed cheese. Bake at 350° for 25 to 30 minutes. Makes 6 servings.

Potato Fluff Topper:

5 med. potatoes, cooked	1 beaten egg
¼ cup warm Superior milk	

Mash potatoes while hot, add milk and egg. Season. Drop in mounds over casserole.

Mildred Porter, Hebron

Sweet & Sour Cabbage Rolls

1½ lbs. hamburg	1 lemon (juice)
½ cup raisins	1 stalk celery (diced)
½ cup brown sugar	salt
1 med. head cabbage	pepper
1 lg. tin whole tomatoes	

Mix hamburger, and peel about 12 leaves of cabbage. Parboil cabbage about 10 minutes. Roll medium size meat balls in a cabbage leaf and secure with a toothpick. Continue until all is used up. Put rolls in deep pot, add tomatoes, celery, raisins and half of lemon. Add more salt and pepper over rolls, also brown sugar and other half of lemon. Bake 2 hours in oven at 325°.

Corinne Pink

Cabbage Rolls

1 lb. hamburg
½ tsp. cinnamon
salt and pepper to taste
1 lg. head cabbage

1½ cups uncooked rice
1 tsp. allspice
1 lg. tin tomatoes

Steam cabbage about five minutes. Drain juice from tomatoes. Mix in order listed and add pulp from tomatoes. Roll a small amount of mixture and put in cabbage leaf. Close the leaf with tooth pick. Place rolls in large pot and cover with juice from tomatoes, plus one can of cream of tomato soup and one can water. Simmer over low heat about 2 hours. Serve with green peas. These are very good warmed over.

Lauretta (Mrs. Arie) Vanderdonk

Chop Suey Burgers

12 hamburger rolls
½ cup butter
5 cups chicken (cooked and cut in strips)
2 cups chopped onion
6 cups diced celery
1 tbsp. salt
¼ tsp. pepper
2 cans mushrooms

3½ cups hot broth (or water)
3 cans Chinese mixed vegetables or bean sprouts
Thickening:
¼ cup cold water
¼ cup cornstarch
4 teaspoons Soy Sauce
2 tsp. brown gravy sauce if desired

Cook meat and onion in butter for 5 minutes. Add celery, salt, pepper and broth. Cover and simmer 10 minutes. Add remainder of vegetables. Mix thickening and add to meat mixture. Should be ready to serve in 2 minutes.

To Serve: Open warm hamburger roll. Cover bottom roll with hot chop suey. Replace top of the roll, and cover generously.

Served with egg noodles and salad, this makes a quick and easy luncheon for 12 people.

Betty Churchill

Easy Chinese Egg Rolls

Filling:

4 cups uncooked cabbage
   shredded
1 cup cooked chicken, minced
¼ cup finely shredded onion
½ cup finely shredded celery

¼ tsp. Accent
1 tbsp. corn oil (Mazola)
2 tsp. salt
1 tbsp. Soya sauce

Place everything but cabbage in large bowl. Mix until thoroughly blended. Add cabbage, stir gently.

"Skins":

2 cups flour
1 beaten egg

1 tsp. salt
½ cup cold water

Place flour in deep bowl. Add egg and salt. Add water and stir until forms a ball. Roll paper thin, cut in 6" squares. Place spoonful of filling in center of square. Brush edges with beaten egg and fold over, pressing ends firmly to close openings.

Cook 1 min. in hot Mazola oil. Keep refrigerated until ready to use. When needed cook in oil till golden brown. Serve with Plum Sauce.

Arlene Stuart

Chinese Fried Rice

½ lb. roasted or fried ham or bacon (a can of lobster or shrimp may
   be substituted or even a can of luncheon meat.)

3 cups cooked rice
1 tbsp. chopped onions
2 tbsp. Soy Sauce

2 eggs
¼ tsp. salt, pepper

Cut ham or bacon in small strips and fry. Not necessary to heat or fry cold roasted meats, canned lobster or shrimp. Simply cut small. Fresh shrimp or lobster should be sauted in butter 3 minutes. Fry onions. Add salt, pepper, meat or seafood, and mix with rice. Add beaten eggs and stir thoroughly while cooking about 3 minutes. Remove from fire, add Soy Sauce and stir. Serve while hot.

Mary Churchill

Deluxe Mushroom Chop Suey Or Chow Mien

¼ cup butter
1½ cup (¾ lb.) beef tenderloin or lean veal, cut in thin strips
1 cup onions, cut fine
1 tsp. salt
1½ cups hot water
1¼ cups canned or fresh mushrooms cut in ¼" pieces
1 can bean sprouts
1/16 tsp. pepper
2 cups celery

FLAVORING AND THICKENING

2 tbsp. cold water
2 tbsp. cornstarch
1 tbsp. brown gravy sauce if

Chop Suey is desired
2 tbsp. Soy Sauce
1 tsp. sugar

Heat fat in skillet, add meat and sear quickly (without burning) Add onions and fry for 5 minutes. Add celery, salt, pepper and hot water. Cover and cook for 5 minutes. Add mushrooms. Add drained bean sprouts. Mix thoroughly and bring to boil. Combine and add thickening and flavoring ingredients. Mix lightly and cook for 1 minute. Serve piping hot over cooked rice for Chop Suey or over noodles for Chow Mien. More Soy Sauce may be needed, according to taste.

Mrs. Leland Trask

Chinese Beef

2 lb. round steak cut in long
   strips
3 whole tomatoes
2 green peppers
2 tbsp. salad oil
1 clove garlic
1 tsp. salt

dash pepper
¼ tsp. ground ginger
¼ cup Soya Sauce
1 tsp. sugar
1 can bean sprouts
1 tbsp. cornstarch
¼ cup water

Place steak, oil, garlic, salt, pepper, ginger, soya sauce, salt and sugar in small roasting pan. Place in 350° oven about ¾ hour or until meat is soft. Remove to pot, and add tomatoes which have been quartered, green peppers cut in pieces and bean sprouts which have been well drained. Cook on top of stove over medium heat for 15 minutes. Make paste of cornstarch and water. Add to meat, cook 15 minutes longer over low heat, stirring constantly. Delicious served with fried rice.

Mrs. Jerry Star

Chicken Marengo

2 broilers, cut up	1 8-oz. can tomato sauce
¼ cup salad oil	1 3-oz. bottle stuffed olives
3 cloves garlic, minced	½ cup sherry
1 tsp. salt	⅓ cup toasted almonds
½ tsp. basil	grated cheese
1 lb. mushrooms, sliced	

Coat chicken pieces lightly with a mixture of flour, pepper and paprika. Brown chicken in hot oil. Drain oil except for spoonful or so. Add seasonings, mushrooms and tomato sauce. Cover and simmer for 15 minutes. Add olives with liquid, sherry and almonds. Transfer chicken to a casserole, sprinkle with grated cheese and bake for forty minutes in a 350° oven.

Mrs. Laurie Mushkat

Chinese Chicken

1 broiler

Cut into pieces. cover each piece with pepper, Accent and fresh garlic.

Mix together:	3 tbsp. Soy Sauce
¾ cup brown sugar	juice of 1 lemon

Pour over chicken and marinate overnight. Bake 1 hour (½ hour on each side in 350° oven). Recipe can easily be doubled. Serve on white rice.

Corinne Pink

Chicken Casserole

Cover and simmer until tender in salted water, a boiling fowl. Remove chicken and put broth in double boiler and add 1 pkg. (or ½ pkg.) small noodles. Cook until soft. Cut up one large onion and fry in butter until transparent. Combine 2 cans of mushroom soup, 1 cup Superior cream, noodles, onion and cut-up chicken. Place in casserole, sprinkle with cornflakes and bake at 350° for ¾ hour.

Mary Clulee

Baked Chicken And Prunes

3 tbsp. vegetable oil	2 frying chickens, cut up
3 medium onions sliced ¼ " thick	1½ lbs. prunes, pitted
2 tbsp. flour	2 8-oz. cans tomato sauce
	salt, pepper

Put oil in bottom of large deep casserole. Add onions and sprinkle with flour. Add half the pieces of chicken and sprinkle with salt and pepper. Add half the prunes. Repeat layers of chicken, seasoning and prunes. Pour tomato sauce over all. Cover and bake in moderate over 350° F. 2 hours.

Bernice Trask

Chicken Dressing

1 10-oz. ready mixed stuffing	2½ cups diced cooked chicken
1 can condensed cream of mush-room soup	½ cup Superior milk
	2 tbsp. chopped pimiento
2 cups chicken broth (if no broth, use chicken soup base)	1 tsp. sweet basil
	1 tsp. thyme
2 well beaten eggs	1 tsp. oregano

Toss stuffing with soup and broth, milk and eggs. Add chicken, pimiento and herbs. Place in a 12 x 8 baking dish covered with foil. Bake at 350 degrees 45 minutes, or until set.

Mrs. D. F. Macdonald

Poultry Stuffing

4 tbsp. butter	⅓ cup chopped celery
2 tsp. summer savoury	1 tbsp. chopped onion
⅛ tsp. pepper	⅓ cup Superior milk
½ tsp. salt	1½ cups soft bread, cubed
1½ cups hot mashed potatoes	

Add butter, summer savoury, salt and pepper to potatoes and mix well. Then add celery and onion. Mix. Add milk, then bread cubes. Use as stuffing for poultry, or as a dressing with meat.

Mrs. Leland Trask

Lemon Dumplings

Combine:	¼ tsp. salt
2/3 cup sifted flour	1 tsp. lemon juice
1 tsp. baking powder	⅓ cup Superior milk
½ tsp. grated lemon rind	

Stir lemon juice into milk. (Doesn't matter if it curdles). Add all at once to dry ingredients, stir just until flour mixture is moistened completely. Drop batter on top of hot chicken stew. Cover tightly. Cook 20 minutes.

Mrs. John R. Robbins

Roast Duck

1 duck prepared for roasting	with orange juice
1 cup orange juice	2 strips bacon
1 apple, peeled and soaked	orange slices

Place apple inside duck. Lay bacon strips on duck and roast — using orange juice for basting purposes. Cooking time — to suit individual, depending on taste for rare or well cooked duck.

Decorate the platter with orange slices, using one or two slices for each serving.

Mrs. E. H. Spinney

Veal Mozzarella

(6 Good Servings)

1½ lbs. veal steak ½ in. thick
1 egg, beaten
2 tbsp. Superior milk
½ tsp. salt
½ cup fine dry bread crumbs
¼ cup cooking oil
¼ cup chopped onion
¼ cup diced green pepper

8-oz. can tomato sauce
¼ cup broth or white wine
garlic salt, to taste
pepper
⅛ tsp. marjoram
⅛ tsp. oregano
4 oz. mozzarella cheese

Dip individual servings of meat into combined eggs, milk, and salt, then into crumbs. Brown on both sides in heated oil in fry pan. Remove veal to large shallow baking dish (11" x 7") in a single layer.

Cook onion and green pepper for 3 minutes in same pan meat was cooked in. Stir in remaining ingredients, except cheese, and simmer for 10 minutes. Pour this sauce over meat in baking dish. Cover and bake in oven 350° until meat is tender (about ½ hour). Cut cheese into slices, arrange over meat. Continue to bake, uncovered, till cheese melts (2 - 3 minutes).

Marion Gardner

Veal Chop Suey

1½ lbs. veal steak (¾" thick)
1½ lbs. pork steak (¾" thick)
1 cup celery
1 green pepper
2/3 cup sliced onion

2 tins mushrooms, 1 tin liquid
1 tin bean sprouts
1 tin pineapple tid-bits
4 cups beef stock, consomme, etc.

Cut meat in cubes, brown well in oil or bacon fat, add 1 cup water, 3 tsp. salt, ½ tsp. pepper, celery, green pepper and onions. Cook 8 - 10 minutes. Add meat stock. Simmer 1 - 1½ hours. Blend ¾ cup flour with enough water to make thick paste, add to meat and cook until thickened.

Add:
½ cup vinegar, cider

4 tbsp. soya sauce
2 tbsp. brown sugar

Add pineapple and juice, bean sprouts (drained. Serves 12 - 14.

Mary Sinclair

Veal Exotic

2 lbs. veal cut into small cubes
2 tsp. kitchen bouquet
2 tbsp. fat
¾ cup chopped onions
1 can sliced mushrooms
1 cup water
2 tbsp. brown sugar
¼ cup vinegar
1 tsp. ground ginger

1 tsp. dry mustard
1 tsp. salt
¼ tsp. pepper
1 tbsp. cornstarch
2 tbsp. water
1½ cups flaked coconut
1 5-oz. can water chestnuts, thinly sliced
3 cups hot cooked rice

Brush veal with the bouquet. Melt fat in a large skillet. Add veal and brown on all sides. Then add onions and mushrooms and cook until onions are brown. Add 1 cup water, sugar and seasonings. Bring to a boil, stirring constantly. Lower heat and simmer uncovered 1 hour or until meat is tender. Mix cornstarch with 2 tbsp. water and add to meat mixture. Stir until thick. Stir in coconut, water chestnuts with their liquid. When hot serve over boiled rice.

Mrs. Irving Pink

Savory Veal Roll

Simmer meat in a spicy sauce, then serve with horseradish gravy.

(Makes 6 servings)

3 to 4 lbs. rolled boned veal shoulder
6 tbsp. flour
1 tbsp. dry mustard
1 tbsp. brown sugar
2 tsp. salt
1 tsp. poultry seasoning
⅛ tsp. pepper

2 tbsp. salad oil
1 lg. onion, chopped (1 cup)
¼ cup chopped celery
2 tbsp. chopped parsley
2 tbsp. vinegar
½ cup water
2 tsp. prepared horseradish

1. Rub veal well with mixture of 2 tbsp. flour, mustard, brown sugar, salt, poultry seasoning, and pepper. (Save remaining flour for gravy in Step 5.)

2. Brown meat slowly in salad oil in heavy kettle or Dutch oven. Add onion, celery, parsley, and vinegar; cover.

3. Simmer 2½ hours, or until meat is tender. Remove to carving board or heated serving platter; keep hot.

4. Strain stock into a 2-cup measure; let fat rise to top; skim off all fat. Add water to stock, if needed, to make 2 cups; return to kettle.

5. Smooth saved 4 tablespoons flour to a paste with water in a cup; stir into stock in kettle. Cook, stirring all the time, until gravy thickens and boils 1 minute. Stir in prepared horseradish.

Almond Veal

4 lbs. veal shoulder, cubed. **Marinate overnight** with garlic cloves, covered, in refrigerator.

Dip in batter of 3 eggs, mixed with 3 tbsp. cornstarch. Deep fry 10 minutes. Drain. ½ hour before serving, put veal in pot of hot brown chicken or roast gravy. Place on platter and smother with chopped, toasted almonds.

Mrs. S. Chernin, Halifax

Superb Veal Chops

Coat 6 rib veal chops with a mixture of
⅓ cup flour
1 tsp. salt
1 tsp. paprika and brown in hot fat
Drain off excess fat from pan and sprinkle meat with
⅓ cup chopped onion   **2 tbsp. lemon juice**
2 tbsp. brown sugar
Pour over meat
1 cup canned mixed vegetable juices and 1 cup water

Cover and simmer until chops are tender — about 50 minutes. Arrange chops on heated platter, thicken gravy, if desired, and pour over meat. Sprinkle with a few sliced olives before serving.

Phyllis Churchill

Rulla Pylsa

(Icelandic)

2 lb. lamb flank, boned   **¾ tsp. ground allspice**
2 tbsp. salt   **1 medium sized onion, chopped**
½ tsp. salt petre   **¾ tsp. pepper**
¾ tsp. ground cloves

Ask butcher to bone the meat, but leave in one piece. Lay this piece flat on the table with boned side up. Mix the salt, salt petre, cloves, allspice and pepper and spread over the flank. Salt petre is necessary, for it makes the meat turn pink in color, otherwise it will be brown. Chop onion and sprinkle over flank. Then roll it up as you would a jelly roll.

Sew up both ends and the loose edge with needle and thread. Then wind string tightly all over the roll. Salt outside of flank. Roll in wax paper. Set in the refrigerator and leave for 3 to 7 days, no less than 3. The spices must work through.

At the end of that time place in cooking pot. Cover with water. Bring to boil and then turn heat down and let simmer for 1½ hours. Remove and cool.

Place between two surfaces and place a heavy weight on top. Leave overnight. Next day remove string, slice and serve cold.

Eleanor Russell

Planked Ham With Vegetables

1 slice ham 2 ins. thick
8 medium potatoes
1 can asparagus

1 bunch carrots
2 15-oz. cans peas

Cover ham with cold water, bring to boil, then simmer for 40 minutes. Drain, place on plank. Stick whole cloves around edge. Brown in oven at 350° for 30 minutes.

Remove from oven, add a border of mashed potatoes, garnishing with the peas and carrots alternately, with the stalks of asparagus separating them. Spread vegetables with butter. Return plank to oven until potatoes are browned. (I always use cookie sheet.) Serves 6.

Mrs. Clifford Deveau

Cranberry Glazed Ham

1 smoked ham (8 to 10 lbs.)
2 doz. long stemmed cloves
1 can (1 lb.) jellied cranberry

sauce
½ cup brown sugar

Bake ham according to manufacturer's directions. One half hour before end of baking time, remove from oven. Score fat with sharp knife, stud with cloves; return to baking pan. (Any fat that has collected in bottom of pan should be poured off before placing ham back in oven.) Crush cranberry sauce with fork; combine crushed cranberry sauce and brown sugar. Spread half of mixture over ham. Bake half hour longer, basting occasionally. Heat remaining cranberry mixture to serve on ham slices.

Hilda Zellers

Glazed Ham Balls

1½ lbs. ground lean pork
1 lb. ground ham
2 cups soft bread crumbs
1 tsp. salt
1 cup Superior milk

1 20-oz. can pineapple
chunks
1 cup brown sugar, firmly packed
½ cup cider vinegar
1 tsp. dry mustard

Heat oven to 350° F. Have butcher grind the pork and ham together. Mix meat, bread crumbs, salt and milk. Shape level tablespoonfuls of mixture into balls. Arrange balls in single layer in a large baking pan. Bake uncovered 30 minutes. While meat is baking, drain pineapple and reserve ½ cup of the juice. Place juice, brown sugar, vinegar, mustard in a saucepan; heat to boiling. Remove ham balls to a 3 qt. casserole, discarding the fat. Pour juice mixture over balls. Bake uncovered 30 minutes, stirring occasionally. Add pineapple chunks and bake 15 minutes longer. Serve with rice, and a crisp mixed salad, with cucumber, and ripe tomatoes in it, and hot crusty rolls. Serves 8 to 10.

Clara Harris

Ham Casserole

1½ cup cooked ham (cut up)
1 cup grated cheese (sharp
  cheddar)
1 can mushroom soup
1 cup Superior milk
½ cup onion, chopped

2 tsp. prepared mustard
dash of cayenne
4 cups cooked rice
1 cup cracker crumbs
2 tbsp. butter

Combine in pan ham, cheese, soup, milk, onion, mustard and cayenne. Heat until blended.

Put a layer of rice in bottom of casserole. Top with layer of ham mixture, then layer of rice, continue until all are used, ending with layer of ham. Sprinkle with crumbs. Dot with butter. Bake 375° oven, 30 - 40 minutes, or until bubbling and browned on top. Serves 6 - 8.

Dot (Mrs. E. L.) Brown

Tasty Raisin Sauce For Baked Ham

¾ cup brown sugar
½ tbsp. mustard
1 tbsp. flour

¼ cup raisins
¼ cup vinegar
1¾ cups water

Mix dry ingredients, add raisins, vinegar and water. Bring to boil and serve hot over baked ham.

Mrs. George Blackadar

Spicy Frankfurters

1 lb. frankfurters
2 tbsp. flour
3 tbsp. water
1 cup water

¾ cup ketchup
3 tbsp. vinegar
1 tbsp. sugar
1 tsp. prepared mustard

Cut frankfurters in half lengthwise. Place in deep covered skillet. Combine flour with 3 tablespoons water, add remaining ingredients. Pour this sauce over the frankfurters. Cover and bring to a boil and simmer 20 minutes.

Mrs. Irving Pink

Canadian Pork Pies

1½ lb. lean pork	⅛ tsp. pepper
1 medium onion	2 cups water
3 or 4 celery tops	pastry
1 tsp. salt	

Cut pork into small pieces and chop onion fairly fine. Place in saucepan along with celery tops, salt and pepper. Cover with water, bring to a boil then simmer over low heat until pork can be pierced easily with fork. Continue cooking until a cup of liquid remains. Remove from stove, take out celery tops and cool. Make enough pastry to cover tops and line bottoms and sides of 12 - 2 inch muffin tins. Fill pastry lined tins with pork mixture and cover with pastry. Bake 30 minutes until crust is a delicate brown. Remove from pans. Cool. May be served hot or cold. Good for picnics.

Mrs. John Robbins

Pork Chops Supreme

6 lean pork chops	6 thin slices lemon
¼ to ½ cup brown sugar	½ cup tomato catsup

Place chops in a baking dish and on each place a thin slice of lemon. Sprinkle generously with brown sugar. Add catsup. Cover and bake at 350 deg. F. about three quarters of an hour. Uncover during last 15 minutes of baking.

GRAVY: Remove chops, pour all but 2 tbsp. fat from pan, add 2 tbsp. flour and stir till well browned. Add 1½ cups water. Stir till smooth. Season with salt and pepper.

Dot Kirk

Casserole Liver Pie

1 lb. beef liver	3 tbsp. flour
4 slices bacon	2 tsp. salt
5 average potatoes	2 cups boiling water
1 small onion	

Wipe liver, cut in strips and parboil 5 minutes in boiling water to cover. Drain and roll in flour. Fry bacon until crisp, then saute the liver in the bacon fat until nicely browned. Arrange liver in casserole, add boiling water to gravy in pan. Lay strips of bacon in casserole, chop the potatoes and onions, mix with the remainder of flour and salt, spread over the meat, pour in the gravy. Cover and bake in hot oven about 1 hour.

Mrs. Winslow Gates

Southern Casserole

4 oz. spaghetti
8 pork sausages (about ½ lb.)
½ cup chopped green pepper
¼ cup chopped onion
¼ tsp. salt
¼ tsp. chili powder

1 cup cream corn
1½ cups shredded cheddar
   cheese
⅓ cup Superior milk
2 tbsp. chopped pimiento

Cook spaghetti in salted water.

Brown sausages in skillet. Drain on absorbent paper. Pour off all but 2 tbsp. of dripping from skillet.

Add green pepper, onion and brown lightly. Season with salt and chili powder. Add corn, cheese, milk and pimiento, mixing until cheese is melted. Add spaghetti to this mixture, mixing well.

Turn into 1 qt. casserole. Arrange sausages on top of spaghetti. Bake in 350° oven about 20 minutes.

Mrs. G. M. Macdonald

Rapee Pie (Tarte A La Rapure) - Acadian Dish

12 large potatoes
5 lb. chicken or black duck
   or rabbit

3 large onions
½ lb. pure lard
salt and pepper

Boil meat in enough water to have about 1¼ gallons of broth. Meat should not be completely cooked. Remove meat from broth and break up with fork. After potatoes are peeled, scrape them, and squeeze in a bag, letting the starchy water drain into a bowl. Allow this water to set. Drain off clear fluid and add the starchy sediment to the potatoes. Pack tightly in a bowl and cover it for a few minutes with a cold wet cloth.

Place potatoes and sliced raw onions in a warm dish. Add the boiling broth gradually, beating continually, and add salt and pepper. Put in a dish previously greased with hot melted lard. Place 1 layer of potatoes, 1 layer of hot meat, then 1 layer of potatoes. Bake in hot oven of 500° F. for 10 minutes, then reduce oven temperature to 300° for 1 hour, then grease top with 2 or 3 teaspoons hot pure lard. Chow-chow adds to the taste. Serves 12.

Mrs. W. M. Phinney

Partridge Or Woodcock

Have birds halved or quartered and thoroughly clean and dry.

Mix:

1 cup pancake flour
1 tsp. salt
½ tsp. pepper
¼ tsp. sage

Place this mixture in a strong paper bag and add bird halves. Shake well until birds are well powdered.

Melt small amount of butter or salad oil or salt pork scraps in heavy skillet.

To this add:

3 tbsp. chopped onion
3 tbsp. chopped celery
3 tbsp. chopped green or sweet red peppers or both

Cook for 5 minutes and move over to side of pan. Brown bird halves well on both sides in this fat. Then add enough boiling water to simmer gently for ¾ to 1 hour. Cover pan tightly while simmering. During the last 15 minutes doughboys may be added. Try sage or poultry seasoning in these.

Remove partridge to hot platter, thicken gravy (do not strain). Pour over bird and serve immediately.

Mrs. Pauline Ring (Birchdale)

Wild Rice Stuffing For Wild Or Domestic Fowl

1½ cups wild rice

Wash thoroughly and boil 10 to 15 minutes (half cooked).

3 tbsp. chopped celery
2 tbsp. chopped onions
4 tbsp. butter
2 tbsp. chopped green pepper
(optional)
2 tbsp. pimiento
¼ tbsp. sage
salt and pepper to taste

Melt butter. Add all seasonings and cook slowly five minutes. Mix with wild rice and stuff fowl 2/3 full. This will serve 16 to 18 people.

Mrs. Pauline Ring (Birchdale)

Roast Loin Of Venison

4 to 5 lbs. loin of venison
1 clove garlic
3 tbsp. prepared mustard
1 tbsp. flour
¼ tsp. salt
½ cup crabapple jelly
1 tbsp. water
green grapes
pickled peach halves

Preheat oven to 350 deg. F. Wipe venison with damp cloth. Cut small slits in top of roast with sharp knife. Pare garlic; cut in tiny slivers. Place garlic in slits of roast. Put roast in shallow pan. Spread with prepared mustard; sprinkle with flour and salt. Roast for 2½ hours. Combine jelly and water. Drizzle over roast. Roast ½ hour longer. Remove to platter. Garnish with tiny bunches of grapes and peach halves. Yield: eight to 10 servings.

Gourmet Venison Pot Roast

4 to 5 lb. shoulder roast venison
1½ tsp. salt
¼ tsp. dry mustard
⅛ tsp. pepper
2 cups dry red wine
2 tbsp. flour
3 tbsp. bacon fat

3 tbsp. snipped parsley
1 cup canned tomatoes
¼ cup minced onion
1 cup sliced celery
1 cup sliced carrots
¼ cup minced green pepper
2 tbsp. flour

Wipe roast with damp cloth. Sprinkle with ½ teaspoon salt, mustard and pepper. Place in deep bowl. Pour in wine. Refrigerate for 24 hours. Drain off marinade; reserve. Wipe meat dry.

Preheat oven to 325° F. Dredge meat with flour; brown on all sides in bacon fat. Place in heavy roaster; add one cup marinade and remaining salt. Cover. Roast two hours.

Remove meat and vegetables to hot platter. Thicken liquid with flour; if needed add remaining marinade to make thin gravy. Serve meat and vegetables and gravy with hot baking powder biscuits, wild cranberry jelly and baked squares of Hubbard squash. Yield: eight to 10 servings.

SUPPER DISHES

Bean Almondine Casserole

½ cup onions (sliced)
1 pkg. frozen French style beans
1 cup celery (chopped)

1 can cream of mushroom soup
1 green pepper (chopped)
almonds (slivered)

Cook beans, celery, onions until tender. Add soup and pepper. Put in casserole. Sprinkle slivered almonds on top. Bake 350° oven 25-30 mins.

Dot (Mrs. E. L.) Brown

Turnip Au Gratin

Peel and cube 4 cups turnip. Boil in salted water, until just tender. Drain. Put it in a baking dish.

Sauce:

Melt 3 tbsp. butter. Beat 2 egg yolks, add 1 tbsp. lemon juice, salt and pepper, and melted butter a little at a time. Mix well. Pour over cooked turnip. Sprinkle bread crumbs on top. Bake 15 minutes. Serve as a vegetable.

Mary Churchill

Mushroom Paprihash

1 lb. firm white mushrooms, sliced
1 medium-sized onion, minced
4 tbsp. butter
2 tbsp. flour

1 cup Superior commercial sour cream
1 tsp. paprika
salt and pepper to taste
1 tbsp. minced fresh parsley

Wash mushrooms carefully under cold running water. Sponge them dry. Slice the mushrooms, but do not peel them. Sprinkle a little lemon juice over them. Saute minced onion in butter until light golden. Add mushrooms, cover, and cook gently for 5 minutes. Drain off liquid and combine it with flour, blending until smooth. If necessary, add 1 to 2 tbsp. cold water. Add to sour cream and paprika and season mixture with salt and pepper. Heat gently until the sauce thickens. Add mushrooms to the sauce and simmer over very low heat for 5 minutes. Sprinkle with minced fresh parsley. Serve very hot on thick slices of buttered toast. Excellent supper dish. Serves 6.

M. Ozvegy

Mushrooms Creole

¼ cup oil
1 lg. onion, sliced or chopped
1 green pepper, sliced or chopped
1 lb. fresh mushrooms, quartered, or
2 to 3 cans (4 ozs. each) button mushrooms

1 can (16 to 19 oz.) whole tomatoes
1 can (6 oz.) tomato paste
⅛ tsp. marjoram
salt and pepper to taste
4 to 6 cups hot cooked rice

Heat oil in heavy saucepan. Add onion and pepper; saute without browning, about 3 minutes, turning often. Add mushrooms, tomatoes, tomato paste, and seasonings. Cover and simmer for 5 to 8 minutes, or until the fresh mushrooms are tender. Press hot rice into oiled ring mold and turn onto serving platter. Fill center with Mushrooms Creole. Yield: 6 servings.

Tested by Y Auxiliary

Bean Salad

1 can green beans
1 can wax beans

1 can kidney beans
1 can lima beans

Drain all beans well (also rinsing kidney beans). Combine in bowl and cover with following:

⅓ cup salad oil
2/3 cup vinegar
1 cup sugar

1 tsp. salt
½ tsp. pepper
½ tsp. dry mustard

Shake ingredients well and pour over bean mixture. Allow to stand at least overnight. Toss before serving. Very nice for barbecues.

Ruth Urquhart

Broccoli Casserole

2 pkgs. frozen broccoli (chopped)

Cook according to directions, but just enough to thaw and separate.

1¼ cups chopped onion

Saute in 4 tbsp. butter. Make white sauce by adding 2 tbsp. flour. Stir few minutes. Add ½ cup water.

Add: 8 oz. jar Cheese Whiz

Add above sauce to the broccoli. Beat 3 eggs and mix in lightly. Put in casserole. Top with buttered bread crumbs. Bake 350° oven 30 minutes.

Myra Sutherland

Beets With Pineapple

1 no. 2 can pineapple chunks, drained
1 large can diced beets

Blend 2 tbsp. pineapple syrup with 2 tbsp. cornstarch. Mix beet juice with ½ cup pineapple syrup and cornstarch mixture. Heat juices, stirring constantly until thickened. Add 1 tbsp. vinegar, ¾ tsp. salt, 1½ cups drained pineapple and then beets. Heat thoroughly and serve.

Ruth Pink

Auxiliary Bean Casserole

1 lb. can green beans	**½ tsp. worcestershire sauce**
1½ tsp. flour	**2 tsp. pimiento**
1½ tsp. butter	**½ cup grated cheese**
1 can mushroom soup	**⅓ cup bread crumbs**
¼ cup bean liquid	**1 tbsp. melted butter**

Melt butter in saucepan, add flour, quickly add bean liquid. Stir in soup, stir until smooth, add worcestershire sauce, cheese and pimiento. Place beans in 10" casserole. Pour sauce over all. Mix bread crumbs and melted butter. Sprinkle over top. Bake 350° 25 minutes.

Carrot Mould With Peas

3 tbsp. fat	**dash of pepper and nutmeg**
1 onion, finely chopped	**4 cups cooked carrots, sieved**
¼ cup sifted all-purpose flour	**1 tbsp. brown sugar**
2 eggs	**1 tbsp. vinegar**
1 tsp. salt	

Heat fat in heavy pan. Add diced onion; cook and stir until tender. Blend in flour; toss and turn for another two minutes. Remove from heat.

To lightly beaten egg yolk add seasonings, sieved carrots, sugar and vinegar. Beat until smooth; add onion mixture. Then beaten egg whites.

Pat into place in oiled 9 inch ring mould. Bake in shallow pan of hot water in 350° oven until set (about 25 minutes). Unmould; fill centre with fast frozen green peas, heated with a sprig of mint. Serves 6.

Tested Y Auxiliary

Carrot Casserole

2 lbs. carrots, peeled, cut and
   boiled 10 minutes
2/3 cup brown sugar
2 cups carrot juice
2 tins mandarin oranges

2 tbsp. flour
3 tbsp. honey
2 tbsp. lemon juice
rind of 1 orange

Boil sugar and carrot juice for 5 minutes. Over layers of drained carrots and oranges, sprinkle rind, honey and lemon juice. Sprinkle with flour. Pour syrup over all. Bake 325° for 2 hours.

Mary Sinclair

Corn Souffle ✔

1 cup soft bread crumbs
1 cup cream style corn
1 cup Superior milk
1 cup sharp cheese, grated

1 tbsp. melted butter
½ tsp. salt
¼ tsp. pepper
3 egg yolks, beaten well

Combine above. Add 3 egg whites beaten until stiff. Fold in. Put in greased baking dish. Bake 1 hour in moderate oven or until firm or in individual dishes a shorter time. Serve at once. Serves 6.

Mrs. B. A. Cleveland

Cheese Corn Puff

3 eggs (separated)
¼ cup flour
2 tsp. sugar
½ tsp. salt
¼ tsp. dry mustard
¾ cup Superior milk

3 tbsp. melted butter
½ lb. pkg. velveeta cheese
   (grated)
1 can corn niblets (drained)
2 tbsp. green pepper

Beat egg yolks. Mix flour, sugar, salt and mustard together. Add milk and melted butter. Mix till smooth, then add cheese, corn niblets and pepper. Fold in beaten egg yolks. Lastly fold in well beaten egg whites. Put in greased baking dish. Bake 350° oven 1 hour.

Allie (Mrs. J. M.) Hayman

Stuffed Green Peppers

Sauce:
2 tins tomato soup

1 tin water
1 tbsp. sugar

Mix and put on stove. Cover and bring to a boil.

Meat Mixture:
¾ or 1 lb. ground meat
small onion chopped fine

¼ cup regular rice
1 egg

Mix with a little water until soft.

Scoop out insides of green peppers. Stuff with meat mixture. Put in sauce in pan. Cover and simmer for 1½ hours. Serve with baked potatoes.

Mrs. Loran (Nella) Greenwood

Stuffed Peppers

1 tsp. salt
3 cloves garlic
6 or 7 medium sized green peppers
½ cup Minute rice
1 can cream of mushroom soup
juice of 1 lemon

black pepper to taste
2 tbsp. finely chopped onion
2 tbsp. butter
2 5-oz. cans shrimp
1 cup grated cheese
paprika

Put salt and garlic in 2 qts. water, bring to boil. Meanwhile cut tops off peppers and scoop them out. Put them in boiling water and cook for five minutes. Cook rice. Combine mushroom soup, lemon juice, pepper, cheese, onion, butter in saucepan, and cook over low heat till butter melts and is well mixed. To this add rice and cleaned shrimp. Stuff peppers almost to top — top with cheese, butter and paprika. Place in casserole with about ¼" water in bottom. Bake about forty minutes.

Mrs. J. T. Balmanno

Pizza Pie

Crust:
2 cups flour
1 tsp. salt

4 tsp. baking powder
2 tbsp. shortening
¾ cup Superior milk

Sift together flour, salt and baking powder. Cut in shortening and add milk slowly. Roll out very thin and place on greased pizza pie plate, broiler pan or several small pie plates, turning up edges slightly.

Spread over 1 small tin tomato sauce and place on top any one or combination of the following: tomato wedges, sliced green peppers, mushrooms, shrimp, salami, olives, sardines. Sprinkle with grated cheese and bake 15 - 20 minutes at 425°. Cut into pie-shaped wedges or squares.

Ruth M. Rideout

Cheese Snacks

Cut thin slices of bread. Trim off crusts. Sprinkle thin slices of cheese with salt, paprika. Put between two slices of bread. Cut in half. Dip in mixture of:

1 beaten egg
½ cup Superior milk

¼ tsp. salt

Melt some butter in hot frying pan, and brown both sides of sandwich. Serve with an individual salad.

Eleanor Symonds

Cheese Fondue

1½ cups Superior milk
2 cups bread crumbs
1½ cups grated cheese
1 tbsp. butter

1 tsp. salt
⅛ tsp. paprika
3 eggs, separated

Heat milk, bread crumbs, cheese, butter, salt, and paprika in top of double boiler until cheese is melted. Cool slightly. Add to beaten egg yolks. Fold in stiffly beaten egg whites. Pour into greased baking dish. Set in pan of hot water and bake in moderate oven (350) for 30 - 40 minutes or until firm. Serve immediately.

Vera Cain

Quiche Lorraine

Line 9 x 9" pie plate with pastry.

6 slices bacon, fried
3 oz. Swiss cheese, sliced
1 tbsp. flour
¼ tsp. salt
⅛ tsp. pepper

1 lg. can undiluted evaporated
milk
4 eggs, beaten
1 tbsp. grated onion

Crumble fried bacon in unbaked pie shell. Cover with cheese slices. Combine flour and seasonings, gradually add milk. Add beaten eggs to milk mixture. Blend well, stir in grated onion. Pour into pie shell. Bake 400°F. 25 - 30 minutes or until knife inserted comes out clean. Garnish with additional bacon if desired. Serve at once.

Maude Churchill

Cheese Souffle

4 tbsp. butter
2 tbsp. flour
1 cup scalded Superior milk
½ tsp. salt
few grains cayenne

½ cup grated cheese (packed)
medium or old
4 egg yolks, beaten very light
4 egg whites, beaten stiff

Melt butter, add flour. Add gradually, hot milk. Stir until thick and smooth. Add salt and pepper, cheese and beaten yolks. Remove from fire. Cool. Fold in egg whites. Pour in well-oiled large casserole and bake in 350 degrees oven 45 minutes. If you prefer a soft souffle bake 30 minutes.

Marjorie Strong

Golden French Toast

Mix and sift 6 tbsp. flour with ½ tsp. salt.

Separate 2 eggs, beat yolks with ½ cup Superior milk, add this to dry ingredients and 1 tbsp. melted butter, then fold in beaten egg whites.

Spread mixture on slices of bread and fry until golden brown Serve hot with maple syrup or jam. (Plenty to coat 6 slices of bread.)

Mrs. Irving Pink

Luncheon Eggs

6 hard boiled eggs, chopped
fine
½ cup grated cheese

1½ cups white sauce
1 cup salmon or tuna
(optional)

Put chopped eggs in casserole in layers with grated cheese between. Cover with white sauce. Sprinkle buttered crumbs on top. Bake in moderate oven until cheese melts and crumbs brown. Also good served over Chinese noodles in individual casseroles.

Mrs. T. A. M. Kirk

Luncheon Egg Rolls

4 shelled hard boiled eggs
4 tbsp. minced parsley
1 cup grated cheese
¼ cup ketchup
1 tbsp. minced onion

salt
6 chopped stuffed olives
(optional)
6 frankfurter rolls
melted butter

Chop eggs and combine with all the rest of the ingredients except rolls and butter. Cut tops off rolls and hollow out centres. Brush with melted butter and fill with egg mixture. Replace tops. Wrap in waxed paper and chill. At lunch or supper time, unwrap, place on baking sheet and bake in moderate oven for 25 - 30 minutes, or until hot and crisp.

Tested

Creamy Egg Scramble On Savory Toast

buttered toast slices
4 eggs slightly beaten
½ tsp. salt
seasoned anchovy, sardine or

fish paste
cayenne
½ to 2/3 cup Superior milk
butter

Add salt, cayenne, milk and butter to eggs. Place over gently boiling water. When sides and bottom set, draw away from pan, letting liquid run under. Cook until all is lightly set. Turn onto hot platter. Border with fingers of toast, trimmed of crusts, and spread with savory fish paste.

Mrs. John Robbins

Corn Pancakes With Maple Syrup

½ tin cream style corn
1 egg
1 cup Superior milk
1½ tsp. baking powder

½ tsp. salt
1 tbsp. sugar
1½ cups flour

Beat egg until light. Add milk. Sift dry ingredients and add gradually to mixture. Add corn last. Drop by spoonfuls on hot greased frying pan or ungreased skillet. When bubbles form in cakes, turn and brown on other side. Serve immediately with butter and maple syrup. Makes 18-20 cakes.

Tested

Waffles

1½ cups flour
3 tsp. baking powder
¼ tsp. salt
2 tbsp. sugar

1 cup Superior milk
2 egg yolks
4 tbsp. melted shortening
2 egg whites

Measure, mix and sift the first four dry ingredients; add the milk gradually then egg yolks and melted shortening and mix thoroughly. Lastly fold in stiffly beaten egg whites.

Mrs. D. F. Macdonald

Gingerbread Waffles

2 cups sifted flour
1½ tsp. soda
1½ tsp. ginger
½ tsp. cinnamon
½ tsp. salt
1 egg yolk, beaten

1 cup molasses
½ cup Superior sour milk or buttermilk
⅓ cup butter, melted
1 egg white, stiffly beaten

Sift flour, measure, add soda, spices and salt. Combine egg yolk, molasses, milk and butter. Add to flour mixture, beating until smooth. Fold in egg white. Bake in waffle iron — not too hot. Serve with Superior whipped cream sweetened and flavored as desired.

Mrs. John R. Robbins

Lasagne

½ lb. (1 pkg.) lasagne or broau noodles
2 cans Catelli meat sauce
2 eggs, beaten

1 pt. (1 pkg.) cottage cheese
2 pkg. Mozzarella cheese, sliced (one can use Swiss cheese)
¼ cup grated Parmesan cheese

Blend beaten eggs with cottage cheese in bowl.

In a baking pan 9 x 13 x 2 put a thin layer of meat sauce, half the noodles (cooked as directed on pkg.), all the cottage cheese and egg mixture and half of the mozzarella cheese slices. Repeat with half the remaining meat sauce, rest of noodles, remainder of meat sauce and other half of mozzarella cheese. Sprinkle with Parmesan cheese. Bake in moderate oven, 350° for 30 minutes. Let cool 10 minutes before serving. This can be made in the morning and just heated up at supper time. Is also good reheated next day. Whole recipe will serve 9 or 10 people.

Joyce (Mrs. E. R.) Syvertsen

Potato And Sausage Casserole

6 medium size potatoes
4 tbsp. melted butter
½ tsp. caraway seeds
6 hard-cooked eggs, sliced
½ lb. sausage or
  ½ lb. knockwurst or
  ½ lb. csabai (Hungarian saus-

age), sliced
salt and pepper to taste
8 tbsp. Superior sour cream
paprika
2 tbsp. bread crumbs
1 tbsp. minced parsley
¼ tsp. caraway seeds

Boil potatoes in slightly salted water with jackets on. Peel them when tender and still warm. Cut into thick slices and arrange a layer in a deep well-buttered casserole. Drizzle a little melted butter over the potatoes and sprinkle lightly with caraway seeds. Arrange a layer of sliced hard-cooked eggs on top of potatoes, then a layer of sliced sausage or whatever you have on hand. Season with salt and pepper to taste. Add another layer of sliced potatoes, 4 tbsp. sour cream, a light sprinkling of caraway seeds. Repeat layers of eggs, sausage and potatoes, ending with a layer of potatoes. Cover top with remaining 4 tbsp. sour cream. Sprinkle with paprika, bread crumbs, parsle and caraway seeds. Cover tightly and bake in a pre-heated moderate (350°F.) oven for 30 - 35 minutes. Uncover and bake 10 minutes longer until top is lightly browned. Serves 6 - 8.

M. Ozvegy

Chicken Spiral Loaf

Chicken Filling:
1 cup diced cooked chicken
1 cup chopped celery
¼ cup chopped green peppers
1 tbsp. chopped onion
½ tsp. salt

Pastry:
1½ cups flour
½ cup corn meal
1 tsp. baking powder
1 tsp. salt
½ cup shortening
½ cup Superior milk

For chicken filling, combine all ingredients, mix well.

For pastry, sift together dry ingredients. Cut in shortening until mixture resembles coarse crumbs. Add milk, tossing lightly with a fork, until mixture will hold together.

Knead gently on floured board. Roll dough out to form a 10"x12" rectangle. Transfer dough to baking sheet. Spoon chicken filling onto dough, spread evenly over the dough. Roll up, beginning on the long side. Place seam ends on underneath side.

Bake in hot oven (425) 20 to 25 minutes. Slice and serve with:

CHEESE SAUCE

¼ cup butter
3 tbsp. flour
1 tsp. finely ground onion

1 cup grated cheese
salt to taste
2 cups Superior milk

Melt butter, add onion. Cook slightly. Add flour and salt. Add ? cup hot milk, stirring constantly until mixture thickens. Add grated cheese, and stir until nice and smooth.

Mary Churchill

Baked Chicken Casserole

1 (6 oz.) can chicken
1 can cream chicken soup
¾ cup mayonnaise
1 cup chopped celery
½ cup chopped walnuts

2 tsp. chopped onion
½ tsp. salt
¼ tsp. pepper
1 tbsp. lemon juice
3 hard-cooked eggs, chopped

Mix together in casserole. Top with crushed potato chips. Bake 15 minutes at 450°. Serve on toast or patty-shell, with a tossed salad.

Mrs. Merle Allen

Chicken Casserole

2 cups chicken (canned or boiled)
2/3 tin chow mein noodles
1 can mushroom soup
1 cup diced celery

½ cup water
¼ cup diced onion
¼ cup cashew nuts
1 can whole or sliced mushrooms

Mix well. Put in casserole dish and cover with remaining ⅓ can noodles. Bake in moderate oven about 50 minutes. If too dry add chicken stock or chicken soup. Minced beef may be substituted for chicken. Cook slightly, pour off fat and add tomato sauce or catsup.

Mrs. H. B. Stackhouse

Hot Chicken Salad ✓

2 cups cut up cooked chicken
2 cups thinly sliced celery
½ cup chopped toasted almonds
½ tsp. salt
2 tsp. grated onion

1 cup mayonnaise
2 tbsp. lemon juice
½ cup grated cheese
1 cup crushed potato chips

Heat oven to 450°. Combine ingredients except cheese and potato chips. Put in casserole, individual baking dishes or sea shells. Sprinkle with cheese and chips. Bake 10 - 15 minutes.

**Mrs. (Capt.) William McMurtry
Margaretville, N.S.**

Ham, Egg And Corn Casserole

1 tin cream style corn
1 cup cubed cooked ham
4 hard-cooked eggs

½ grated onion
2 strips chopped gr. pepper
1 cup buttered crumbs

Mix together. Add seasoning to taste. Bake ¾ hour in 350° oven.

Turkey And Ham Casserole

1 pkg. frozen peas (10 ozs.)	4 tbsp. flour
1 medium onion, chopped	1 cup chicken broth or
1 cup diced celery	1 cube chicken bouillion made
1 can mushrooms (3 or 4 oz.)	into 1 cup broth
5 tbsp. butter	1 cup Superior cream
2 cups diced cooked ham	1 tbsp. soy sauce
2 cups diced cooked turkey	

Place peas (frozen), onion, celery, mushrooms and liquid and tbsp. butter in 8 cup baking dish and cover. Bake in 350° oven 2(minutes. Stir in meats. Cover and bake 20 minutes more. Melt remaining 4 tbsp. butter over low heat in medium-sized saucepan. Blend in flour, cook, stirring all the time until mixture bubbles. Add chicken broth and cream slowly, Continue cooking and stirring until sauce thickens and boils 1 minute. Stir in soy sauce. Pour over meats and vegetables in baking dish. Stir lightly to mix. Bake uncovered 20 minutes longer. Serves 8 generously.

(1 can cream of chicken soup may be used, diluted as directed on can, in place of cream and chicken broth.)

Mary Sperry

Turkey Joes

¼ cup chopped onion	½ cup catsup
2 tbsp. butter or margarine	¼ cup water
2 cups finely diced cooked	1 tsp. worcestershire sauce
turkey meat	1 tsp. prepared mustard
1 can chicken gumbo soup,	½ tsp. salt
undiluted	

Cook onion in butter or margarine in a 10-inch skillet until tender but not brown. Add remaining ingredients and blend well. Cover and simmer 30 minutes. Serve immediately on toasted buns. Makes 6 to 8 servings.

Mrs. Loran (Nella) Greenwood

English Style Curry

with rice, chicken or any lean meat

1½ tsp. curry powder	1 green apple
2 tsp. flour blended with cold	1 small onion
water	½ cup raisins
1 tbsp. vinegar	1 tbsp. brown sugar

Peel and cut up apple and onion. Put apple, onion, raisins and brown sugar in pot to boil tender. Add meat, blended curry mixture. This should be sweet - sour, hot and tasty.

Serve with rice, peas, etc. Any left over meat — chicken, lamb, beef — can be used.

Annie Fox

Palacsinta Pancakes

Yield: about 24 pancakes

2 cups sifted flour
2 tbsp. sugar
1 tsp. salt

4 eggs, well beaten
2 cups Superior milk

Mix flour, sugar and salt. Combine eggs and milk. Add gradually to flour mixture, beating to a thin smooth batter. Spoon 3 tbsp. of batter onto hot, lightly greased 6 to 7 inch skillet, tilting pan so batter is distributed to edges. Brown lightly on both sides. Repeat, making cakes until batter is used up. Stack on warm plate. Spread pancakes with your favorite filling, roll up or fold and serve very hot. Serve it either as a dessert or as a main dish, depending upon the filling.

FILLINGS: FOR DESSERT

COTTAGE CHEESE:

1 lb. dry cottage cheese
1 egg, well beaten

¼ to ½ cup sugar
¼ cup raisins

Mix all ingredients thoroughly. Spread on pancakes. Roll up, place in baking dish. Sprinkle with confectioners sugar. Heat thoroughly in 300°F. oven. Serve topped with sour cream.

JAM FILLING:

Spread hot pancakes lightly with your favorite jam. Roll up, heat as above.

MAIN DISHES

MUSHROOM FILLING:

dash of pepper
½ cup Superior sour cream
1 egg, slightly beaten

1½ cups finely chopped mushrooms
2 tbsp. butter
½ tsp. salt

Brown mushrooms in butter; cool slightly, then combine with the salt and pepper, sour cream and egg. Place a freshly baked pancake on a buttered baking dish; spread with 1 tbsp. of filling, and repeat until you have many layers. Butter the top cake and place in moderate oven 300 - 350° F. until filling is set, about 20 minutes. Cut pie-fashion and serve hot.

HAM FILLING:

1 lb. chopped, boiled ham
2 egg yolks

1 cup Superior sour cream

Combine the ham, egg yolks and cream. Using this filling proceed as for mushroom pancakes.

LOBSTER FILLING:

½ cup **mushrooms, finely
  chopped**
1 tbsp. **butter**
1 cup **cooked lobster or
  crab meat or any fish**
1 tbsp. chopped **fresh** parsley

½ **tsp. salt**
dash of **pepper**
½ cup **Superior sour cream**
1 **baker's roll or 1 slice white
  bread softened in milk**

Brown mushrooms lightly in butter and allow to cool. Combine all ingredients. Use this filling, follow procedure as above.

Use your imagination for fillings. Any left over meat can be used up this way.

M. Ozvegy

Farmer's Breakfast

Good Supper Dish

Cut 4 slices bacon into small pieces and fry over low heat until just brown and crisp. Drain off all but 2 tbsp. fat. Add 4 large boiled potatoes, cubed, 1 tbsp. finely chopped onion, salt and pepper, to the bacon. Cook gently until the potatoes are a deep ivory color. Sprinkle ½ cup grated cheddar cheese over potatoes. Break 4 eggs into pan over potatoes and cook over low heat, stirring constantly until eggs are set. Decorate with parsley. Serve at once.

IMPORTANT — Do not beat eggs beforehand.

Mrs. John R. Robbins

FISH AND FISH SAUCES

Goose Hills Lobster Chowder

1 tsp. sugar	10 lbs. lobster in shell or
salt	2 lbs. meat
pepper	¼ lb. butter
1 lb. potatoes	1½ qts. Superior milk
¼ lb. onions	½ tin canned milk

Dice potatoes and cut onion fine. Put in pot with enough water to cook. Put ½ the butter in frying pan, cut lobster in small pieces and fry in butter until red. When potato is cooked, add the milk, sugar, lobster, salt, pepper and remaining butter.

Mr. Henry Hensey

Lobster Chowder

6 cups cut-up lobster	½ pt. Superior heavy cream
¼ lb. butter	Superior milk
1 tbsp. vinegar	salt
4 medium sized potatoes	pepper
1 medium sized onion	

Melt butter in frying pan, and add lobster. Simmer gently for five minutes, and add vinegar, simmering a minute or two longer. Add cream. Meanwhile boil potatoes and onions, which have been diced, in just enough boiling salted water to cover. When done drain and add lobster mixture. Season according to taste, and add sufficient milk to cover chowder. Heat and serve.

Mrs. J. T. Balmanno

Oyster Stew

1 pt. oysters with liquid	1½ tsp. salt
½ cup butter, melted	⅛ tsp. pepper
1 qt. Superior milk, scalded	

Add oysters with their liquid to melted butter in a saucepan. Simmer over low heat until oysters plump and their edges begin to curl, about 3 minutes. Combine with scalded milk and seasonings. Serve immediately.

Maude Churchill

Creamed Fried Lobster

Heat slowly 1 quart lobster meat in —

½ cup butter   Add:
    ⅓ cup vinegar
    season to taste

When ready to serve add 1 cup Superior cream.

**Mrs. Bernard Outhouse,
Port Maitland**

Lobster Casserole

1 can cream of mushroom soup
½ cup Superior milk
½ lb. lobster
1¼ cups crushed potato chips
1 cup peas
3 cooked eggs (chopped)

Mix soup and milk well. Add lobster, 1 cup potato chips, peas and chopped eggs. Sprinkle ¼ cup potato chips on top before baking. Bake 20 - 30 minutes at 350°.

Mrs. Flo (Bill) MacConnell

Scalloped Lobster

2 cups cut up lobster
1 egg well beaten
1 cup Superior milk
2 tbsp. melted butter
1 cup soft bread crumbs
1 tsp. lemon juice
1 tbsp. finely chopped onion
1 tsp. salt
a few buttered crumbs for top

Break lobster into bite size pieces. Combine beaten egg, milk and melted butter, pour over the soft bread crumbs, add lemon juice, onion, salt and mix well. Fold in the lobster. Spoon into 1 qt. baking dish (buttered) and top with the buttered crumbs. Bake in 375° oven until top is well browned, about 20 minutes.

Mrs. Loran Crowell

Baked Lobster

1 can lobster (not frozen kind)
4 tbsp. melted butter
4 tbsp. flour
½ tsp. salt
1½ cups Superior milk
2 large eggs separated

Melt butter and add flour and salt. Add milk, cook until thick, let cool. Prepare lobster in bottom of casserole, sprinkle with Accent. Add egg yolks to cool white sauce mixture. Beat egg whites and fold into sauce and add to lobster. Sprinkle with paprika. Bake one half hour in 375° oven. Do not open oven until half hour is up.

Vera Cain

Lobster In Aspic

2 cups lobster, cooked or canned
2 cups boiling water
½ cup cold water
4 tbsp. sugar
1 cup blanched almonds
1 cup lobster liquid or water
2½ tbsp. gelatine
4 tbsp. lemon juice
1½ tsp. salt

Soak gelatine in cold water for 5 minutes. Add sugar, salt, lemon juice and boiling water. Stir and cool. Add lobster liquid, diced lobster, and chopped almonds. Place in mould previously rinsed in cold water. Chill until set. Almond may be omitted. 1 avocado pear, diced and added, is delicious. (Serves 6)

Dot Lonergan

Easy Shrimp Creole

¼ cup finely chopped celery
1 medium onion, chopped
3 tbsp. salad oil
½ cup water
¾ cup tomato soup

¼ tsp. garlic salt
1 tsp. vinegar
1 7-oz. can shrimp
2 cups cooked rice

Cook celery and onion in salad oil until soft. Blend in the water, soup, salt and vinegar. Simmer about 10 minutes. Add shrimp; heat. Serve over hot rice. Makes 4 servings.

Phyllis Churchill

Scalloped Oysters

1 pint oysters
2 cups coarse cracker crumbs
¼ cup butter

½ tsp. salt
dash of pepper
½ cup Superior milk

Chop oysters coarsely cutting in 3 or 4 pieces with kitchen shears and combine with their liquor. Mix cracker crumbs and melted butter and arrange a layer of half the buttered crumbs in bottom of a 9 inch round shallow baking dish. Pour oysters over them in layers and sprinkle with salt and pepper. Cover with remaining crumbs and pour milk over all. Bake in oven of 400° for 20 minutes. Serves 5.

Mrs. D. F. Macdonald

Seafood Fritters

1½ cups finely chopped lobster
  or shrimp or
  1 pt. oysters or clams
  (1 tin clams may be used)
2 eggs

⅓ cup Superior milk
1⅓ cups flour
2 tsp. baking powder
½ tsp. salt
few grains pepper

Drain oysters or clams. Remove any bits of shell and cut in pieces. Beat eggs, add milk.

Sift together flour, baking powder, salt and pepper. Add milk mixture. Add oysters or clams. Mix well.

Drop by spoonfuls into shallow fat or salad oil heated to 375° F. Fry 3 minutes or until brown. They may have to be turned to brown the top. Drain on absorbent paper. Serve with any desired fish sauce.

Mrs. John Ryan

Spanish Crab Meat

Put butter size of an egg in top of double boiler, 1 green pepper (cut fine). Cook in butter till tender. Add 2 tbsp. flour (cook smooth), 1 cup Superior milk, 1 egg beaten, 1 cup grated cheese, can tomato soup, can crabmeat, dash cayenne. Let set over hot water for at least 1 hour until thick.

Serve on patty shells or crackers.

Helen Clarke

Barbecued Shrimpwiches

¼ lb. fresh shrimp or
1 4-oz. can shrimp
¾ cup shredded cheddar cheese
¼ cup mayonnaise

1 tsp. vinegar
¼ tsp. pepper
½ tsp. worcestershire sauce
6 hotdog rolls

Rinse and drain shrimp. Mash slightly. Add and mix in cheese, mayonnaise, vinegar, pepper and worcestershire sauce. Split rolls, butter and spread with shrimp mixture. Wrap securely in foil and refrigerate until ready to use. Barbecue near hot coals 20 - 25 minutes, or bake 350° 15 - 20 minutes. Serves 6.

Doris Cox

Scallop Casserole

1 lb. scallops
1 tsp. salt
½ cup chopped onion
1 cup mushrooms or 1 5-oz. can
1 cup chopped green peppers
6 tbsp. butter

¼ cup flour
1 tsp. salt
2 cups Superior milk
1 cup soft bread crumbs
1 tbsp. butter (melted)
¼ cup grated cheese

Separate scallops and sprinkle with salt. Cook vegetables (next 4 ingredients) until tender. Make cream sauce with remainder. Combine scallops, sauce, vegetables, etc. Combine melted butter and bread crumbs. Put on top and sprinkle with grated cheese. Bake 375° - 20 minutes.

Bertha Walsh

Cheese Shrimp Custard

7 slices bread
3 tbsp. butter
½ lb. cheese
2 5¾-oz. cans shrimp

3 eggs well beaten
½ tsp. salt
½ tsp. paprika
2½ cups Superior milk

Spread bread with butter and cut into 1" squares. Cut cheese into thin slices. Clean shrimp. Alternate layers of bread, shrimp and cheese in greased 2 quart casserole.

Combine beaten eggs, salt, paprika and milk. Pour over mixture in casserole. Bake in moderate oven of 325° for 1 hour. Set it in a pan of water for baking. Serves 6.

M. Wyman

Seafood Ragout

¼ cup butter	few drops onion juice
¼ cup flour	¼ tsp. pepper
¾ cup oyster liquid	1 pt. fresh oysters
¾ cup Superior cream	¾ cup cooked lobster, diced
¾ tsp. salt	1 ½ tbsp. Sautern
few grains cayenne pepper	1 tbsp. finely chopped parsley

Cook oysters in their juice, only until they plump up and the edges begin to curl. Drain off the juice and reserve for sauce. Make sauce of the first 8 ingredients. Add oysters, lobster, wine and parsley. Serve as is with cooked rice, or in ramkin or top with cheese buttered crumbs and bake as a casserole. May also be served with toast points.

Clara Harris

Crab Cobbler

Melt ½ cup butter in top of double boiler. Then add:	½ cup chopped green pepper
	½ cup chopped onion

Cook over boiling water until tender (about 10 minutes.)

Blend in:	1 cup Superior milk
½ cup flour	1 cup shredded cheese
1 tsp. dry mustard	(do ¼ cup shredded cheese ex-
¼ tsp. Accent	tra for pastry topping)

Cook, stirring constantly, until cheese is melted and mixture very thick.

Add:	2 tsp. worcestershire sauce
1 tin crab meat	½ tsp. salt
1 ½ cups drained tomatoes	pepper to taste

Blend thoroughly and pour into 2 quart casserole. (Do not fill right to top as mixture bubbles when cooking.

CHEESE BISCUIT TOPPING

Sift together:	
1 cup flour	cut in 2 tbsp. shortening
4 tsp. baking powder	Add:
½ tsp. salt	½ cup Superior milk
Then add:	
¼ cup shredded cheese	

Stir only until moistened. Drop on hot crab mixture. Bake in 450° oven 20 - 25 minutes.

Joyce (Mrs. E. R.) Syvertsen

Seafood Supreme

½ cup finely cut onion
1 4-oz. can mushroom stems and pieces, undrained
2 tbsp. butter or margarine
1 10½-oz. can cream of mushroom soup
⅛ tsp. pepper

1 tsp. worcestershire sauce
2 drops tabasco
1 cup evaporated milk
2/3 cup sliced stuffed olives
1 4½-oz. can shrimp, well drained
1 7-oz. can tuna, well drained

In a 10-inch skillet, brown onion in butter or margarine. Add mushroom stems and pieces, cream of mushroom soup, pepper worcestershire sauce, and tabasco and stir until smooth. Cover and cook over medium heat 1 minute. Remove from heat and stir in evaporated milk gradually. Add olives, shrimp, and tuna. Stir just until combined and heat to steaming hot (do not boil). Serve over toast points, chow mein noodles, or hot rice. Makes 6 servings.

(If shrimp seem quite salt, rinse them well by putting them in a collander or seive, and running cold water over them. Lobster may be used instead of shrimp, and any fresh cooked fish, or canned salmon instead of the tuna.)

Clara Harris

Gefilte Fish (Fish Balls)

3 lbs. haddock or halibut
2 onions
3 tbsp. cracker crumbs
2 tsp. salt
¼ cup water

3 carrots
3 eggs
¼ tsp. pepper
2 tsp. sugar

Clean, fillet and salt fish. Keep skin and large bones. Prepare in large pot 1 sliced onion, 3 sliced carrots, 1 tsp. salt and 1 tsp. sugar, skin and bones. Add 3 glasses of water and bring to boil.

Chop or grind one onion, fish. add eggs, ¼ cup water, 1 tsp. salt, cracker crumbs, pepper and 1 tsp. sugar. Mix well. Mixture should feel sticky. Form into small balls, and place in pot carefully. Water should about cover fish balls. Boil slowly for 1¼ hours. Cool and remove from pot.

Mrs. Danny Star

Fish Rolls

Baking powder biscuit dough using 2 cups flour
1½ cups cooked fish
½ tsp. salt

1 small onion chopped
1 green pepper chopped
or ½ cup peas
Superior milk

Roll biscuit dough to ¼ inch thickness, on floured board. Combine fish with seasonings. Moisten slightly with milk. Mix well and spread on biscuit dough. Roll as for a jelly roll and cut in ½ inch slices. Bake on greased pan in hot oven 400 degrees ½ hour. Serve with a cheese or tomato sauce.

Mrs. Earl Churchill

Salmon Scallop ✓

2 eggs
1 small can salmon (skin and
  bones removed)
½ tsp. salt
⅛ or ¼ tsp. pepper

¾ cup soft bread crumbs
scraping of onion
finely chopped celery
  (optional)
2/3 cup Superior milk

Beat eggs, add remaining ingredients. Put in casserole and cover with the following:

TOPPING:— ¾ - 1 cup bread crumbs, stirred into 3 tbsp. melted butter. Spread over top of scallop. Bake in fairly hot oven. Crumbs need to be brown and crispy. Serves 4 - 5.

Mrs. Dick Sweeny

Fish Loaf

2 tbsp. melted butter
3 cups rice (already cooked)
1 cup cooked or canned salmon
  or flaked tuna
1 tsp. chopped parsley

1 tbsp. minced onion
1 lg. tsp. dark curry powder
1 cup medium cream sauce
1 egg slightly beaten
½ tsp. worcestershire sauce

Combine melted butter and rice. Grease 1½ quart mold or loaf pan and line with rice, reserving ½ cup of rice for top.

Mix together remaining ingredients. Fill the rice mold with this mixture and spread remaining rice on top. Place in pan of hot water. Bake 350 oven about 40 minutes.

This dish does not need a sauce, but may be served with tomatoes or a parsley sauce.

Kay Ladd

Baked Tuna and Cheese Casserole

1 cup macaroni
2 cans (7-oz.) tuna, drained
1 8-oz. can diced carrots
¼ cup slivered olives
5 tbsp. butter or margarine
½ cup seasoned bread crumbs

¼ cup sliced onion
¼ cup flour
1½ tsp. salt
⅛ tsp. pepper
2½ cups Superior milk
¾ cup sharp cheddar cheese

1. Cook macaroni and drain. Preheat oven to 375°.
2. In 2 qt. casserole toss macaroni with tuna, carrots and olives, mix well.
3. Melt butter in medium saucepan. Toss 1 tbsp. melted butter with bread crumbs in small bowl. Set aside. In rest of butter, saute onions until golden brown (5 minutes.)
4. Remove from heat. Add flour, salt and pepper. Stir until smooth. Gradually stir in milk.
5. Bring to boiling. Boil 1 minute. Reduce heat and add cheese,

stirring until melted.

6. Pour cheese sauce over tuna mixture. Toss to mix well.

7. Sprinkle with buttered crumbs over top. Bake 20 minutes or until golden brown and bubbly.

Makes 6 - 8 servings. Delicious with cole slaw.

Mrs. James Wallace

Tuna Casserole

1 can cream of mushroom soup	1½ cups potato chips
½ cup Superior milk	1 cup peas
1 can (7 oz.) tuna, drained and flaked	1 tbsp. lemon juice
	3 tsp. chopped green pepper

Mix soup and Superior milk. Add tuna and 1 cup potato chips, peas, lemon juice and green pepper. Stir well. Sprinkle top with remaining ½ cup potato chips.

Bake 25 - 30 minutes in 350° oven.

(Same recipe can be used omitting potato chips but topping with cheese biscuits!)

Mrs. Flo (Bill) MacConnell

Budget Tuna Bake

4 cups peeled raw potatoes, thinly sliced	¾ cup thinly sliced onion
3 tbsp. butter	1 tsp. salt
¼ cup flour	dash of pepper
2 tbsp. catsup	2 cups Superior milk
	1 7-oz. can flaked tuna

Cook potatoes in slightly salted water for 10 minutes. Drain. While potatoes are cooking, melt butter in saucepan, stir in flour, catsup, salt and pepper. Add milk gradually while stirring. Cook over low heat until thickened. Arrange potatoes, tuna and onions in buttered 2 quart casserole. Pour sauce over and bake in moderate 375° oven until potatoes are tender, about 45 minutes. Makes six servings.

Ruth Trefry

Tuna Casserole

1 tin tuna or chicken	¼ cup water
1 cup celery (chopped)	¼ lb. cashew nuts
1 cup onion (chopped)	1 can chow mein noodles
1 can mushroom soup	

Put all in casserole (reserve some noodles for top). Bake 30 - 35 minutes in 350° oven. Garnish with mandarin oranges and parsley when serving. Serves 6.

Almond Fish Fillets

2 lb. fresh or frozen fish fillets
(cod, halibut, ocean perch or
sole)
6 tbsp. butter, divided
salt and pepper

⅛ cup water
2 tbsp. flour
½ cup Superior milk
½ cup slivered toasted almonds

Let fillets thaw in refrigerator until they can be separated, if frozen fish is used.

Melt 4 tbsp. butter in frying pan or skillet. Sprinkle fish fillets with salt and pepper; place in pan with butter. Add water. Cover pan; let simmer gently about 10 minutes or until fish flakes easily when tested with fork. Carefully remove fish to heatproof serving platter. Cook liquid left in pan until reduced about one-third. Cream remaining butter and flour. Add with milk to liquid in pan. Let simmer, stirring occasionally, until thickened. Sprinkle the almonds around fish. Pour sauce over fish and reheat for a minute or two in hot oven or, if desired, brown quickly under broiler. Serve immediately. Serves six.

Hilda Zellers

Baked Halibut with Mushrooms

5 halibut steaks
½ sq. butter
1 can mushroom soup

¼ onion (chopped)
½ cup Superior milk

Put butter in bottom of baking dish. Lay steaks on top. Pour over rest of ingredients. Bake in a moderately hot oven for ¾ hour.

Mrs. David L. Garson

Jiffy Baked Fish

Lay heavy foil in baking pan. Spread haddock or halibut fillets generously with Miracle Whip salad dressing, salt, pepper. Sprinkle corn flake crumbs over all, and dot with butter. Bring edges of foil up over fish, to prevent scorching. Bake in 400° oven 15 minutes.

Phyllis Churchill

Tuna Buns

1 6-oz. can tuna
2 hard boiled eggs
½ cup small pieces cream cheese
(may use a few sprinkles of
grated cheese instead)

¼ tsp. salt
dash of pepper
3 tbsp. grated onion
¼ tsp. mustard
enough mayonnaise to moisten

Fill hamburg rolls with mixture. Wrap each in aluminum foil. Heat in oven 325°, for 20 minutes.

Mrs. Paul Cleveland

Baked Tuna Roll

2 cups all purpose flour
¼ tsp. salt
4 tsp. baking powder
¼ cup shortening
1 beaten egg
½ cup Superior milk

FILLING:
1 cup flaked tuna
¼ cup Superior milk
2 tsp. chopped onion
1½ tbsp. dehydrated parsley
¼ cup chopped sweet pickles
½ tsp. salt

Sift flour, salt and baking powder. Cut in shortening. Mix to resemble coarse crumbs. Add egg and ½ cup milk. Mix and roll ¼ inch thick. Combine remaining ingredients, spread over dough. Roll and bake on cookie sheet 350° 30 minutes. Serve with cheese sauce: 3 tbsp. fat, 3 tbsp. flour. Stir in 1½ cups milk until thick. Add ½ pkg. Velvetta cheese or your favorite kind. Stir until melted.

Mrs. Russell Cleveland
Mrs. Herman Shapiro

Haddock Savory

1 small haddock (skinned and
  boned)
1 green pepper
¾ tsp. salt
¼ tsp. paprika

1 small onion
1½ cups Superior milk
2 tbsp. chopped parsley
4 tbsp. butter

Place fish in baking dish with butter dotted over top. Sprinkle with onion and seeded pepper, chopped fine, the chopped parsley, paprika and salt. Cover with milk and bake in 375 degree oven for one hour, basting frequently as milk evaporates. Serve at once.

Miss Connie Jolly

Sunset Scallop

1 lb. haddock fillets
2 hard boiled eggs
white sauce

2 cups mashed potatoes
grated cheese
1 onion

Cut up onion and fry golden brown in butter. Remove onions and fry fillets. Put fillets in casserole, slice eggs over it. Add white sauce, then well seasoned potatoes and sprinkle with grated cheese. Bake in moderate oven until potatoes are well browned.

Mrs. Esther Amirault

Quick Fresh Haddock Fillets

1 lb. haddock fillets
½ tsp. salt

⅛ lb. butter
⅛ tsp. pepper

Wash fillets. Put butter in pan with pepper and salt. Lay in fillets and cover pan. Let cook on top of stove on moderate heat, about 30 minutes. Just before serving add ¼ cup to ½ cup top Superior milk or Superior cream, spooning it over fish.

Mrs. C. A. Topple

Baked Halibut Supreme

1 ½ - 2 lbs. halibut in one thick piece	⅓ cup cracker crumbs
1 tsp. lemon juice	2 tbsp. butter
1 cup Superior milk	2 tbsp. green pepper or pimiento

Place halibut in buttered baking dish. Brush with lemon juice. Sprinkle with salt and pepper and peppers. Cover with cracker crumbs. Dot with butter. Bake 1 hour at 350°.

Mrs. A. B. Anthony

Scalloped Halibut and Vegetables

1 ½ - 2 lbs. halibut	4 tbsp. butter
3 small raw carrots	salt and paprika to taste
4 med. raw potatoes	Superior milk
1 small onion	¼ cup cracker crumbs

Slice vegetables thinly. Place in layers in buttered dish. Season, dot with butter. Add milk to cover. Place raw halibut in serving pieces on top. Season fish. Top with cracker crumbs and dots of butter. Bake 40 minutes.

Mrs. J. D Cohen

Broiled Swordfish

Have the swordfish steak cut approximately 1 ½ inches thick. Wipe fish with a damp cloth, sprinkle both sides of fish with pepper, salt and a little lemon juice. Oil a piece of aluminum foil, place fish on foil, dot with butter and put in pre-heated broiler 550 degrees F., about 3 inches from source of heat. Broil 12 minutes, then turn, dot with butter and continue cooking 10 to 12 minutes longer, or until fish is lightly browned. Swordfish is a heavy grained fish, thus may be difficult to cook through. Always try your fish with a fork before removing from the broiler. If fork comes out of fish easily, fish is done.

Clara Harris

Pan Fried Swordfish

Cut fish approximately 1 ½ inches thick, and dip in flour, then in egg and Superior milk beat up together, then in cracker meal. Fry in pure vegetable oil in skillet. Fry slowly until fish is golden brown. Then turn and fry slowly until other side is brown. Pepper and salt each side as it cooks. Always try with fork for doneness before serving. Serve with a wedge of lemon and some tartar sauce, if desired.

Another delicious way to prepare swordfish is to put fish in a baking pan, dot with butter, pepper and salt, and cover with Superior milk. Bake in a moderate hot oven 400 F. until fork tender.

Clara Harris

Halibut Loaf with Lobster Sauce

2 cups Superior milk
2½ cups soft bread crumbs
1 tbsp. butter

1 - 1½ lbs. chopped uncooked
  halibut
4 egg whites
salt and celery salt to taste

Scald milk. Add crumbs, butter and seasonings. Add chopped halibut, mix well. Cook gently until fish is thoroughly heated. Fold in stiffly beaten egg whites. Place in greased casserole or loaf pan. Set in pan of hot water and bake for 1½ hours in 375° oven.

LOBSTER SAUCE
1½ cups freshly cooked or
  canned lobster
3 tbsp. butter
3 tbsp. flour

1 tsp. salt
½ tsp. pepper
1 cup Superior milk and
  ½ cup Superior cream

Melt butter. Add flour and seasonings. Gradually add hot milk and cream. Boil until thick. Add chunks of lobster. Heat thoroughly, but do not boil. When ready to serve slice halibut loaf and spoon sauce over.

Can serve loaf whole with sauce poured over it, for a glamorous party dish.

Mrs. Herman Slade

Creamed Finnan Haddie

Cover a finnan haddie with water, let come to the boiling point and simmer for a few minutes until the fish is cooked — using the top of the stove or the oven. Drain the fish, lay on a hot platter and place small pieces of butter on top. Return to the oven to heat and just before serving add ½ cup of Superior cream or Superior whole milk heated. Do not let the fish remain too long or the cream may curdle from the smoked fish. Garnish with parsley.

Gloucester Codfish Balls

1 cup salt cod fish
2½ cups cubed potatoes
½ tsp. butter

dash of pepper
1 egg slightly beaten

Soak codfish overnight in cold water. Drain; shred by placing on cutting board and pulling apart with a fork. Peel potatoes; cut into cubes; cook until tender. Drain well and return to kettle in which they were cooked. Shake over heat until thoroughly dry; mash well; add butter and pepper. Beat until light. Add cod fish and beaten egg. Continue beating until light and fluffy. Add salt if necessary. Make balls by dipping with a small ice-cream scoop or drain. Makes about 10 cakes. Allow two cakes for a serving. Serve with Tomato Sauce or occasionally with Mushroom Egg Sauce.

Fish Sauces

STANDARD RECIPE FOR WHITE SAUCE FOR CREAM SOUPS

1 tbsp. butter
1 tbsp. flour
1 cup hot Superior milk

¼ tsp. salt
⅛ tsp. pepper
¼ cup sieved, cooked vegetables

For Vegetables, Meats and Fish

2 tbsp. butter
2 tbsp. flour
⅛ tsp. pepper

¼ tsp. salt
1 cup hot Superior milk or
cream

For Cutlets and Croquettes

4 tbsp. butter
⅓ cup flour
¼ tsp. salt

⅛ tsp. pepper
1 cup hot Superior milk or
white soup stock

For Souffles

3 tbsp. butter
3 tbsp. flour
¼ tsp. salt

⅛ tsp. pepper
1 cup hot Superior milk

GENERAL METHOD:— Scald the milk. Melt the butter in a saucepan. Remove from fire and mix with flour. Cook until it bubbles, then add 2/3 of the hot milk at once and rest gradually and boil, stirring constantly until the mixture thickens. Season and serve.

Delicious Fish Sauce

2 tsp. prepared mustard
¼ tsp. salt

2 tsp. lemon juice
6 tbsp. butter

Mix mustard, salt and butter, cream and heat slowly, stirring constantly. When smooth stir in lemon juice. By adding 1 tbsp. ketchup to this sauce it makes it dandy for meats and roasts.

Mrs. E. B. Robbins

Tartar Sauce for Fish

1 cup mayonnaise
2 tbsp. chopped olives
2 tbsp. chopped gerkins
1 tbsp. chopped parsley
1 tbsp. chopped onions

1 tbsp. chopped green peppers
1 tsp. lemon juice
1 tsp. salt
1 tsp. pepper

Mix all together and serve cold.

Mattie Crowell

Quick Tartar Sauce

1 cup Miracle Whip   1 tsp. lemon juice
¼ cup sweet pickle relish   ½ tsp. grated onion

Mix all ingredients and serve.

Phyllis Churchill

Maitre D'Hotel Butter Sauce For Fish

4 tbsp. butter   1 tsp. salt
2 tbsp. chopped parsley   ¼ tsp. pepper
2 tbsp. lemon juice

Melt butter and add the other ingredients. Mix well and serve hot.

Mattie Crowell

Tomato Creole Sauce

2 tbsp. minced green peppers   1 can tomato soup
1 small onion minced   ¼ cup water
1 tbsp. butter

Cook green pepper and onion in butter until soft. Add soup and water, heat. Makes about 1¾ cups sauce. Excellent with fish, chopped steaks, or fried egg plant.

Moonay Sauce For Fish

1 pint Superior whipping cream   2 egg yolks
salt and cayenne pepper   1 tbsp. grated cheese

Beat cream, salt and pepper together with eggs. Add grated cheese.

Mrs. Omer Milestone

PICKLES AND JAMS

Pepper Haste (Good)

1 large cabbage
6 large onions

6 red peppers
6 green peppers

Remove seeds from peppers. Chop all together (very fine). Add:

½ cup salt

Let sit overnight. In morning drain well and add:

¼ cup mustard seed
1 tbsp. celery seed

1½ pts. sugar (3 cups)
1½ pts. vinegar

Set in warm place (back of stove) until sugar is well dissolved. Do not cook. Bottle.

Mrs. Freeman Tupper

Cucumber Relish

12 ripe cucumbers
4 cups onions (measured after put
thru food chopper)

1 cup coarse salt (scant)

Peel cucumbers, take out seeds. Put thru food chopper. Put all together and let sit overnight. — In morning drain.

Dressing:
3 pts. white vinegar (6 cups)
6 cups white sugar
1 cup flour

1 tsp. mustard seed (heaping)
1 tsp. celery seed
½ tsp. turmeric

Mix and cook dressing till it thickens. Add vegetables and cook 5 minutes. Bottle.

Mary (Mrs. E. P.) Sinclair

Carrot - Cucumber Relish

4 - 6 unpared cucumbers coarsely ground (3½ cups)
6 carrots ground (2 - 2½ cups)
2 medium onions ground
2 tbsp. salt

2½ cups sugar
1½ cups vinegar
1½ tsp. celery seed
1½ tsp. mustard seed

Combine ground vegetables; stir in salt. Let stand 3 hours; drain. Combine remaining ingredients and bring to a boil. Add vegetables; simmer uncovered 20 minutes. Seal at once in sterilized jars.

Ruth Pink

Indian Relish

20 ripe tomatoes
4 large onions
4 large red peppers

3 cups white sugar
3 tbsp. salt
4 cups vinegar

Chop tomatoes, onions and peppers finely. Add sugar, salt and vinegar. Boil gently for 3 hours. Bottle hot in sterilized jars.

Tested

Fruit Chutney

13 red tomatoes
6 pears
6 peaches

6 onions
3 green peppers
3 bunches celery

Peel and dice all fruit and vegetables and add:

4 cups sugar
2 tbsp. salt

1 qt. cider vinegar
1 oz. allspice

Simmer 2 hours.

Phyllis Churchill

Gooseberry Relish

2 qts. cleaned gooseberries
4 - 5 cups brown sugar
⅓ cup mixed spice tied in bag

4 cups ground onions
1 cup cider vinegar

Grind berries, add all other ingredients. Simmer until thick and red in color.

Marion Gardner

Calico Pepper Relish

1 lb. carrots scraped
4 large green peppers
4 large red peppers
4 large onions

1½ cups white sugar
2 tbsp. salt
1½ cups vinegar

Quarter and seed peppers, put through grinder on coarse blade, grind carrots and onions (there should be 10 cups of vegetables.) Cover vegetables with boiling water, let stand 5 minutes; drain well. Return vegetables to kettle, stir in all other ingredients; heat to boiling. Simmer, stirring often for 10 - 15 minutes, or until vegetables are firm but not raw. Seal at once in sterilized jars.

Mrs. Irving Pink

Beet and Horseradish Relish

1 quart crisp white raw cabbage chopped fine
1 quart beets, cooked and chopped
½ cup grated horseradish

Mix ingredients together. Add:—

1 cup brown sugar
1 tbsp. salt
1 tbsp. mustard

1 tsp. white pepper
cider vinegar

Cover with cider vinegar and bottle.

Mrs. Nathan Eaton

Rhubarb Relish

4 lbs. chopped rhubarb
1½ lbs. onion
2 lbs. sugar
1 tsp. cloves

1 tbsp. salt
1 tsp. cinnamon
3 cups vinegar

Cook ½ hour. Cool before sealing.

Mrs. Arthur Cosman

Winter Salad

1 qt. onions
1 qt. cucumbers
1 qt. green tomatoes
1 small cabbage

1 small cauliflower
1 red pepper
1 green pepper

Grind all. Sprinkle ½ cup salt and pour boiling water to cover. Let stand 1 hour on back of stove. Drain well.

Mix together:
6 tbsp. mustard
1 tbsp. turmeric
1 cup flour

6 cups white sugar
Add 2 qts. vinegar
Heat and stir well.

Pour over ground mixture, stirring well, but DO NOT COOK. Bottle.

Mrs. Arnold Moses

Chow Chow

(4 pints)

2 cups cucumber (seeds removed)
2 cups chopped cauliflower
2 cups chopped onions
2 cups sugar
3 tbsp. flour

¼ cup dry mustard
1 tbsp. celery seeds
1 tbsp. mustard seed
2 tsp. turmeric
2¼ cups vinegar

Combine chopped vegetables in a large bowl, cover with a brine (¾ cup pickling salt to 5 cups water). Leave overnight. Drain and rinse. Combine remaining ingredients in a large saucepan. Add vegetables and simmer until tender.

Mrs. Tom Doucette

Green Tomato Pickles (Chow Chow)

4 qts. green tomatoes
2 qts. onions
1 qt. vinegar

4 cups white sugar
½ cup mixed pickling spice
(tied in bag)

Slice the tomatoes at night. Sprinkle with ¾ cup salt. Cover with a weight on top. Drain off brine in morning (drain well). Bring spices, sliced onions and vinegar to boil, then add tomatoes. Add sugar. Cook very slowly until onions and tomatoes are tender. Seal in jars.

Mrs. David Corning

Chili Sauce

6 lbs. red tomatoes
2 lbs. sugar
3 lbs. apples (sour)

1 pint vinegar (scant)
½ cup pickling spice

Peel tomatoes, sprinkle with salt, press down with plate. Let stand overnight. Drain in morning. Put vinegar, sugar and spice in kettle, add peeled and sliced apples. Add 2 or 3 onions, 2 sweet peppers. Cook apples, onions and peppers down a little first, then add tomatoes and cook until done.

Mrs. Arthur Cosman

Quick Chili Sauce

1 cup sugar
1 can tomatoes (large)
½ cup vinegar
2 large onions chopped fine

1 tbsp. salt
½ tsp. cinnamon
½ tsp. pepper
¼ tsp. cloves

Mix all together and simmer slowly for 2 hours.

Mrs. Jack Woods

Mustard Pickles

12 cups cucumbers (6 or 8 lg.)
3 medium cauliflowers
5 cups (2 pts.) "silverskin" onions
1 cup salt
2 sweet red peppers
2 green peppers
½ cup pimientos

1 cup flour
¼ lb. dry mustard
1 tbsp. each turmeric, salt, celery seed
5 cups light brown sugar
3 qts. cider vinegar

Seed cucumbers and cut into one inch cubes. Cut cauliflower into small flowerets. Peel onions and mix vegetables. Sprinkle with the one cup of salt. Just cover with cold water, let stand overnight.

NEXT DAY bring mixture to a boil. Drain well, then add diced peppers and pimientos, cut up. Mix next 6 ingredients and slowly stir until smooth and thick, about 7 minutes. Add vegetables and bring to a boil, then spoon into sterile jars. Seal and store.

Olive Quickfall

Mustard Beans

1 peck beans (wax or green)

Wash, string and remove ends of beans, cut in half inch pieces, boil in salted water 3 - 5 minutes until nearly tender. Drain.

3 lbs. sugar
3 pints vinegar
2 tbsp. celery seed

2 tbsp. turmeric
1 cup mustard
1 cup flour

Heat vinegar; mix dry ingredients in a little cold vinegar; add hot vinegar gradually. Cook, stirring constantly until thick as cream. Add beans, Scald and bottle while hot.

Mrs. Gordon Lawrence

Mustard Pickles

1 quart (about 8) large cucumbers cut in pieces (peeled)
1 quart small cucumbers, not peeled, cut in pieces
1 quart onions cut fine, or can use small ones
1 quart green tomatoes cut in pieces (about 2 lbs.)
1 cauliflower cut in pieces

Cover with cold water and 1 cup coarse salt (scant). Let stand overnight. In morning scald in brine they are in. Drain.

Sauce:	
1 cup flour	1 tsp. turmeric
6 tsp. mustard	2 cups sugar (white)
	1 qt. cider vinegar

Cook slightly. Add vegetables and cook until thick and smooth. Bottle.

Mrs. Freeman Tupper

9-Day Pickles or Icicle Pickles

8 qts. small green cucumbers or cucumber wedges	3 qts. white vinegar
2 cups salt	14 cups white sugar
4 qts. boiling water	¼ cup celery seed
2 tbsp. alum	½ cup mixed pickling spices
2 gallons hot water	tied in bag

Use small whole cucumbers or slice larger cucumbers in wedges. Remove seeds but do not peel. Place in stone crock; make a brine of salt and water; pour over cucumbers; let stand 3 days. Drain brine from cucumbers, heat to boiling; again pour over cucumbers and let stand for 3 days. Drain again. This time rinse cucumbers well in cold water.

Dissolve alum in boiling water; pour over cucumbers; let stand 6 hours. Drain and rinse.

Make a syrup of vinegar, sugar and spices; pour over cucumbers; let stand 1 day.

For the next 2 days drain the syrup; bring to the boil and cover the cucumbers; on the last day pickles are placed in jars. Jars are filled to overflowing with hot syrup, then sealed. Yields 9 pints delectable pickles. They're crisp and crunchy if cucumbers are fresh and firm.

For a variation try this substitution of spices: 1 oz. each cassia buds, allspice buds and celery seed.

**Phyllis Churchill and
Eloise Forbes**

Bread and Butter Pickles

4 qts. cucumbers
6 med. white onions (sliced)
1 sweet green pepper
1 sweet red pepper
3 cloves garlic (optional)
⅓ cup pickling salt

3 cups distilled white vinegar
5 cups white sugar
1½ tsp. turmeric
1½ tsp. celery seed
2 tbsp. mustard seed

Select medium-sized cucumbers. Wash thoroughly but do not peel. Slice thinly. Wash peppers, remove stem ends, seeds and white membranes — cut in thin strips. Place the vegetables in a crock or large crockery bowls, sprinkling the salt over each layer. Add garlic speared on tooth picks. Mix a trayful of ice cubes through the layers and another on top. This treatment makes the cukes crisp. Let stand 3 hours. Drain well. Remove garlic. Divide into two batches for cooking. Combine vinegar and remaining ingredients. Pour over the two batches of vegetables. Heat only to boiling point. Ladle hot pickles into hot sterilized jars. Seal — and store at least a month before using. Yield 8 pints.

Mrs. T. A. M. Kirk

Vinegar Dill Pickles

Bring to a boil:
4 cups vinegar
12 cups water

Add:
¾ cup coarse salt

Pour this over cucumbers packed in sterile jars to which one stalk of dill has been added. One clove garlic and 1 tbsp. mixed spice may be added if desired.

Myra Sutherland

Transparent Fingers

Peel and cut up in finger length pieces without seeds, 4 quarts cukes (about 12). Put in crock.

Make brine of 2 quarts boiling water, 1 cup salt (uniodized). Pour over cukes. Let stand three days — pour off brine. Reboil and pour over cukes again. Repeat at the end of 3 days. On 9th day, drain cukes and wipe well.

Pour over cukes — 2 quarts boiling water and 1 tbsp. of alum (well dissolved). Let stand 6 hours. Drain again, but do not wipe.

Pour following syrup over cukes:

1 qt. cider vinegar
1 cup water
4 lbs. white sugar

1 oz. celery seed (3 tbsp.)
1 oz. whole allspice
1 oz. stick cinnamon

Boil together. Leave in crock.

Mrs. Wilmot Dean

Cold Packs

2 cups white sugar	¼ cup black pepper
1 cup dry mustard	1 gallon vinegar
1 cup salt	

Mix and pour over whole cucumbers. This amount will cover 2 gallons or more of cucumbers. ½ of recipe can be used. Stir often as mustard and pepper settles at bottom.

Mrs. Russell Cleveland

Pickled Beets

Boil small beets. Slip peel off and pack in jars. If large beets are used they may be cut in half or quartered.

1½ cups cider vinegar	1 cup brown sugar
½ cup water	

Make a syrup and boil 5 minutes. Pour over beets. I tsp. mustard seed OR 3 whole cloves may be put in each jar. This amount of syrup makes 5 pints beets.

Mrs. David Corning

Watermelon Rind Pickle

7 lbs. rind (cut green part off)	½ tsp. oil of cloves
7 cups sugar	½ tsp. oil of cinnamon
2 cups vinegar	

Cut rind in cubes. Soak cubes overnight in salt water, ¼ cup salt to 1 qt. water.

In morning drain and rinse with cold water. Cover with cold water and cook until tender, but not mushy.

Combine sugar, vinegar, oil of cloves and oil of cinnamon. Bring to boiling point. Pour over watermelon rind. Let stand overnight, Drain, and heat the syrup.

Repeat this 3 times. On the 4th day heat the cubes in the syrup and bottle.

The oil of cloves and oil of cinnamon keep the watermelon rind cubes transparent.

Nina Slade

Gooseberry Relish

5 lbs. gooseberries (4 1 qt. boxes)	1½ tbsp. cinnamon
4 lbs. sugar	1 tbsp. cloves
2 cups cider vinegar	1 tbsp. allspice

Bring to boiling point and let simmer all of 3 hours. Bottle.

(Sometimes, if gooseberries are quite sour, I have to add more sugar.)

Mrs. D. F. Macdonald

Mincemeat

4 lbs. meat, cooked and ground
10 lbs. apples
1 lb. suet (I use 2 if made of deer meat) ground
4 lbs. sugar
1 qt. Silver Lasses molasses
1 pt. cider vinegar
1 qt. liquid, meat was boiled in
3 tbsp. cloves
10 tbsp. cinnamon
3 tbsp. mace
1 tbsp. pepper
2 tbsp. nutmeg
Juice and rind of:
2 lemons
2 oranges
3 or 4 lbs. raisins

Mix in order given, and cook slowly, stirring often, to keep from sticking, until apple is cooked. You may want to add more lemon, orange or vinegar, also spices, if this doesn't suit your taste.

**Mrs. Glenna (Victor) King
Brooklyn**

New Brunswick Mincemeat

4 lbs. beef
2 lbs. suet (ground)
1 pk. apples, peeled and ground
2 lbs. raisins
1 lb. currants
1 lb. mixed peel
1 lb. brown sugar
2 tbsp. cinnamon
1 tsp. allspice
2 tsp. salt
½ gallon apple cider

Grind meat which has been cooked till tender. Add suet and ground apples, then add the remaining ingredients, mixing well. Add apple cider last. Canned apple juice might be substituted for cider. Simmer over very low heat from 2 to 3 hours — stir often to prevent sticking on the bottom of pan.

Mrs. Wilmot Dean

Pickled Onions

5 lbs. silverskin onions
1 gal. white vinegar
1 cup salt
1 cup dry mustard
1 cup brown sugar
½ cup pepper
¼ tsp. powdered alum
(spices if desired)

Pour over onions. Let stand one week, stirring every day. Small cukes can be used instead of onions, if preferred.

Mary Deeks

Silverskin Onions

Peel onions and cover with brine as follows:
2 quarts boiling water to 1 cup salt.
(1) Let stand two days — drain.
(2) Cover with another brine — let stand two days — drain.
(3) Make more of same brine — heat to boiling point, put in onions and scald 2 minutes.
(4) Put onions in sterile jars with red pepper (about 2), bit of bay leaf and mace. Fill jars to overflowing with scalded vinegar, allowing 1 cup sugar to 1 gallon vinegar. Cover while hot. These stay crisp and delicious.

Mrs. D. J. Urquhart

Pickled Cherries

1 cup water
1 cup malt vinegar

1 tbsp. salt
3 tbsp. white sugar

Pour cold mixture over large dark red cherries on which the stems have been left. Bottle. No cooking needed. Let stand 1 - 2 months before using.

Mrs. Roger Rand

Quick - As - A - Wink Cranberry Jelly

4 cups cranberries (1 qt.)   2 cups water

Boil till cranberries are soft and put through sieve. Add:—
2 cups sugar to strained mixture and let boil until thick (about 10 minutes.)

Pour into jelly glasses that have been rinsed in water.

Mrs. Clement Crowell

Mint Jelly

1¾ cups mint infusion
2 tbsp. lemon juice
green food coloring

3½ cups sugar
½ bottle Certo

To prepare mint infusion: Wash large bunch of fresh mint (leaves and stems) and crush thoroughly (about 2 cups full). Add 2½ cups water and bring to a boil. Remove from heat, cover and let stand 15 minutes. Strain, measure 1¾ cups into saucepan. Add lemon juice and green coloring.

To make jelly: Add sugar to mint juice, bring to a boil over high heat, stirring constantly. Stir in Certo and boil hard 1 minute, stirring constantly. Remove from heat, skim, pour into jelly glasses and seal with wax.

Ruth M. Rideout

Rose Hip Jelly

2 cups prepared juice
  (4 cups prepared fruit)
3½ cups sugar

juice 2 lemons
½ bottle Certo

To prepare juice: Remove stems, seeds, etc., from fresh rose hips. To 4 cups prepared fruit, add 3 cups water. Bring to a boil and simmer covered ½ hour. Strain through jelly bag. Measure 2 cups juice into large saucepan, adding extra water if necessary.

To make jelly: Add sugar and lemon juice to fruit juice. Place over high heat and bring to a boil, stirring constantly. Add Certo, bring to a full rolling boil and boil hard 1 minute, stirring constantly. Remove from heat, skim, pour into glasses and seal with wax.

(Rose Hip Jelly is exceptionally rich in vitamin C).

Ruth M. Rideout

Strawberry Marmalade

2 oranges
2 lemons
1 qt. strawberries
½ cup water

⅛ tsp. soda
7 cups sugar
½ bottle Certo

Peel oranges and lemons. Remove white membrane, slice rind very thinly and simmer in ½ cup water and ⅛ tsp. soda for 10 minutes. Add orange and lemon pulp and simmer 20 minutes longer. Wash, hull and crush strawberries. Combine fruit and rind and measure. There should be 4 cups. Add 7 cups sugar and bring to boil and boil 5 minutes. Remove from heat and stir in Certo fruit pectin. Let stand 5 minutes, then skim. Pour into hot sterilized glasses. Cover while hot with wax. Yield: 8 six oz. jelly jars.

Mrs. John R. Robbins

Grape Conserve

1 lg. basket concord grapes
4 oranges

2 pkgs. seeded raisins
6 to 10 apples

Peel oranges, dice peeling and take seeds out of pulp. Separate skins from pulp of grapes, put pulp and apples (unpeeled and cut in quarters) on to cook until apples are real soft and seeds are out of grapes. Remove and put through strainer. Add orange pulp and peel, raisins and one scant cup of sugar for every cup of pulp. Cook about half an hour.

Mrs. Ernest Syvertsen

Homemade Marmalade

2 oranges   2 lemons
2 grapefruit

Put through food chopper and pour over mixture 2 quarts cold water. Let stand overnight.

Bring to boil and add 7 cups white sugar. Boil till marmalade thickens (to test, put on a saucer to cool). Bottle while hot.

Mrs. Clement Crowell

Marmalade

3 lbs. oranges   Save seeds and blossoms and
1 pound lemons   cover with water
Cut fruit up in small pieces,   Sugar
should be four lbs. prepared fruit Water

Add 2 pints of water for each pound of fruit and let stand overnight. In morning put in a thick bottomed kettle and add 2 pounds of sugar for each pound of fruit, tie the seeds in a muslin bag and boil slowly with the fruit 4 or 5 hours, stirring frequently, remove bags. — Put in sterile jars and seal.

For ginger marmalade, add —
2 oz. of bruised or crushed Jamaica ginger tied in a bag and cooked along with the marmalade.

Some chopped crystalized ginger may also be added. Yield about 12 lbs.

Mrs. Austin Drummond

Heavenly Peach Marmalade

4 lbs. peaches (about 24 medium) small bottle maraschino cherries
3 lbs. sugar   rind and juice of an orange

Skin peaches in boiling water. Pit. Cut up fine. Cut up cherries fine, grind rind of oranges. Put everything in kettle and boil. Test syrup often till it jells.

Mrs. Joseph Pink

Pear Marmalade

5 lbs. pears (cut fine)   3 oranges (put in grinder)
4 lbs. sugar

Mix sugar wtih 1 cup water. When it comes to a boil add fruit. Cook till it thickens.

Mrs. Grace Clark

CANDY

Cocoanut Ice Candy

4 cups white sugar
1 cup Superior milk
Mix and boil 6 mins. Add:

1 cup cocoanut
1 tsp. vanilla

Leave and boil at high speed for 1 minute. Put pot into pan of cold water, beat continually till it thickens. Pour ½ in a damp pan (8 x 8) OR a bit smaller. Add pink coloring to rest and pour over first half.

Tested

Carnation 5-Minute Fudge

(Makes 2 lbs.)

2/3 cup undiluted Carnation milk
1 2/3 cup sugar
½ tsp. salt
1½ cups (1½ 6 oz. pkg. Bakers) chocolate chips

16 medium diced marshmallows (1½ cups)
1 tsp. vanilla
½ cup chopped nuts

Mix Carnation milk, sugar, salt in saucepan over medium heat. Heat to boiling, then cook for 5 minutes, stirring constantly. Remove from heat. Add remaining ingredients. Stir 1 to 2 minutes, till marshmallows melt. Pour into buttered 9 in. square pan. Cool. Cut in squares.

Tested

Panocha

2½ cups brown sugar
dash salt
1 tbsp. light corn syrup
1 tbsp. butter

¾ cup Superior milk
1 tsp. vanilla
½ cup broken nuts

Combine sugar, salt, corn syrup, butter and milk; cook, stiring till sugar dissolves, to soft-ball stage (238°). Cool at room temp. without stirring, till lukewarm.

Add vanilla. Beat until mixture holds its shape. Add nuts. Quickly spread in greased pan. Cool. Cut in squares.

Lois L. Sweeny

Maple Cream

3 cups brown sugar
1 cup rich Superior milk
2 tbsp. butter

1 tsp. vanilla and nuts
2 tsp. corn syrup

Boil to soft ball stage and beat until creamy.

Tested

Swedish Nuts

1½ cups blanched almonds
2 cups walnut halves
1 cup sugar

dash salt
2 egg whites, beaten stiff
½ cup butter

Toast nuts until light brown. Fold sugar, salt into whites, beat until stiff. Fold nuts in meringue. Melt butter in cookie pan. Spread nuts in butter. Bake in slow oven. Stir every ten minutes until nuts are coated with brown covering and no butter remains. Cool. Any combination or mixture of nuts may be used.

Mrs. Irving Pink

Chocolate Fudge

Melt in heavy saucepan:
2 tbsp. butter
2 sqs. Bakers chocolate
4 tbsp. corn syrup
Blend, keeping over low heat.

Gradually stir in:
2/3 cup hot water
Add:
2 cups white sugar

Boil very slowly until it reaches the soft ball stage, when dropped in cold water. Remove from heat and cool in pan of cold water. Add vanilla and nuts.

Helen Filliter

Chocolate Fudge

1 cup white sugar
1 cup brown sugar
½ cup Superior milk
¼ cup butter

pinch salt
7 tbsp. Bakers cocoa
OR 2½ sqs. Bakers bitter
    chocolate

Put all the ingredients into a pot on high temperature on stove. When all the ingredients have melted and blended together, keep on high temperature until boiling. Once it has boiled turn stove to low heat and keep boiling for three (3) minutes. When this has been completed, take off stove and add a capful of vanilla. Then begin to hand beat, and do this until thick. Pour into a square pan and let stand until hard. Cut into squares.

Annette Abraham

Brown Sugar Fudge

3 cups brown sugar
1 cup white sugar
¾ cup canned milk
3 tbsp. corn syrup
½ tsp. salt

1 tsp. vanilla
nuts or ½ cup peanut butter
    (optional)
1 tbsp. butter

Mix first five ingredients together and boil for 5 minutes (time of first boil), stirring constantly. Remove from heat, add butter and vanilla. Do not stir. Let cool for 20 minutes, then beat until it loses it's gloss. Pour into prepared 8 x 8 pan.

Mrs. Hope Langille

Peanut Butter Fudge

2 cups white sugar
¾ cup Superior milk

4 tbsp. peanut butter
vanilla, salt

Stir 'till sugar is dissolved. Cook to soft ball stage without stirring. Set in pan of cold water 'till it cools a little. Add 4 tablespoons peanut butter, vanilla and salt. Beat until creamy.

Mrs. Charles Robbins

Peanut Cluster

½ lb. Bakers semi-sweet
    chocolate

½ cup sweetened condensed milk
1 cup whole unsalted peanuts

Melt chocolate in top of double boiler. Remove from fire and add condensed milk and peanuts, stirring constantly. As soon as mixture thickens, drop from a teaspoon on a greased baking sheet to cool. Chill thoroughly in refrigerator. If desired, washed seedless raisins may be added or substituted for peanuts. Makes about 3 doz.

Tested

Glazed Nuts and Fruits

2 cups sugar
1 cup water
2/3 cup corn syrup

½ to 1 cup cherries, pineapple
    wedges
½ to 1 cup brazils, pecans, walnuts, etc.

Heat slowly sugar, water and syrup until sugar is dissolved. Then cook moderately until brittle (about 290°). Pour over fruits and nuts and drop by spoonfuls.

Mrs. Douglas Foster

Gingery Ginger Fudge

¼ lb. candied ginger
¾ cup Superior milk
2 cups white sugar
1 cup brown sugar

2 tbsp. light corn syrup
2 tbsp. butter or margarine
1 tsp. vanilla extract

Cut ginger in small chunks. Cook white sugar, brown sugar, milk and corn syrup over medium heat until a little dropped in cold water forms a soft ball or candy thermometer reaches 238°. Stir occasionally. Remove from range, add butter or margarine and cool. When candy is cool, add ginger and vanilla extract, then beat hard until fudge begins to thicken. Pour onto buttered platter.

Mrs. Charles Robbins

Molasses Taffy

1 cup molasses (Silver Lasses)
1½ cups sugar
½ cup water
1½ tbsp. vinegar

¼ tsp. cream tartar
4 tbsp. melted butter
⅛ tsp. soda

Cook molasses, sugar, water and vinegar in heavy pan, stirring constantly. When boiling point is reached add cream tartar. Boil until mixture is brittle when tried in cold water, 256°F. Stir constantly during last part of cooking. When nearly done add butter and soda. Turn on buttered shallow pan and when cool, pull until porous and light coloured. While pulling add 1 tsp. vanilla or few drops oil of peppermint. Cut in small pieces and wrap in wax paper.

Y. Auxiliary

PARTY FARE

Cheese Spread

1 cup white sugar
½ cup butter
1 pkg. Velveeta cheese

3 eggs (well beaten)
3 tsp. mustard

Cook above mixture in double boiler until thick. Cool and add: 1 cup vinegar, mixed with 4 tbsp. flour and salt to taste. Heat again, then cool and add: ¼ pt. heavy Superior cream, small bottle olives and small can of pimientos (cut in small pieces). Bottle and store in frig.

Mrs. C. L. Brown, Amherst

Dip For Chips

3 eggs (beaten)
3 tbsp. sugar
3 tbsp. vinegar
1 tsp. butter
½ lb. cream cheese

1 small onion (chopped)
3 tbsp. green relish
1 sweet red pepper
Add seasoning and ketchup to taste

Combine beaten eggs, sugar, vinegar. Cook over hot water, stirring constantly until mixture thickens. Add butter, cream cheese, beat until smooth. Add finely chopped onion, relish, pepper and ketchup.

Doris Tufts

Cheese Puffs

2 cups grated cheese (cheddar)
½ cup soft butter
1 cup flour (sifted)

½ tsp. salt
½ tsp. paprika
48 stuffed olives

Blend cheese, butter, salt and paprika. Stir in flour, mix well. Take 1 tsp. mix, put olive in centre, roll in ball. Bake 15 minutes in 400° oven. Let stand 5 minutes before serving.

Allie (Mrs. J. M.) Hayman

Cheese Puffs

grate 1 cup sharp cheese
beat 2 egg whites until stiff
fold in ½ tsp. baking powder

dash cream of tartar, salt
Fold all together

Cut thick bread slices, about 9 squares to a slice. Put blobs of mixture, entirely covering tops of squares. Bake in 350° oven until lightly brown, 10-15 minutes. Prepare mixture just before serving. Does not keep. Serves 6-8 persons.

Phyllis Churchill

Beer Cheese

1 lb. sharp cheese	1 tsp. salt
1 lb. mild cheese	1 tsp. dry mustard
3 cloves garlic OR garlic juice	dash of tobasco sauce
3 tbsp. worcestershire sauce	1 cup beer

Grate cheese, put in mixmaster with garlic, worcestershire, salt, mustard and tobasco sauce. Beat well. Gradually beat in 1 cup beer. Mix till smooth. Line a loaf pan with waxed paper. Pack in cheese mixture. Put in frig overnight. Serve with crackers.

Allie (Mrs. J. M.) Hayman

Yule Log Patte

(Serve with wheat thins OR salted crackers)

1 lb. chicken livers	2 tbsp. lemon juice
4 lg. onions	4 eggs (hard boiled)
2 tsp. salt	½ cup butter (melted)
¼ tsp. pepper	

Cook livers 5 minutes in small amount of water. (Drain). Put all but lemon juice and butter thru food chopper, then add lemon juice and mix well. When smooth add butter. Form into log and roll in finely chopped parsley. Chill thoroughly.

Allie (Mrs. J. M.) Hayman

Tasty Tuna

(For biscuits or rolls)

1 can tuna (7 oz.)	2 tbsp. pickle relish
2 tbsp. chopped onion	2 tbsp. mayonnaise

Mix together, put on biscuits, grated cheese on top. Broil 3-5 minutes.

Dot (Mrs. E. L.) Brown

Celery Rolls In Loaf

½ cup butter	½ tsp. celery seeds
¼ tsp. salt	1 loaf regular or sandwich bread
dash of cayenne	unsliced
¼ tsp. paprika	

Allow butter to stand at room temperature until soft. Add remaining ingredients, except bread, and blend. Remove all crusts from unsliced loaf of bread. Cut down the middle lengthwise, a little over half through the loaf. Then cut half through loaf crosswise at 2" intervals. Spread butter mixture generously over entire surface and cuts in loaf. Place in baking pan and bake in moderately hot oven, 375° for about 20 minutes or until golden brown. Serve hot on plate. Serves 6 - 8. (Nice with a casserole).

Joyce (Mrs. E. R.) Syvertsen

Parsley-Cheese Ball

Makes 12 to 16 servings

2 pkgs. (8 oz. each) cream cheese
4 oz. blue cheese, crumbled
(about 1 cup)
1 tsp. grated onion

3 drops red-pepper seasoning
¼ cup finely chopped parsley
1 pimiento (from a 4-oz. can)

1. Soften cream cheese in a medium-size bowl; blend in blue cheese, onion, and red-pepper seasoning. Chill until firm enough to handle.

2. Spoon out onto waxed paper or foil; shape with hands into a large ball.

3. To decorate with parsley, cut 6 strips of white paper, 12x¾; fold each in half lengthwise, then trim ends to taper to about ¼ inch.

4. Unfold strips and place flat, spoke fashion, on clean waxed paper or foil; place cheese ball in center; fold strips up and around ball. Roll ball in parsley to coat uncovered sections generously. Chill again until very firm.

5. When ready to serve, carefully peel off paper. Decorate plain sections with tiny stars cut from pimiento, and top with a stem of pimiento. Serve with an assortment of your favorite crackers.

Y Auxiliary

Hot Spiced Tea

(Serves 3 - 4)

Combine:
¼ cup granulated sugar
1 tsp. grated lemon rind
1 tsp. grated orange rind
½ cup water (use well water)
1 2" stick cinnamon
⅛ tsp. powdered cloves

Boil above for ten minutes
Remove cinnamon stick.
Add:
2 tbsp. fresh lemon juice
¼ cup fresh orange juice
¼ cup pineapple juice (canned)

Place over low heat. (Use earthen or glass teapot, not metal). In earthen teapot steep ¼ cup oolong tea in 3 cups (well water), freshly boiled . . . for 10 minutes. Strain onto fruit juices and serve immediately, very hot. (Add a dash or two of aromatic bitters.)

Norma Crowell

Fruit Punch

Serves 150

4 doz. oranges
2 doz. lemons
sugar to taste (¼ to ½ cup)
6 bottles lg. Sussex Ginger Ale

6 bottles lg. Sussex Orange
2 bottles Grape Juice
½ bottle strawberry or raspberry syrup

Mrs. Johnny Green

Fruit Punch

Serves 75

10 cups water
10 cups sugar (boil 10 min.)
Add juice 3 doz. lemons

1 doz. oranges
1 lg. tin pineapple juice
1 lg. tin apple juice

Juice from 2 tins of whole beets for color. Do not add beets. When ready to serve, add 6 large bottles of Ginger Ale.

Mrs. Johnny Green

Party Coffee

For every cup of coffee desired, place 1 cup water in large pot. In cheese cloth bag or flour bag, mix 1 heaping tbsp. coffee per cup — 2 eggs, shells and all, pinch of salt and mustard. Mix to thick paste with ½ cup cold water. Immerse bag in water. Bring to boil. Boil 20 minutes. Serve at once.

Mr. Laird Farin, Halifax

Cold Water Coffee

In cloth bag place 1 heaping tbsp. coffee per cup desired. Soak this bag in cold water, one cup per person. Soak 12 hours. Before needed bring to a simmer. Immediately remove bag. Keep coffee hot until ready to serve.

Mr. Laird Farin, Halifax